A DISCLAIMER

✗ ✗ ✗

LOOK, WE TRIED OUR BEST.

WE FILLED THIS PLANNER WITH ALL OF THE
EXTRA LITTLE DETAILS THAT WE COULD, JUST
BECAUSE WE LOVE THAT KIND OF THING...AND
WE HOPE THAT YOU DO TOO.

THAT SAID, WE PROBABLY MADE A FEW
MISTAKES...EVEN THOUGH WE TRIED REALLY
HARD TO AVOID THEM. WE'RE JUST THREE
TIRED DESIGNERS THAT LOVE TO BITE OFF
MORE THAN THEY CAN CHEW...AND HONESTLY,
THIS PLANNER REQUIRED THE HEIMLICH
MORE THAN A FEW TIMES.

SO, IF IT TURNS OUT THAT 'NATIONAL
TOASTER APPRECIATION DAY' ISN'T OFFICIALLY
RECOGNIZED IN TENNESSEE, WELL WE'RE REALLY
SORRY FOR THE PAIN THAT IT MAY HAVE
CAUSED YOU. SEND US AN EMAIL ABOUT IT IF
IT HELPS YOU SLEEP AT NIGHT.

✖

PART-TIME ADULT

✖

IF FOUND:

. . . .

. . . .

. . . .

IS REALLY SAD.

BRASSMONKEYGOODS.COM

MAY 10 (EXAMPLE)

WRITE IN THE DATES BELOW (AND SHADE IN TODAY)

MONDAY	TUESDAY	WEDNESDAY	THURSDAY	FRIDAY	SATURDAY
5/7/29	5/8/29	5/9/29	5/10/29	5/11/29	
☐ TODAY	☐ TODAY	☐ TODAY	☒ TODAY	☐ TODAY	☐ SUNDA'

IT'S NATIONAL SHRIMP DAY
THE PISTOL SHRIMP CAN PRODUCE SOUNDS LOUDER THAN A GUNSHOT.

FRED ASTAIRE WAS BORN IN 1899   KENAN THOMPSON WAS BORN IN 19'

7 AM

8:30 coffee w/ ALEX @ ODDLY   8 A

9 AM   ↳ bring B-DAY CARD

                                                                10 A

11 AM   *UPDATE Master list BY EOD*

                                                                NOO

1 PM

MEETING w/ PRODUCTION   *ZOOM call 834 0134 079 10 9235   2 P

3 PM

                                                                4 P

5 PM   7:00 dinner w/ TOBE & AMBER @ Novel

                                                                6 P

ON THIS DAY IN 1877: THE FIRST TELEPHONE WAS INSTALLED IN THE WHITE HOUSE.

NOTES AND/OR LIMERICKS

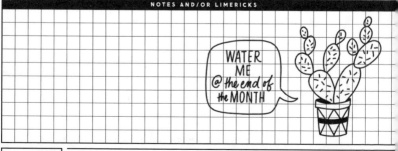

WATER ME @ the end of the MONTH

YEAR: 2029 | 130 DAYS DOWN. 235 DAYS LEFT (UNLESS IT'S A LEAP YEAR [131/235])

HOW TO USE A DAILY PLANNER
THIS ONE — SPECIFICALLY

✖

UNDATED?
MORE LIKE UNYEARED.

WE PUT IN ALL THE DATES, THE FIXED HOLIDAYS, AND A BUNCH OF EXTRA STUFF. ALL OF THE HARD WORK IS DONE.

ALL YOU HAVE TO DO IS FILL IN THE YEAR, AND WHAT DAY OF THE WEEK EACH DAY IS ON.

SIMPLE. IF YOU WANT, YOU CAN BUY THIS PLANNER IN 2023 AND STILL PUT OFF USING IT UNTIL 2054.

VISUAL LEARNER?
LOOK LEFT.

WE FILLED OUT A SAMPLE PAGE OVER THERE FOR YOU TO SEE.

IS JANUARY 19TH ON A TUESDAY THIS YEAR? FILL IN THE BLOCK. NOW FOLLOW SUIT FOR THE REST OF THE PLANNER. DECIDE TO START USING THE PLANNER IN AUGUST? JUST USE THE BOOKMARK AND START THERE. WHEN YOU GET BACK AROUND TO JANUARY, MOVE ON TO THE NEXT YEAR.

✖

A FEW THINGS TO KEEP IN MIND
ALSO KNOWN AS: CALENDARS ARE WEIRD

✖

MOST HOLIDAYS
FLOAT. FEW ARE FIXED.

WE AREN'T TALKING ABOUT 'TAKE YOUR IGUANA TO WORK DAY.' WE MADE A POINT TO ONLY PICK THE RANDOM HOLIDAYS THAT FALL ON SPECIFIC DATES FOR THAT VERY REASON.

WE'RE TALKING THE BIG ONES, YOU KNOW, LIKE THANKSGIVING. SURE, IT ALWAYS FALLS ON THE FOURTH THURSDAY OF NOVEMBER...PROBLEM IS, THAT'S A DIFFERENT DAY EVERY YEAR. SO, WE EXPLAIN THE RULES OF THESE HOLIDAYS IN THE MONTH AT A GLANCE PAGE PRECEDING EACH MONTH.

JUST REMEMBER THAT THEY'RE NOT INCLUDED IN THE DAILY CALENDAR PORTION. YOUR MOM WILL BE MAD IF YOU FORGET TO CALL.

THANKS AGAIN

DON'T FORGET LEAP
DAY. OR ACTUALLY, DO.

ONCE EVERY FOUR YEARS (MOST OF THE TIME ANYWAY...MORE ON THAT LATER) WE HAVE A LEAP YEAR, ADDING FEBRUARY 29TH TO THE CALENDAR.

SO OUR PLANNER HAS TO HAVE IT TOO...WHETHER YOU NEED IT THAT YEAR OR NOT. YOUR JOB IS JUST TO IGNORE IT. UNLESS, WELL, IT'S A LEAP YEAR.

SO WHEN EXACTLY ARE LEAP YEARS? LEAP YEARS ARE ALWAYS EVENLY DIVISIBLE BY 4.

HOWEVER: IF THE YEAR CAN ALSO BE EVENLY DIVIDED BY 100, IT IS NOT A LEAP YEAR.

UNLESS: THE YEAR IS ALSO EVENLY DIVISIBLE BY 400. THEN IT IS A LEAP YEAR.

BLAME JULIUS CAESAR

✖

IT'S OFFICIALLY

 JANUARY

OF THE YEAR

☐ ☐ ☐ ☐

MONTH ONE

. . . .

. . . .

. . . .

CONGRATULATIONS, YOU MADE IT
TO THE MONTH OF JANUARY

✖

CELEBRATE, IT'S

NATIONAL BLOOD DONOR MONTH

NATIONAL BRAILLE LITERACY MONTH

NATIONAL HOBBY MONTH

NATIONAL STAYING HEALTHY MONTH

NATIONAL SOUP MONTH

OFFICIAL SYMBOLS

BIRTHSTONE: GARNET

FLOWERS: CARNATION & SNOWDROP

TREES: FIR, ELM, & CYPRESS

CAPRICORN (DEC 22 / JAN 19)

AQUARIUS (JAN 20 / FEB 18)

✖

A FEW DATES TO KNOW*
LIKE, IMPORTANT ONES.

✖

NEW YEAR'S DAY
JANUARY 1ST

WORLD BRAILLE DAY
JANUARY 4TH

CHRISTMAS
(EASTERN ORTHODOX)
JANUARY 7TH

MAHAYANA NEW YEAR
FIRST FULL MOON OF THE YEAR

WORLD RELIGION DAY
THIRD SUNDAY IN JANUARY

MARTIN LUTHER KING JR. DAY
THIRD MONDAY IN JANUARY

CHINESE NEW YEAR
SECOND NEW MOON AFTER THE
WINTER SOLSTICE (MAY BE IN FEB.)

REPUBLIC DAY
(OF INDIA)
JANUARY 26TH

INTL. HOLOCAUST REMEMBRANCE DAY
JANUARY 27TH

MARK YOUR CALENDAR ✖ IT'S RIGHT OVER THERE

---

*A DISCLAIMER OF SORTS

HEY THERE. WE HERE AT BRASS MONKEY LIKE TO JOKE AROUND...BUT WE ALSO WANT TO TAKE A MINUTE TO RECOGNIZE JUST A FEW OF THE MANY HOLIDAYS & EVENTS THAT ARE IMPORTANT TO OUR FRIENDS AROUND THE GLOBE (AND AT HOME). YOU MAY BE DIFFERENT THAN US. WE MAY HAVE NEVER MET. BUT WE LOVE YOU ALL THE SAME.

SO, WITH ALL OF THAT SAID, IF YOU HAVEN'T HEARD OF A DAY, PLEASE LOOK IT UP. LEARNING ABOUT AND APPRECIATING CULTURES DIFFERENT THAN YOURS IS REALLY IMPORTANT...WAY MORE SO THAN POSTING A FEW 'STRAWBERRY JAM DAY' VIDEOS ON TIKTOK. DON'T GET US WRONG, THERE IS PLENTY OF ROOM FOR BOTH. JUST PLEASE DO BOTH.

JANUARY AT A GLANCE

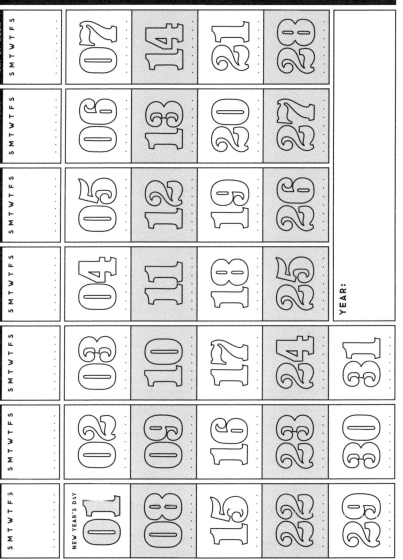

SMTWTFS	SMTWTFS	SMTWTFS	SMTWTFS	SMTWTFS	SMTWTFS	SMTWTFS
07	06	05	04	03	02	NEW YEAR'S DAY 01
14	13	12	11	10	09	08
21	20	19	18	17	16	15
28	27	26	25	24	23	22
				31	30	29

YEAR:

WELL, WHAT ARE YOU WAITING FOR?

✗ START PLANNING. IN THE CALENDAR ABOVE, WE'VE MARKED THE MORE COMMON U.S. HOLIDAYS ALREADY (THE ONES THAT ARE DATED, THAT IS). SO USE THE LIST TO THE LEFT TO FILL IN THE REST...LIKE ALL OF THE ONES THAT CHANGE DATES FROM YEAR TO YEAR, FOR EXAMPLE. ✗

LISTS, NOTES & MEMOIRS

MILLION DOLLAR IDEAS
OR SOME BORING TO-DO LIST

1
2
3
4
5
6
7
8
9
10
11
12
13
14

TEN DOLLAR IDEAS
OR A GROCERY LIST OR SOMETHING

1
2
3
4
5
6
7
8
9
10
11
12
13
14

ILLNESSES BETTER THAN A CHAMPAGNE HANGOVER
USE FIGURE 1 FOR ANY NECESSARY VISUAL AIDS

FIG. 1

1   4
2   5
3   6

JANUARY 1

MONDAY	TUESDAY	WEDNESDAY	THURSDAY	FRIDAY	SATURDAY ☐
. . . . ☐ TODAY	. . . . ☐ TODAY	. . . . ☐ TODAY	. . . . ☐ TODAY	. . . . ☐ TODAY	☐ SUNDAY

IT'S NEW YEAR'S DAY
THE FIRST TIMES SQUARE BALL DROP WAS IN 1908.

J.D. SALINGER BORN IN 1919   VERNE TROYER WAS BORN IN 1969

7 AM

8 AM

9 AM

10 AM

11 AM

NOON

1 PM

2 PM

3 PM

4 PM

5 PM

6 PM

ON THIS DAY IN 1984: NYC TRANSIT FARE ROSE FROM 75 CENTS TO 90 CENTS.

BRILLIANT AND/OR TERRIBLE IDEAS

1 DAY DOWN, 364 DAYS LEFT (UNLESS IT'S A LEAP YEAR [1/365])

YEAR:

JANUARY 2

MONDAY	TUESDAY	WEDNESDAY	THURSDAY	FRIDAY	SATURDAY ☐
. . . .	. . . .	. . . .	. . . .	. . . .	
☐ TODAY	☐ TODAY	☐ TODAY	☐ TODAY	☐ TODAY	☐ SUNDAY

IT'S NATIONAL SCIENCE FICTION DAY
REESE'S PIECES SALES TRIPLED IN THE EARLY 1980s AFTER THE RELEASE OF 'E.T.'

ISAAC ASIMOV WAS BORN IN 1920   TAYE DIGGS WAS BORN IN 1971

7 AM
. . . .
8 AM
. . . .
9 AM
. . . .
10 AM
. . . .
11 AM
. . . .
NOON
. . . .
1 PM
. . . .
2 PM
. . . .
3 PM
. . . .
4 PM
. . . .
5 PM
. . . .
6 PM

ON THIS DAY IN 1973: THE 55 MPH SPEED LIMIT WAS INTRODUCED.

NOTES AND/OR LIMERICKS

YEAR: 2 DAYS DOWN, 363 DAYS LEFT (UNLESS IT'S A LEAP YEAR [2/364])

JANUARY 3

MONDAY	TUESDAY	WEDNESDAY	THURSDAY	FRIDAY	SATURDAY ☐
. . . .	. . . .	. . . .	. . . .	. . . .	
☐ TODAY	☐ TODAY	☐ TODAY	☐ TODAY	☐ TODAY	☐ SUNDAY

IT'S FESTIVAL OF SLEEP DAY
HUMANS ARE THE ONLY ANIMALS THAT WILLINGLY PUT OFF SLEEP.

J.R.R. TOLKIEN WAS BORN IN 1892   FLORENCE PUGH WAS BORN IN 1996

7 AM

8 AM

9 AM

10 AM

11 AM

NOON

1 PM

2 PM

3 PM

4 PM

5 PM

6 PM

ON THIS DAY IN 2009: BITCOIN WAS INVENTED.

BRILLIANT AND/OR TERRIBLE IDEAS

3 DAYS DOWN, 362 DAYS LEFT (UNLESS IT'S A LEAP YEAR [3/363])   YEAR:

JANUARY 4

IT'S NATIONAL TRIVIA DAY
ALEX TREBEK HOSTED OVER 8,200 EPISODES OF 'JEOPARDY!' IN HIS CAREER.

DAVE FOLEY WAS BORN IN 1963   CHARLYNE YI WAS BORN IN 1986

7 AM

. . . .

8 AM

. . . .

9 AM

. . . .

10 AM

. . . .

11 AM

. . . .

NOON

. . . .

1 PM

. . . .

2 PM

. . . .

3 PM

. . . .

4 PM

. . . .

5 PM

. . . .

6 PM

ON THIS DAY IN 1903: TOPSY THE ELEPHANT WAS ELECTROCUTED AT LUNA PARK IN NYC.

NOTES AND/OR LIMERICKS

YEAR: 4 DAYS DOWN, 361 DAYS LEFT (UNLESS IT'S A LEAP YEAR [4/362])

JANUARY 5

		WRITE IN THE DATES BELOW (AND SHADE IN TODAY)			
MONDAY	**TUESDAY**	**WEDNESDAY**	**THURSDAY**	**FRIDAY**	**SATURDAY** ☐
. . . .	. . . .	. . . .	. . . .	. . . .	
☐ TODAY	☐ TODAY	☐ TODAY	☐ TODAY	☐ TODAY	☐ SUNDAY

IT'S NATIONAL WHIPPED CREAM DAY
IT WAS ORIGINALLY KNOWN AS 'MILK SNOW' UNTIL THE 17TH CENTURY.

DIANE KEATON WAS BORN IN 1946   BRADLEY COOPER WAS BORN IN 1975

7 AM

8 AM

9 AM

10 AM

11 AM

NOON

1 PM

2 PM

3 PM

4 PM

5 PM

6 PM

ON THIS DAY IN 1933: WORK STARTED ON THE GOLDEN GATE BRIDGE.

BRILLIANT AND/OR TERRIBLE IDEAS

5 DAYS DOWN, 360 DAYS LEFT (UNLESS IT'S A LEAP YEAR [5/361])   YEAR:

JANUARY 6

MONDAY	TUESDAY	WEDNESDAY	THURSDAY	FRIDAY	SATURDAY ☐
. . . .	. . . .	. . . .	. . . .	. . . .	
☐ TODAY	☐ TODAY	☐ TODAY	☐ TODAY	☐ TODAY	☐ SUNDAY

IT'S NATIONAL TECHNOLOGY DAY
MORE THAN 570 NEW WEBSITES ARE CREATED EVERY MINUTE.

FOR EXAMPLE: BRASSMONKEYGOODS.COM

KATE MCKINNON WAS BORN IN 1984   EDDIE REDMAYNE WAS BORN IN 1982

7 AM
. . . .
8 AM
. . . .
9 AM
. . . .
10 AM
. . . .
11 AM
. . . .
NOON
. . . .
1 PM
. . . .
2 PM
. . . .
3 PM
. . . .
4 PM
. . . .
5 PM
. . . .
6 PM

ON THIS DAY IN 1975: 'WHEEL OF FORTUNE' DEBUTED ON NBC.

NOTES AND/OR LIMERICKS

YEAR: 6 DAYS DOWN, 359 DAYS LEFT (UNLESS IT'S A LEAP YEAR [6/360])

JANUARY 7

MONDAY	TUESDAY	WEDNESDAY	THURSDAY	FRIDAY	SATURDAY ☐
. . . . ☐ TODAY	. . . . ☐ TODAY	. . . . ☐ TODAY	. . . . ☐ TODAY	. . . . ☐ TODAY	☐ SUNDAY

IT'S NATIONAL BOBBLEHEAD DAY
THE BIGGEST ONE ON RECORD IS A 15 FOOT TALL SAINT BERNARD.

NICOLAS CAGE WAS BORN IN 1964   BLUE IVY CARTER WAS BORN IN 2012

7 AM

8 AM

9 AM

10 AM

11 AM

NOON

1 PM

2 PM

3 PM

4 PM

5 PM

6 PM

ON THIS DAY IN 1990: THE TOWER OF PISA CLOSED AFTER LEANING TOO FAR.

BRILLIANT AND/OR TERRIBLE IDEAS

7 DAYS DOWN, 358 DAYS LEFT (UNLESS IT'S A LEAP YEAR [7/359])   YEAR:

JANUARY 8

MONDAY	TUESDAY	WEDNESDAY	THURSDAY	FRIDAY	SATURDAY ☐
. . . .	. . . .	. . . .	. . . .	. . . .	
☐ TODAY	☐ TODAY	☐ TODAY	☐ TODAY	☐ TODAY	☐ SUNDAY

IT'S BUBBLE BATH DAY
MARILYN MONROE WAS KNOWN FOR BATHING IN CHAMPAGNE.

ELVIS PRESLEY WAS BORN IN 1935   DAVID BOWIE WAS BORN IN 1947

7 AM
. . . .
8 AM
. . . .
9 AM
. . . .
10 AM
. . . .
11 AM
. . . .
NOON
. . . .
1 PM
. . . .
2 PM
. . . .
3 PM
. . . .
4 PM
. . . .
5 PM
. . . .
6 PM

ON THIS DAY IN 1998: MR. ROGERS RECEIVED A STAR ON THE WALK OF FAME.

NOTES AND/OR LIMERICKS

YEAR:	8 DAYS DOWN, 357 DAYS LEFT (UNLESS IT'S A LEAP YEAR [8/358])

JANUARY 9

MONDAY	TUESDAY	WEDNESDAY	THURSDAY	FRIDAY	SATURDAY ☐
. . . .	. . . .	. . . .	. . . .	. . . .	
☐ TODAY	☐ TODAY	☐ TODAY	☐ TODAY	☐ TODAY	☐ SUNDAY

IT'S NATIONAL STATIC ELECTRICITY DAY
AROUND SEVENTY PERCENT OF THOSE STRUCK BY LIGHTNING SURVIVE.

KATE MIDDLETON WAS BORN IN 1982   NICOLA PELTZ WAS BORN IN 1995

7 AM

8 AM

9 AM

10 AM

11 AM

NOON

1 PM

2 PM

3 PM

4 PM

5 PM

6 PM

ON THIS DAY IN 2007: STEVE JOBS ANNOUNCED THE FIRST iPHONE.

BRILLIANT AND/OR TERRIBLE IDEAS

9 DAYS DOWN, 356 DAYS LEFT (UNLESS IT'S A LEAP YEAR [9/357])   YEAR:

JANUARY 10

WRITE IN THE DATES BELOW (AND SHADE IN TODAY)

MONDAY	TUESDAY	WEDNESDAY	THURSDAY	FRIDAY	SATURDAY ☐
. . . .	. . . .	. . . .	. . . .	. . . .	
☐ TODAY	☐ TODAY	☐ TODAY	☐ TODAY	☐ TODAY	☐ SUNDAY

IT'S HOUSEPLANT APPRECIATION DAY
SPIDER PLANTS ARE A MILD HALLUCINOGENIC FOR CATS.

GEORGE FOREMAN WAS BORN IN 1949   PAT BENATAR WAS BORN IN 1953

7 AM
. . . .
                                                                              8 AM
. . . .
9 AM
. . . .
                                                                             10 AM
. . . .
11 AM
. . . .
                                                                              NOON
. . . .
1 PM
. . . .
                                                                              2 PM
. . . .
3 PM
. . . .
                                                                              4 PM
. . . .
5 PM
. . . .
                                                                              6 PM

ON THIS DAY IN 1983: 'FRAGGLE ROCK' PREMIERED ON HBO.

NOTES AND/OR LIMERICKS

YEAR:	10 DAYS DOWN, 355 DAYS LEFT (UNLESS IT'S A LEAP YEAR [10/356])

WRITE IN THE DATES BELOW (AND SHADE IN TODAY)					
MONDAY	TUESDAY	WEDNESDAY	THURSDAY	FRIDAY	SATURDAY ☐
. . . .	. . . .	. . . .	. . . .	. . . .	
☐ TODAY	☐ TODAY	☐ TODAY	☐ TODAY	☐ TODAY	☐ SUNDAY

IT'S NATIONAL MILK DAY
A GALLON OF MILK WEIGHS 8.59 LBS.

MARY J. BLIGE WAS BORN IN 1971   AMANDA PEET WAS BORN IN 1972

7 AM

8 AM

9 AM

10 AM

11 AM

NOON

1 PM

2 PM

3 PM

4 PM

5 PM

6 PM

ON THIS DAY IN 1970: THE KANSAS CITY CHIEFS WON THE SUPERBOWL IV.

BRILLIANT AND/OR TERRIBLE IDEAS

JANUARY 12

MONDAY	TUESDAY	WEDNESDAY	THURSDAY	FRIDAY	SATURDAY ☐
. . . .	. . . .	. . . .	. . . .	. . . .	☐
☐ TODAY	☐ TODAY	☐ TODAY	☐ TODAY	☐ TODAY	☐ SUNDAY

IT'S WORK HARDER DAY
PROCRASTINATING ON A PROJECT CAN INCREASE FOCUS AND EFFICIENCY.

KIRSTIE ALLEY WAS BORN IN 1951   ZAYN MALIK WAS BORN IN 199

7 AM
. . . .
8 AM
. . . .
9 AM
. . . .
10 AM
. . . .
11 AM
. . . .
NOON
. . . .
1 PM
. . . .
2 PM
. . . .
3 PM
. . . .
4 PM
. . . .
5 PM
. . . .
6 PM

ON THIS DAY IN 2019: MISSY ELLIOTT JOINED THE SONGWRITERS HALL OF FAME.

NOTES AND/OR LIMERICKS

YEAR: 12 DAYS DOWN, 353 DAYS LEFT (UNLESS IT'S A LEAP YEAR [12/354])

JANUARY 13

		WRITE IN THE DATES BELOW (AND SHADE IN TODAY)			
MONDAY	**TUESDAY**	**WEDNESDAY**	**THURSDAY**	**FRIDAY**	**SATURDAY** ☐
☐ TODAY	☐ TODAY	☐ TODAY	☐ TODAY	☐ TODAY	☐ SUNDAY

IT'S NATIONAL STICKER DAY
THE STICKERS ON FRUIT ARE EDIBLE AND CONTROLLED BY THE FDA.

LIAM HEMSWORTH WAS BORN IN 1990   ORLANDO BLOOM WAS BORN IN 1977

7 AM

8 AM

9 AM

10 AM

11 AM

NOON

1 PM

2 PM

3 PM

4 PM

5 PM

6 PM

ON THIS DAY IN 1999: MICHAEL JORDAN RETIRED (FOR THE SECOND TIME).

BRILLIANT AND/OR TERRIBLE IDEAS

13 DAYS DOWN, 352 DAYS LEFT (UNLESS IT'S A LEAP YEAR [13/353])   YEAR:

JANUARY 14

WRITE IN THE DATES BELOW (AND SHADE IN TODAY)

MONDAY	TUESDAY	WEDNESDAY	THURSDAY	FRIDAY	SATURDAY ☐
. . . . ☐ TODAY	. . . . ☐ TODAY	. . . . ☐ TODAY	. . . . ☐ TODAY	. . . . ☐ TODAY	☐ SUNDAY

IT'S NATIONAL DRESS UP YOUR DOG DAY
DOGS SEND MESSAGES WITH THEIR URINE—LIKE GROSS EMAIL.

FAYE DUNAWAY WAS BORN IN 1941   JASON BATEMAN WAS BORN IN 196

7 AM
. . . .
8 AM
. . . .
9 AM
. . . .
10 A M
. . . .
11 AM
. . . .
NOO
. . . .
1 PM
. . . .
2 P
. . . .
3 PM
. . . .
4 P
. . . .
5 PM
. . . .
6 P

ON THIS DAY IN 1954: MARILYN MONROE MARRIED JOE DIMAGGIO.

NOTES AND/OR LIMERICKS

YEAR: 14 DAYS DOWN, 351 DAYS LEFT (UNLESS IT'S A LEAP YEAR [14/352])

JANUARY 15

MONDAY	TUESDAY	WEDNESDAY	THURSDAY	FRIDAY	SATURDAY ☐
☐ TODAY	☐ TODAY	☐ TODAY	☐ TODAY	☐ TODAY	☐ SUNDAY

WRITE IN THE DATES BELOW (AND SHADE IN TODAY)

IT'S NATIONAL BAGEL DAY
IN 2008, ASTRONAUT GREGORY CHAMITOFF TOOK 18 OF THEM TO SPACE.

MARTIN LUTHER KING JR. WAS BORN IN 1929   CHARO WAS BORN IN 1951

7 AM

8 AM

9 AM

10 AM

11 AM

NOON

1 PM

2 PM

3 PM

4 PM

5 PM

6 PM

ON THIS DAY IN 2009: SULLY SULLENBERGER LANDED A PLANE ON THE HUDSON.

BRILLIANT AND/OR TERRIBLE IDEAS

15 DAYS DOWN, 350 DAYS LEFT (UNLESS IT'S A LEAP YEAR [15/351])   YEAR:

JANUARY 16

MONDAY	TUESDAY	WEDNESDAY	THURSDAY	FRIDAY	SATURDAY ☐
. . . .	. . . .	. . . .	. . . .	. . . .	☐
☐ TODAY	☐ TODAY	☐ TODAY	☐ TODAY	☐ TODAY	☐ SUNDAY

IT'S NATIONAL FIG NEWTON DAY
OVER 1 BILLION ARE EATEN A YEAR, AND YET WE'VE NEVER HAD ONE.

LIN MANUEL MIRANDA WAS BORN IN 1980   KATE MOSS WAS BORN IN 1974

7 AM
. . . .
                                                                                    8 AM
. . . .
9 AM
. . . .
                                                                                    10 AM
. . . .
11 AM
. . . .
                                                                                    NOON
. . . .
1 PM
. . . .
                                                                                    2 PM
. . . .
3 PM
. . . .
                                                                                    4 PM
. . . .
5 PM
. . . .
                                                                                    6 PM

ON THIS DAY IN 1939: THE SUPERMAN DAILY COMIC STRIP DEBUTED.

NOTES AND/OR LIMERICKS

YEAR:	16 DAYS DOWN, 349 DAYS LEFT (UNLESS IT'S A LEAP YEAR [16/350])

JANUARY 17

MONDAY	TUESDAY	WEDNESDAY	THURSDAY	FRIDAY	SATURDAY ☐
. . . . ☐ TODAY	. . . . ☐ TODAY	. . . . ☐ TODAY	. . . . ☐ TODAY	. . . . ☐ TODAY	☐ SUNDAY

IT'S NATIONAL BOOTLEGGER'S DAY
DURING PROHIBITION, CONGRESS HAD THEIR OWN PRIVATE SMUGGLER.

AMES EARL JONES WAS BORN IN 1931   ZOOEY DESCHANEL WAS BORN IN 1980

7 AM

AM

9 AM

⊃ AM

11 AM

⌐OON

1 PM

PM

3 PM

PM

5 PM

PM

ON THIS DAY IN 1949: THE FIRST VW BEETLE ARRIVED IN THE U.S. FROM GERMANY.

BRILLIANT AND/OR TERRIBLE IDEAS

17 DAYS DOWN, 348 DAYS LEFT (UNLESS IT'S A LEAP YEAR [17/349])   YEAR:

JANUARY 18

MONDAY	TUESDAY	WEDNESDAY	THURSDAY	FRIDAY	SATURDAY ☐
. . . .	. . . .	. . . .	. . . .	. . . .	☐
☐ TODAY	☐ TODAY	☐ TODAY	☐ TODAY	☐ TODAY	SUNDAY

IT'S NATIONAL PEKING DUCK DAY
THE CHARACTER DONALD DUCK WAS BASED OFF OF A PEKIN DUCK.

CARY GRANT WAS BORN IN 1904   KEVIN COSTNER WAS BORN IN 195

7 AM
. . . .
8 A
. . . .
9 AM
. . . .
10 A
. . . .
11 AM
. . . .
NOO
. . . .
1 PM
. . . .
2 P
. . . .
3 PM
. . . .
4 P
. . . .
5 PM
. . . .
6 P

ON THIS DAY IN 1993: MARTIN LUTHER KING JR. DAY BECAME A FEDERAL HOLIDAY.

NOTES AND/OR LIMERICKS

YEAR: ___   18 DAYS DOWN, 347 DAYS LEFT (UNLESS IT'S A LEAP YEAR [18/348])

WRITE IN THE DATES BELOW (AND SHADE IN TODAY)

MONDAY	TUESDAY	WEDNESDAY	THURSDAY	FRIDAY	SATURDAY ☐
. . . . ☐ TODAY	. . . . ☐ TODAY	. . . . ☐ TODAY	. . . . ☐ TODAY	. . . . ☐ TODAY	☐ SUNDAY

IT'S NATIONAL POPCORN DAY
POPCORN KERNELS CAN POP UPWARDS OF THREE FEET HIGH.

DOLLY PARTON WAS BORN IN 1946   EDGAR ALLAN POE WAS BORN IN 1809

7 AM

8 AM

9 AM

10 AM

11 AM

NOON

1 PM

2 PM

3 PM

4 PM

5 PM

6 PM

ON THIS DAY IN 2013: LANCE ARMSTRONG ADMITTED TO DOPING.

BRILLIANT AND/OR TERRIBLE IDEAS

19 DAYS DOWN, 346 DAYS LEFT (UNLESS IT'S A LEAP YEAR [19/347])   YEAR:

JANUARY 20

MONDAY	TUESDAY	WEDNESDAY	THURSDAY	FRIDAY	SATURDAY ☐
. . . .	. . . .	. . . .	. . . .	. . . .	☐
☐ TODAY	☐ TODAY	☐ TODAY	☐ TODAY	☐ TODAY	SUNDAY

IT'S NATIONAL CHEESE LOVER'S DAY
MICE DON'T EVEN REALLY LIKE CHEESE. BUT WE DO.

BUZZ ALDRIN WAS BORN IN 1930   QUESTLOVE WAS BORN IN 197°

7 AM
. . . .
                                                                              8 AM
. . . .
9 AM
. . . .
                                                                              10 AM
. . . .
11 AM
. . . .
                                                                              NOON
. . . .
1 PM
. . . .
                                                                              2 PM
. . . .
3 PM
. . . .
                                                                              4 PM
. . . .
5 PM
. . . .
                                                                              6 PM

ON THIS DAY IN 2009: BARACK OBAMA BECAME THE 44TH PRESIDENT.

NOTES AND/OR LIMERICKS

YEAR: 20 DAYS DOWN, 345 DAYS LEFT (UNLESS IT'S A LEAP YEAR [20/346])

JANUARY 21

MONDAY	TUESDAY	WEDNESDAY	THURSDAY	FRIDAY	SATURDAY ☐
· · · · · · · · · ☐ TODAY	· · · · · · · · · ☐ TODAY	· · · · · · · · · ☐ TODAY	· · · · · · · · · ☐ TODAY	· · · · · · · · · ☐ TODAY	☐ SUNDAY

IT'S ONE-LINERS DAY

SOMEONE STOLE OUR PLANNER—THEY GOT TWELVE MONTHS.

GEENA DAVIS WAS BORN IN 1956   GRIGORI RASPUTIN WAS BORN IN 1869

7 AM

8 AM

9 AM

10 AM

11 AM

NOON

1 PM

2 PM

3 PM

4 PM

5 PM

6 PM

ON THIS DAY IN 1796: THE SMALLPOX VACCINE WAS INTRODUCED.

BRILLIANT AND/OR TERRIBLE IDEAS

21 DAYS DOWN, 344 DAYS LEFT (UNLESS IT'S A LEAP YEAR [21/345])

YEAR:

JANUARY 22

IT'S NATIONAL HOT SAUCE DAY
GENERALLY, THE SMALLER THE CHILI, THE HOTTER IT IS.

GUY FIERI WAS BORN IN 1968   CAPTAIN HIKARU SULU WAS BORN IN 2231

7 AM
. . . .
                                                                                            8 AM
. . . .
9 AM
. . . .
                                                                                           10 AM
. . . .
11 AM
. . . .
                                                                                            NOON
. . . .
1 PM
. . . .
                                                                                            2 PM
. . . .
3 PM
. . . .
                                                                                            4 PM
. . . .
5 PM
. . . .
                                                                                            6 PM

ON THIS DAY IN 1959: BUDDY HOLLY RECORDED MUSIC FOR THE FINAL TIME IN HIS NYC APARTMENT.

NOTES AND/OR LIMERICKS

YEAR:	22 DAYS DOWN, 343 DAYS LEFT (UNLESS IT'S A LEAP YEAR [22/344])

JANUARY 23

MONDAY	TUESDAY	WEDNESDAY	THURSDAY	FRIDAY	SATURDAY ☐
. . . .	. . . .	. . . .	. . . .	. . . .	
☐ TODAY	☐ TODAY	☐ TODAY	☐ TODAY	☐ TODAY	☐ SUNDAY

IT'S NATIONAL HANDWRITING DAY
SMALL HANDWRITING CAN INDICATE SHYNESS IN A PERSON.

MARISKA HARGITAY WAS BORN IN 1964   RUTGER HAUER WAS BORN IN 1944

7 AM

AM

9 AM

10 AM

11 AM

NOON

1 PM

PM

3 PM

PM

5 PM

PM

ON THIS DAY IN 1979: WILLIE MAYS JOINED THE BASEBALL HALL OF FAME.

BRILLIANT AND/OR TERRIBLE IDEAS

23 DAYS DOWN, 342 DAYS LEFT (UNLESS IT'S A LEAP YEAR [23/343])   YEAR:

JANUARY 24

WRITE IN THE DATES BELOW (AND SHADE IN TODAY)

MONDAY	TUESDAY	WEDNESDAY	THURSDAY	FRIDAY	SATURDAY ☐
. . . . ☐ TODAY	. . . . ☐ TODAY	. . . . ☐ TODAY	. . . . ☐ TODAY	. . . . ☐ TODAY	☐ SUNDAY

IT'S NATIONAL PEANUT BUTTER DAY
IN 1901 THE FIRST RECIPE FOR A PB&J SANDWICH WAS PUBLISHED.

ED HELMS WAS BORN IN 1974   JOHN BELUSHI WAS BORN IN 194█

7 AM
. . . .
                                                                              8 A
. . . .
9 AM
. . . .
                                                                             10 A
. . . .
11 AM
. . . .
                                                                             NOO
. . . .
1 PM
. . . .
                                                                              2 P
. . . .
3 PM
. . . .
                                                                              4 P
. . . .
5 PM
. . . .
                                                                              6 P

ON THIS DAY IN 2011: THE ALBUM '21' BY ADELE WAS RELEASED.

NOTES AND/OR LIMERICKS

YEAR: 24 DAYS DOWN, 341 DAYS LEFT (UNLESS IT'S A LEAP YEAR [24/342])

JANUARY 25

MONDAY	TUESDAY	WEDNESDAY	THURSDAY	FRIDAY	SATURDAY ☐

WRITE IN THE DATES BELOW (AND SHADE IN TODAY)

☐ TODAY	☐ TODAY	☐ TODAY	☐ TODAY	☐ TODAY	☐ SUNDAY

IT'S NATIONAL OPPOSITE DAY

OPPOSITES RARELY ATTRACT—UNLESS YOU'RE PAULA ABDUL.

ALICIA KEYS WAS BORN IN 1981   VIRGINIA WOOLF WAS BORN IN 1882

7 AM

8 AM

9 AM

10 AM

11 AM

NOON

1 PM

2 PM

3 PM

4 PM

5 PM

6 PM

ON THIS DAY IN 2003: SERENA WILLIAMS WON A 5TH GRAND SLAM SINGLES TITLE.

BRILLIANT AND/OR TERRIBLE IDEAS

25 DAYS DOWN, 340 DAYS LEFT (UNLESS IT'S A LEAP YEAR [25/341])   YEAR:

JANUARY 26

		WRITE IN THE DATES BELOW (AND SHADE IN TODAY)			
MONDAY	TUESDAY	WEDNESDAY	THURSDAY	FRIDAY	SATURDAY ☐
. . . . ☐ TODAY	. . . . ☐ TODAY	. . . . ☐ TODAY	. . . . ☐ TODAY	. . . . ☐ TODAY	☐ SUNDAY

IT'S NATIONAL PEANUT BRITTLE DAY
CREATED BY MISTAKE IN 1890, BY A WOMAN TRYING TO MAKE TAFFY.

MARIA VON TRAPP WAS BORN IN 1905   MIKE SAYRE WAS BORN IN 198

7 AM
. . . .
8 AM
. . . .
9 AM
. . . .
10 A
. . . .
11 AM
. . . .
NOO
. . . .
1 PM
. . . .
2 P
. . . .
3 PM
. . . .
4 P
. . . .
5 PM
. . . .
6 P

ON THIS DAY IN 1998: BILL CLINTON DENIED HAVING SEX WITH MONICA LEWINSKY.

NOTES AND/OR LIMERICKS.

YEAR: ☐   26 DAYS DOWN, 339 DAYS LEFT (UNLESS IT'S A LEAP YEAR [26/340])

JANUARY 27

MONDAY	TUESDAY	WEDNESDAY	THURSDAY	FRIDAY	SATURDAY ☐
☐ TODAY	☐ TODAY	☐ TODAY	☐ TODAY	☐ TODAY	☐ SUNDAY

IT'S BUBBLE WRAP APPRECIATION DAY
IT WAS ORIGINALLY INTENDED TO BE A TEXTURED WALLPAPER.

PATTON OSWALT WAS BORN IN 1969   ROSAMUND PIKE WAS BORN IN 1979

7 AM

8 AM

9 AM

10 AM

11 AM

NOON

1 PM

2 PM

3 PM

4 PM

5 PM

6 PM

ON THIS DAY IN 1948: THE FIRST AUDIO TAPE RECORDER WAS SOLD.

BRILLIANT AND/OR TERRIBLE IDEAS

27 DAYS DOWN, 338 DAYS LEFT (UNLESS IT'S A LEAP YEAR [27/339])

YEAR:

JANUARY 28

MONDAY	TUESDAY	WEDNESDAY	THURSDAY	FRIDAY	SATURDAY ☐
. . . .	. . . .	. . . .	. . . .	. . . .	☐
☐ TODAY	☐ TODAY	☐ TODAY	☐ TODAY	☐ TODAY	SUNDAY

IT'S NATIONAL KAZOO DAY
THERE'S A MUSEUM DEDICATED TO THEM IN BEAUFORT, SOUTH CAROLINA.

ELIJAH WOOD WAS BORN IN 1981   ALAN ALDA WAS BORN IN 193

7 AM
. . . .
                                                                            8 AM
. . . .
9 AM
. . . .
                                                                            10 AM
. . . .
11 AM
. . . .
                                                                            NOON
. . . .
1 PM
. . . .
                                                                            2 PM
. . . .
3 PM
. . . .
                                                                            4 PM
. . . .
5 PM
. . . .
                                                                            6 PM

ON THIS DAY IN 1986: THE SPACE SHUTTLE 'CHALLENGER' EXPLODED.

NOTES AND/OR LIMERICKS

YEAR: 28 DAYS DOWN, 337 DAYS LEFT (UNLESS IT'S A LEAP YEAR [28/338])

JANUARY 29

WRITE IN THE DATES BELOW (AND SHADE IN TODAY)					
MONDAY	TUESDAY	WEDNESDAY	THURSDAY	FRIDAY	SATURDAY ☐
. . . .	. . . .	. . . .	. . . .	. . . .	
☐ TODAY	☐ TODAY	☐ TODAY	☐ TODAY	☐ TODAY	☐ SUNDAY

IT'S NATIONAL PUZZLE DAY

PEOPLE WHO ENJOY PUZZLE'S ARE KNOWN AS DISSECTOLOGISTS.

OPRAH WINFREY WAS BORN IN 1954   TOM SELLECK WAS BORN IN 1945

7 AM
. . . .
8 AM
. . . .
9 AM
. . . .
10 AM
. . . .
11 AM
. . . .
NOON
. . . .
1 PM
. . . .
2 PM
. . . .
3 PM
. . . .
4 PM
. . . .
5 PM
. . . .
6 PM

ON THIS DAY IN 1959: WALT DISNEY'S 'SLEEPING BEAUTY' WAS RELEASED.

BRILLIANT AND/OR TERRIBLE IDEAS

29 DAYS DOWN, 336 DAYS LEFT (UNLESS IT'S A LEAP YEAR [29/337])   YEAR:

JANUARY 30

WRITE IN THE DATES BELOW (AND SHADE IN TODAY)

MONDAY	TUESDAY	WEDNESDAY	THURSDAY	FRIDAY	SATURDAY ☐
. . . .	. . . .	. . . .	. . . .	. . . .	
☐ TODAY	☐ TODAY	☐ TODAY	☐ TODAY	☐ TODAY	☐ SUNDAY

IT'S YODEL FOR YOUR NEIGHBORS DAY
BLAME IT ON US.

CHRISTIAN BALE WAS BORN IN 1974   OLIVIA COLMAN WAS BORN IN 197̄

7 AM

. . . .

8 AM

. . . .

9 AM

. . . .

10 AM

. . . .

11 AM

. . . .

NOON

. . . .

1 PM

. . . .

2 PM

. . . .

3 PM

. . . .

4 PM

. . . .

5 PM

. . . .

6 PM

ON THIS DAY IN 1973: KISS PLAYED THEIR FIRST SHOW IN QUEENS, NEW YORK.

NOTES AND/OR LIMERICKS

YEAR: 30 DAYS DOWN, 335 DAYS LEFT (UNLESS IT'S A LEAP YEAR [30/336])

JANUARY 31

MONDAY	TUESDAY	WEDNESDAY	THURSDAY	FRIDAY	SATURDAY ☐
. . . .	. . . .	. . . .	. . . .	. . . .	
☐ TODAY	☐ TODAY	☐ TODAY	☐ TODAY	☐ TODAY	☐ SUNDAY

IT'S EAT BRUSSELS SPROUTS DAY
RESEARCH SHOWS THAT EATING BRUSSELS SPROUTS CAN BOOST YOUR LIBIDO.

JACKIE ROBINSON WAS BORN IN 1919   FRANZ SCHUBERT WAS BORN IN 1797

7 AM

8 AM

9 AM

10 AM

11 AM

NOON

1 PM

2 PM

3 PM

4 PM

5 PM

6 PM

ON THIS DAY IN 1865: CONGRESS PASSED THE 13TH AMENDMENT.

BRILLIANT AND/OR TERRIBLE IDEAS

31 DAYS DOWN, 334 DAYS LEFT (UNLESS IT'S A LEAP YEAR [31/335])   YEAR:

IT'S OFFICIALLY

× FEBRUARY ×

OF THE YEAR

☐ ☐ ☐ ☐

MONTH TWO

. . . .

. . . .

. . . .

FEBRUARY AT A GLANCE

CONGRATULATIONS, YOU MADE IT
TO THE MONTH OF FEBRUARY

✖

CELEBRATE, IT'S

BLACK HISTORY MONTH

NATIONAL CAT HEALTH MONTH

NTL. HOT BREAKFAST MONTH

GREAT AMERICAN PIE MONTH

NATIONAL SNACK FOOD MONTH

OFFICIAL SYMBOLS

BIRTHSTONE: AMETHYST

FLOWERS: VIOLET & PRIMROSE

TREES: POPLAR, CEDAR, & PINE

AQUARIUS (JAN 20 / FEB 18)

PISCES (FEB 19 / MAR 20)

✖

A FEW DATES TO KNOW*
LIKE, IMPORTANT ONES.

✖

LEAP DAY
(APPROX. EVERY 4 YEARS)
FEBRUARY 29TH
(SEE OUR 'GET STARTED'
PAGE FOR THE RULES)

GROUNDHOG DAY
FEBRUARY 2ND

VALENTINE'S DAY
FEBRUARY 14TH

MARDI GRAS
47 DAYS BEFORE EASTER
(SORRY ABOUT THE MATH)

PURIM
(JUDAISM)
14TH DAY OF ADAR IN THE JEWISH
CALENDAR (MAY FALL IN MARCH)

SUSAN B. ANTHONY DAY
FEBRUARY 15TH

PRESIDENTS' DAY
THIRD MONDAY IN FEBRUARY

ASH WEDNESDAY
(CHRISTIANITY)
46 DAYS BEFORE EASTER
(SORRY AGAIN)

MARK YOUR CALENDAR ✖ IT'S RIGHT OVER THERE

---

*A DISCLAIMER OF SORTS

HEY THERE. WE HERE AT BRASS MONKEY LIKE TO JOKE AROUND...BUT WE ALSO WANT TO TAKE A MINUTE TO RECOGNIZE JUST A FEW OF THE MANY HOLIDAYS & EVENTS THAT ARE IMPORTANT TO OUR FRIENDS AROUND THE GLOBE (AND AT HOME). YOU MAY BE DIFFERENT THAN US. WE MAY HAVE NEVER MET. BUT WE LOVE YOU ALL THE SAME.

SO, WITH ALL OF THAT SAID, IF YOU HAVEN'T HEARD OF A DAY, PLEASE LOOK IT UP. LEARNING ABOUT AND APPRECIATING CULTURES DIFFERENT THAN YOURS IS REALLY IMPORTANT...WAY MORE SO THAN POSTING A FEW 'STRAWBERRY JAM DAY' VIDEOS ON TIKTOK. DON'T GET US WRONG, THERE IS PLENTY OF ROOM FOR BOTH. JUST PLEASE DO BOTH.

FEBRUARY AT A GLANCE

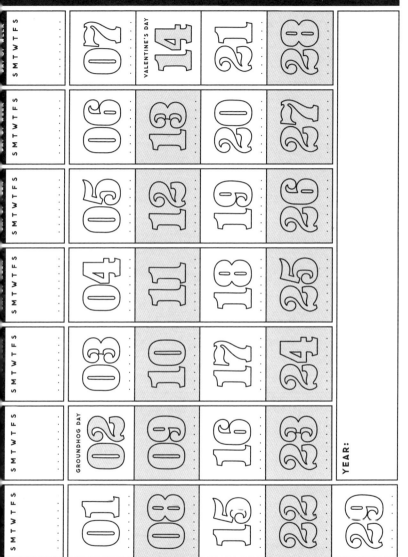

S M T W T F S	S M T W T F S	S M T W T F S	S M T W T F S	S M T W T F S	S M T W T F S	S M T W T F S
01	02 GROUNDHOG DAY	03	04	05	06	07
08	09	10	11	12	13	14 VALENTINE'S DAY
15	16	17	18	19	20	21
22	23	24	25	26	27	28
29						

YEAR:

WELL, WHAT ARE YOU WAITING FOR?

✖ START PLANNING. IN THE CALENDAR ABOVE, WE'VE MARKED THE MORE COMMON U.S. HOLIDAYS ALREADY (THE ONES THAT ARE DATED, THAT IS). SO USE THE LIST TO THE LEFT TO FILL IN THE REST...LIKE ALL OF THE ONES THAT CHANGE DATES FROM YEAR TO YEAR, FOR EXAMPLE. ✖

LISTS, NOTES & MEMOIRS

COMFORT FOODS
OR SOME BORING TO-DO LIST

1
2
3
4
5
6
7
8
9
10
11
12
13
14

UNCOMFORTABLE FOODS
OR A GROCERY LIST OR SOMETHING

1
2
3
4
5
6
7
8
9
10
11
12
13
14

FIRST PURCHASES AFTER WINING THE LOTTERY
USE FIGURE 1 FOR ANY NECESSARY VISUAL AIDS

FIG. 1

1   4
2   5
3   6

FEBRUARY 1

WRITE IN THE DATES BELOW (AND SHADE IN TODAY)

MONDAY	TUESDAY	WEDNESDAY	THURSDAY	FRIDAY	SATURDAY ☐
☐ TODAY	☐ TODAY	☐ TODAY	☐ TODAY	☐ TODAY	☐ SUNDAY

IT'S CHANGE YOUR PASSWORD DAY
ABOUT THIRTY PERCENT OF ALL PHISHING EMAILS ARE OPENED.

BRANDON LEE WAS BORN IN 1965   HARRY STYLES WAS BORN IN 1994

7 AM

8 AM

9 AM

10 AM

11 AM

NOON

1 PM

2 PM

3 PM

4 PM

5 PM

6 PM

ON THIS DAY IN 1982: 'LATE NIGHT WITH DAVID LETTERMAN' DEBUTED.

BRILLIANT AND/OR TERRIBLE IDEAS

32 DAYS DOWN, 333 DAYS LEFT (UNLESS IT'S A LEAP YEAR [32/334])

YEAR:

FEBRUARY 2

MONDAY	TUESDAY	WEDNESDAY	THURSDAY	FRIDAY	SATURDAY ☐
☐ TODAY	☐ TODAY	☐ TODAY	☐ TODAY	☐ TODAY	☐ SUNDAY

IT'S GROUNDHOG DAY
WHILE FILMING 'GROUNDHOG DAY,' BILL MURRAY WAS BIT 3 TIMES.

FARRAH FAWCETT WAS BORN IN 1947   SHAKIRA WAS BORN IN 1977

7 AM

. . . .

8 AM

. . . .

9 AM

. . . .

10 AM

11 AM

. . . .

NOON

. . . .

1 PM

. . . .

2 PM

. . . .

3 PM

. . . .

. . . .

4 PM

5 PM

. . . .

6 PM

ON THIS DAY IN 2020: THE KANSAS CITY CHIEFS WON SUPER BOWL LIV.

NOTES AND/OR LIMERICKS

YEAR: 33 DAYS DOWN, 332 DAYS LEFT (UNLESS IT'S A LEAP YEAR [33/333])

FEBRUARY 3

MONDAY	TUESDAY	WEDNESDAY	THURSDAY	FRIDAY	SATURDAY ☐
☐ TODAY	☐ TODAY	☐ TODAY	☐ TODAY	☐ TODAY	☐ SUNDAY

IT'S INTERNATIONAL GOLDEN RETRIEVER DAY
THE BREED WAS DEVELOPED BY LORD TWEEDMOUTH IN THE LATE 1800s.

(YES, THAT'S ACTUALLY A REAL PERSON)

NATHAN LANE WAS BORN IN 1956   ISLA FISHER WAS BORN IN 1976

7 AM

8 AM

9 AM

10 AM

11 AM

NOON

1 PM

2 PM

3 PM

4 PM

5 PM

6 PM

ON THIS DAY IN 1959: BUDDY HOLLY DIED IN A PLANE CRASH.

BRILLIANT AND/OR TERRIBLE IDEAS

34 DAYS DOWN, 331 DAYS LEFT (UNLESS IT'S A LEAP YEAR [34/332])   YEAR:

FEBRUARY 4

MONDAY	TUESDAY	WEDNESDAY	THURSDAY	FRIDAY	SATURDAY ☐
. . . .	. . . .	. . . .	. . . .	. . . .	
☐ TODAY	☐ TODAY	☐ TODAY	☐ TODAY	☐ TODAY	☐ SUNDAY

IT'S ROSA PARKS DAY
THE FOUNDER OF LITTLE CAESAR'S PAID HER RENT FOR MANY YEARS.

ROSA PARKS WAS BORN IN 1913   GEORGE ROMERO WAS BORN IN 1940

7 AM
. . . .
8 AM
. . . .
9 AM
. . . .
10 AM
. . . .
11 AM
. . . .
NOON
. . . .
1 PM
. . . .
2 PM
. . . .
3 PM
. . . .
4 PM
. . . .
5 PM
. . . .
6 PM

ON THIS DAY IN 2004: MARK ZUCKERBERG LAUNCHED FACEBOOK.

NOTES AND/OR LIMERICKS

YEAR: 35 DAYS DOWN, 330 DAYS LEFT (UNLESS IT'S A LEAP YEAR [35/331])

FEBRUARY 5

MONDAY	TUESDAY	WEDNESDAY	THURSDAY	FRIDAY	SATURDAY ☐
☐ TODAY	☐ TODAY	☐ TODAY	☐ TODAY	☐ TODAY	☐ SUNDAY

IT'S NATIONAL FART DAY

FART JOKES HAVE BEEN AROUND SINCE AT LEAST 1900 BC.

CHRIS PARNELL WAS BORN IN 1967   CRISTIANO RONALDO WAS BORN IN 1985

7 AM

8 AM

9 AM

10 AM

11 AM

NOON

1 PM

2 PM

3 PM

4 PM

5 PM

6 PM

ON THIS DAY IN 1971: THE APOLLO 14 ASTRONAUTS LANDED ON THE MOON.

BRILLIANT AND/OR TERRIBLE IDEAS

36 DAYS DOWN, 329 DAYS LEFT (UNLESS IT'S A LEAP YEAR [36/330])

YEAR:

FEBRUARY 6

MONDAY	TUESDAY	WEDNESDAY	THURSDAY	FRIDAY	SATURDAY ☐
. . . .	. . . .	. . . .	. . . .	. . . .	☐
☐ TODAY	☐ TODAY	☐ TODAY	☐ TODAY	☐ TODAY	☐ SUNDAY

IT'S NATIONAL FROZEN YOGURT DAY
THE FIRST SOFT-SERVE FROZEN YOGURT WAS CALLED 'FROGURT.'

KATHY NAJIMY WAS BORN IN 1957   BOB MARLEY WAS BORN IN 1945

7 AM
. . . .
                                                                              8 AM
. . . .
9 AM
. . . .
                                                                             10 AM
. . . .
11 AM
. . . .
                                                                              NOON
. . . .
1 PM
. . . .
                                                                              2 PM
. . . .
3 PM
. . . .
                                                                              4 PM
. . . .
5 PM
. . . .
                                                                              6 PM

ON THIS DAY IN 1943: FRANK SINATRA MADE HIS RADIO SINGING DEBUT.

NOTES AND/OR LIMERICKS

YEAR:	37 DAYS DOWN, 328 DAYS LEFT (UNLESS IT'S A LEAP YEAR [37/329])

FEBRUARY 7

MONDAY	TUESDAY	WEDNESDAY	THURSDAY	FRIDAY	SATURDAY ☐
☐ TODAY	☐ TODAY	☐ TODAY	☐ TODAY	☐ TODAY	☐ SUNDAY

WRITE IN THE DATES BELOW (AND SHADE IN TODAY)

IT'S NATIONAL PERIODIC TABLE DAY
LESS THAN THIRTY GRAMS OF FRANCIUM EXIST ON EARTH AT ANY TIME.

JAMES SPADER WAS BORN IN 1960   CHARLES DICKENS WAS BORN IN 1812

7 AM

8 AM

9 AM

10 AM

11 AM

NOON

1 PM

2 PM

3 PM

4 PM

5 PM

6 PM

ON THIS DAY IN 1985: 'NEW YORK, NEW YORK' BECAME NYC'S OFFICIAL SONG.

BRILLIANT AND/OR TERRIBLE IDEAS

38 DAYS DOWN, 327 DAYS LEFT (UNLESS IT'S A LEAP YEAR [38/328])   YEAR:

FEBRUARY 8

MONDAY	TUESDAY	WEDNESDAY	THURSDAY	FRIDAY	SATURDAY ☐
. . . .	. . . .	. . . .	. . . .	. . . .	☐
☐ TODAY	☐ TODAY	☐ TODAY	☐ TODAY	☐ TODAY	SUNDAY

IT'S OPERA DAY
THE FIRST OPERA WRITTEN WAS 'DAFNE' BY JACOPO PERI IN 1598.

JAMES DEAN WAS BORN IN 1931   SETH GREEN WAS BORN IN 197

7 AM
. . . .
                                                                              8 AM
. . . .
9 AM
. . . .
                                                                             10 AM
. . . .
11 AM
. . . .
                                                                              NOON
. . . .
1 PM
. . . .
                                                                              2 PM
. . . .
3 PM
. . . .
                                                                              4 PM
. . . .
5 PM
. . . .
                                                                              6 PM

ON THIS DAY IN 1992: THE SONG 'I'M TOO SEXY' TOPPED THE U.S. CHARTS.

NOTES AND/OR LIMERICKS

YEAR:	39 DAYS DOWN, 326 DAYS LEFT (UNLESS IT'S A LEAP YEAR [39/327])

FEBRUARY 9

MONDAY	TUESDAY	WEDNESDAY	THURSDAY	FRIDAY	SATURDAY ☐
☐ TODAY	☐ TODAY	☐ TODAY	☐ TODAY	☐ TODAY	☐ SUNDAY

IT'S PIZZA PIE DAY
AMERICANS EAT ABOUT 100 ACRES OF IT EVERY DAY.

(CUMULATIVELY—DON'T TRY TO DO THIS ALONE)

JOE PESCI WAS BORN IN 1943   TOM HIDDLESTON WAS BORN IN 1981

7 AM

8 AM

9 AM

10 AM

11 AM

NOON

1 PM

2 PM

3 PM

4 PM

5 PM

6 PM

ON THIS DAY IN 2020: 'PARASITE' WAS THE FIRST NON-ENGLISH FILM TO WIN BEST PICTURE.

BRILLIANT AND/OR TERRIBLE IDEAS

40 DAYS DOWN, 325 DAYS LEFT (UNLESS IT'S A LEAP YEAR [40/326])   YEAR:

FEBRUARY 10

MONDAY	TUESDAY	WEDNESDAY	THURSDAY	FRIDAY	SATURDAY ☐
. . . .	. . . .	. . . .	. . . .	. . . .	☐
☐ TODAY	☐ TODAY	☐ TODAY	☐ TODAY	☐ TODAY	SUNDAY

IT'S NATIONAL FLANNEL DAY
THE UNOFFICIAL UNIFORM OF THE 1990s.

EMMA ROBERTS WAS BORN IN 1991   CHLOË GRACE MORETZ WAS BORN IN 199

7 AM
. . . .
8 AM
. . . .
9 AM
. . . .
10 AM
. . . .
11 AM
. . . .
NOO
. . . .
1 PM
. . . .
2 P
. . . .
3 PM
. . . .
4 P
. . . .
5 PM
. . . .
6 P

ON THIS DAY IN 1940: 'TOM AND JERRY' MADE THEIR DEBUT.

NOTES AND/OR LIMERICKS

| YEAR: | 41 DAYS DOWN, 324 DAYS LEFT (UNLESS IT'S A LEAP YEAR [41/325]) |

FEBRUARY 11

MONDAY	TUESDAY	WEDNESDAY	THURSDAY	FRIDAY	SATURDAY ☐
. . . . ☐ TODAY	. . . . ☐ TODAY	. . . . ☐ TODAY	. . . . ☐ TODAY	. . . . ☐ TODAY	☐ SUNDAY

IT'S GET OUT YOUR GUITAR DAY
B.B. KING WAS INSPIRED TO NAME HIS GUITAR 'LUCILLE' FROM A BAR FIGHT.

JENNIFER ANISTON WAS BORN IN 1969   KELLY ROWLAND WAS BORN IN 1981

7 AM

8 AM

9 AM

10 AM

11 AM

NOON

1 PM

2 PM

3 PM

4 PM

5 PM

6 PM

ON THIS DAY IN 1990: NELSON MANDELA WAS RELEASED FROM PRISON.

BRILLIANT AND/OR TERRIBLE IDEAS

42 DAYS DOWN, 323 DAYS LEFT (UNLESS IT'S A LEAP YEAR [42/324])

YEAR:

FEBRUARY 12

MONDAY	TUESDAY	WEDNESDAY	THURSDAY	FRIDAY	SATURDAY ☐
. . . .	. . . .	. . . .	. . . .	. . . .	
☐ TODAY	☐ TODAY	☐ TODAY	☐ TODAY	☐ TODAY	☐ SUNDAY

IT'S NATIONAL LOST PENNY DAY
COPPER PENNIES (PRE-1983, TO BE EXACT) WILL REPEL SLUGS.

CHRISTINA RICCI WAS BORN IN 1980   ABRAHAM LINCOLN WAS BORN IN 1809

7 AM
. . . .
8 AM
. . . .
9 AM
. . . .
10 AM
. . . .
11 AM
. . . .
NOON
. . . .
1 PM
. . . .
2 PM
. . . .
3 PM
. . . .
4 PM
. . . .
5 PM
. . . .
6 PM

ON THIS DAY IN 2023: THE KANSAS CITY CHIEFS WON SUPERBOWL LVII.

NOTES AND/OR LIMERICKS

YEAR: 43 DAYS DOWN, 322 DAYS LEFT (UNLESS IT'S A LEAP YEAR [43/323])

FEBRUARY 13

MONDAY	TUESDAY	WEDNESDAY	THURSDAY	FRIDAY	SATURDAY ☐
. . . . ☐ TODAY	. . . . ☐ TODAY	. . . . ☐ TODAY	. . . . ☐ TODAY	. . . . ☐ TODAY	☐ SUNDAY

IT'S WORLD RADIO DAY

THE FIRST EVER RADIO JINGLE AIRED ON CHRISTMAS EVE 1926—IT WAS FOR WHEATIES.

ETER GABRIEL WAS BORN IN 1950   ROBBIE WILLIAMS WAS BORN IN 1974

7 AM

AM

9 AM

O AM

11 AM

OON

1 PM

PM

3 PM

PM

5 PM

PM

ON THIS DAY IN 2000: THE LAST 'PEANUTS' COMIC STRIP WAS PUBLISHED.

BRILLIANT AND/OR TERRIBLE IDEAS

44 DAYS DOWN, 321 DAYS LEFT (UNLESS IT'S A LEAP YEAR [44/322])

YEAR:

FEBRUARY 14

MONDAY	TUESDAY	WEDNESDAY	THURSDAY	FRIDAY	SATURDAY ☐
. . . . ☐ TODAY	. . . . ☐ TODAY	. . . . ☐ TODAY	. . . . ☐ TODAY	. . . . ☐ TODAY	☐ SUNDAY

IT'S VALENTINE'S DAY
OH, AND IT'S NATIONAL ORGAN DONOR DAY.

(A HEART SEEMS APPROPRIATE)

ROB THOMAS WAS BORN IN 1972   SIMON PEGG WAS BORN IN 197

7 AM
. . . .
8 A
. . . .
9 AM
. . . .
10 A
. . . .
11 AM
. . . .
NOO
. . . .
1 PM
. . . .
2 P
. . . .
3 PM
. . . .
4 P
. . . .
5 PM
. . . .
6 P

ON THIS DAY IN 2005: YOUTUBE WAS LAUNCHED (AND PEWDIEPIE WAS SIX).

NOTES AND/OR LIMERICKS

YEAR:	45 DAYS DOWN, 320 DAYS LEFT (UNLESS IT'S A LEAP YEAR [45/321])

FEBRUARY 15

MONDAY	TUESDAY	WEDNESDAY	THURSDAY	FRIDAY	SATURDAY ☐
. . . .	. . . .	. . . .	. . . .	. . . .	
☐ TODAY	☐ TODAY	☐ TODAY	☐ TODAY	☐ TODAY	☐ SUNDAY

IT'S NATIONAL HIPPO DAY
CONSIDERED THE WORLD'S DEADLIEST (AND HUNGRIEST) LAND MAMMAL.

CHRIS FARLEY WAS BORN IN 1964   SUSAN B. ANTHONY WAS BORN IN 1820

7 AM

AM

9 AM

O AM

11 AM

NOON

1 PM

PM

3 PM

PM

5 PM

PM

ON THIS DAY IN 1965: JOHN LENNON PASSED HIS DRIVING TEST.

BRILLIANT AND/OR TERRIBLE IDEAS

46 DAYS DOWN, 319 DAYS LEFT (UNLESS IT'S A LEAP YEAR [46/320])   YEAR:

FEBRUARY 16

WRITE IN THE DATES BELOW (AND SHADE IN TODAY)

MONDAY	TUESDAY	WEDNESDAY	THURSDAY	FRIDAY	SATURDAY ☐
. . . .	. . . .	. . . .	. . . .	. . . .	
☐ TODAY	☐ TODAY	☐ TODAY	☐ TODAY	☐ TODAY	☐ SUNDAY

IT'S NATIONAL INNOVATION DAY
SAMUEL THOMAS HOUGHTON RECEIVED A PATENT WHEN HE WAS ONLY 5 YEARS OLD.

ICE-T WAS BORN IN 1958   THE WEEKND WAS BORN IN 199

7 AM
. . . .
                                                                         8 A
. . . .
9 AM
. . . .
                                                                        10 A
. . . .
11 AM
. . . .
                                                                        NOO
. . . .
1 PM
. . . .
                                                                         2 P
. . . .
3 PM
. . . .
                                                                         4 P
. . . .
5 PM
. . . .
                                                                         6 P

ON THIS DAY IN 1968: THE FIRST 911 CALL WAS PLACED.

NOTES AND/OR LIMERICKS

YEAR:

47 DAYS DOWN, 318 DAYS LEFT (UNLESS IT'S A LEAP YEAR [47/319])

FEBRUARY 17

MONDAY	TUESDAY	WEDNESDAY	THURSDAY	FRIDAY	SATURDAY ☐
. . . . ☐ TODAY	. . . . ☐ TODAY	. . . . ☐ TODAY	. . . . ☐ TODAY	. . . . ☐ TODAY	☐ SUNDAY

IT'S RANDOM ACT OF KINDNESS DAY
IF YOU COULD 'RANDOMLY' SEND US COOKIES, THAT WOULD BE GREAT.

(1408 W. 12TH STREET, KANSAS CITY, MO 64101)

D SHEERAN WAS BORN IN 1991   MICHAEL JORDAN WAS BORN IN 1963

7 AM

AM

9 AM

O AM

11 AM

OON

1 PM

PM

3 PM

PM

5 PM

PM

ON THIS DAY IN 2014: JIMMY FALLON DEBUTED AS THE HOST OF 'THE TONIGHT SHOW.'

BRILLIANT AND/OR TERRIBLE IDEAS

48 DAYS DOWN, 317 DAYS LEFT (UNLESS IT'S A LEAP YEAR [48/318])   YEAR:

FEBRUARY 18

MONDAY	TUESDAY	WEDNESDAY	THURSDAY	FRIDAY	SATURDAY ☐
. . . .	. . . .	. . . .	. . . .	. . . .	
☐ TODAY	☐ TODAY	☐ TODAY	☐ TODAY	☐ TODAY	☐ SUNDAY

IT'S NATIONAL DRINK WINE DAY
ONE ACRE OF GRAPEVINES PRODUCES APPROX. 800 GALLONS OF WINE.

MOLLY RINGWALD WAS BORN IN 1968   DR. DRE WAS BORN IN 196

7 AM
. . . .
                                                                                            8 A
. . . .
9 AM
. . . .
                                                                                           10 A
. . . .
11 AM
. . . .
                                                                                            NOO
. . . .
1 PM
. . . .
                                                                                            2 P
. . . .
3 PM
. . . .
                                                                                            4 P
. . . .
5 PM
. . . .
                                                                                            6 P

ON THIS DAY IN 1986: THE FIRST ANTI-SMOKING AD AIRED ON TELEVISION.

NOTES AND/OR LIMERICKS

YEAR: 49 DAYS DOWN, 316 DAYS LEFT (UNLESS IT'S A LEAP YEAR [49/317])

FEBRUARY 19

MONDAY	TUESDAY	WEDNESDAY	THURSDAY	FRIDAY	SATURDAY ☐
☐ TODAY	☐ TODAY	☐ TODAY	☐ TODAY	☐ TODAY	☐ SUNDAY

IT'S INTERNATIONAL TUG-OF-WAR DAY
IT WAS AN OFFICIAL OLYMPIC SPORT FROM 1900 TO 1920.

ENICIO DEL TORO WAS BORN IN 1967   MILLIE BOBBY BROWN WAS BORN IN 2004

7 AM

AM

9 AM

AM

11 AM

OON

1 PM

PM

3 PM

PM

5 PM

PM

ON THIS DAY IN 1985: CHERRY COKE WAS INTRODUCED AS A FLAVOR BY COCA-COLA.

BRILLIANT AND/OR TERRIBLE IDEAS

50 DAYS DOWN, 315 DAYS LEFT (UNLESS IT'S A LEAP YEAR [50/316])   YEAR:

FEBRUARY 20

MONDAY	TUESDAY	WEDNESDAY	THURSDAY	FRIDAY	SATURDAY ☐
. . . .	. . . .	. . . .	. . . .	. . . .	
☐ TODAY	☐ TODAY	☐ TODAY	☐ TODAY	☐ TODAY	☐ SUNDAY

IT'S LOVE YOUR PET DAY
FLEAS CAN JUMP OVER 350 TIMES THEIR BODY LENGTH.

KURT COBAIN WAS BORN IN 1967   RIHANNA WAS BORN IN 198

7 AM
. . . .
                                                                          8 A
. . . .
9 AM
. . . .
                                                                          10 A
. . . .
11 AM
. . . .
                                                                          NOO
. . . .
1 PM
. . . .
                                                                          2 P
. . . .
3 PM
. . . .
                                                                          4 P
. . . .
5 PM
. . . .
                                                                          6 P

ON THIS DAY IN 1962: JOHN GLENN MADE THE FIRST AMERICAN ORBIT OF EARTH.

NOTES AND/OR LIMERICKS

YEAR: 51 DAYS DOWN, 314 DAYS LEFT (UNLESS IT'S A LEAP YEAR [51/315])

	WRITE IN THE DATES BELOW (AND SHADE IN TODAY)				
MONDAY	**TUESDAY**	**WEDNESDAY**	**THURSDAY**	**FRIDAY**	**SATURDAY** ☐
· · · · · · · · ☐ TODAY	· · · · · · · · ☐ TODAY	· · · · · · · · ☐ TODAY	· · · · · · · · ☐ TODAY	· · · · · · · · ☐ TODAY	☐ **SUNDAY**

IT'S NATIONAL STICKY BUN DAY
GERMAN SETTLERS IN PENNSYLVANIA ARE TO THANK FOR THEM.

NINA SIMONE WAS BORN IN 1933   ELLIOT PAGE WAS BORN IN 1987

7 AM

8 AM

9 AM

10 AM

11 AM

NOON

1 PM

2 PM

3 PM

4 PM

5 PM

6 PM

ON THIS DAY IN 1986: THE FIRST 'LEGEND OF ZELDA' GAME WAS RELEASED.

BRILLIANT AND/OR TERRIBLE IDEAS

52 DAYS DOWN, 313 DAYS LEFT (UNLESS IT'S A LEAP YEAR [52/314])   YEAR:

FEBRUARY 22

MONDAY	TUESDAY	WEDNESDAY	THURSDAY	FRIDAY	SATURDAY ☐
· · · · · · · ·	· · · · · · · ·	· · · · · · · ·	· · · · · · · ·	· · · · · · · ·	☐
☐ TODAY	☐ TODAY	☐ TODAY	☐ TODAY	☐ TODAY	SUNDAY

IT'S NATIONAL MARGARITA DAY
THE WORD MARGARITA MEANS 'DAISY' IN SPANISH.

STEVE IRWIN WAS BORN IN 1962   DREW BARRYMORE WAS BORN IN 197

7 AM
· ·
                                                                              8 A
· ·
9 AM
· ·
                                                                             10 A
11 AM
· ·
                                                                             NOO
· ·
1 PM
· ·
                                                                              2 P
· ·
3 PM
· ·
                                                                              4 P
· ·
5 PM
· ·
                                                                              6 P

ON THIS DAY IN 2009: 'SLUMDOG MILLIONAIRE' WON EIGHT OSCARS.

NOTES AND/OR LIMERICKS

YEAR:	53 DAYS DOWN, 312 DAYS LEFT (UNLESS IT'S A LEAP YEAR [53/313])

FEBRUARY 23

MONDAY	TUESDAY	WEDNESDAY	THURSDAY	FRIDAY	SATURDAY ☐
☐ TODAY	☐ TODAY	☐ TODAY	☐ TODAY	☐ TODAY	☐ SUNDAY

IT'S CURLING IS COOL DAY
CURLING STONES ARE MADE FROM A RARE TYPE OF MICRO-GRANITE.

EMILY BLUNT WAS BORN IN 1983   DAKOTA FANNING WAS BORN IN 1994

7 AM

8 AM

9 AM

10 AM

11 AM

NOON

1 PM

2 PM

3 PM

4 PM

5 PM

PM

ON THIS DAY IN 1997: NBC AIRED 'SCHINDLER'S LIST' COMPLETELY UNCENSORED.

BRILLIANT AND/OR TERRIBLE IDEAS

54 DAYS DOWN, 311 DAYS LEFT (UNLESS IT'S A LEAP YEAR [54/312])

YEAR:

FEBRUARY 24

IT'S WORLD BARTENDER DAY
GO HAVE A DRINK, IT'S THE LEAST YOU CAN DO.

STEVE JOBS WAS BORN IN 1955   BILLY ZANE WAS BORN IN 196●

7 AM
. . . .
                                                                                              8 AM
. . . .
9 AM
. . . .
                                                                                             10 AM
. . . .
11 AM
. . . .
                                                                                              NOON
. . . .
1 PM
. . . .
. . . .
                                                                                              2 PM
3 PM
. . . .
                                                                                              4 PM
. . . .
5 PM
. . . .
                                                                                              6 PM

ON THIS DAY IN 1972: RICHARD NIXON VISITED THE GREAT WALL OF CHINA.

NOTES AND/OR LIMERICKS

YEAR:	55 DAYS DOWN, 310 DAYS LEFT (UNLESS IT'S A LEAP YEAR [55/311])

FEBRUARY 25

MONDAY	TUESDAY	WEDNESDAY	THURSDAY	FRIDAY	SATURDAY ☐
. . . . ☐ TODAY	. . . . ☐ TODAY	. . . . ☐ TODAY	. . . . ☐ TODAY	. . . . ☐ TODAY	☐ SUNDAY

IT'S NATIONAL CLAM CHOWDER DAY
CLAMS WERE SOMETIMES USED AS CURRENCY BETWEEN NATIVE AMERICANS.

CHELSEA HANDLER WAS BORN IN 1975   GEORGE HARRISON WAS BORN IN 1943

7 AM

8 AM

9 AM

10 AM

11 AM

NOON

1 PM

2 PM

3 PM

4 PM

5 PM

6 PM

ON THIS DAY IN 1964: CASSIUS CLAY BECAME THE HEAVYWEIGHT CHAMPION.

BRILLIANT AND/OR TERRIBLE IDEAS

56 DAYS DOWN, 309 DAYS LEFT (UNLESS IT'S A LEAP YEAR [56/310])

YEAR:

FEBRUARY 26

MONDAY	TUESDAY	WEDNESDAY	THURSDAY	FRIDAY	SATURDAY ☐
. . . .	. . . .	. . . .	. . . .	. . . .	☐
☐ TODAY	☐ TODAY	☐ TODAY	☐ TODAY	☐ TODAY	☐ SUNDAY

IT'S NATIONAL PISTACHIO DAY
THEIR GREEN AND PURPLE HUES ARE DUE TO ANTIOXIDANTS.

JOHNNY CASH WAS BORN IN 1932   ERYKAH BADU WAS BORN IN 197

7 AM
. . . .
                                                                                         8 AM
. . . .
9 AM
. . . .
                                                                                        10 AM
. . . .
11 AM
. . . .
                                                                                         NOON
. . . .
1 PM
. . . .
                                                                                          2 PM
. . . .
3 PM
. . . .
                                                                                          4 PM
. . . .
5 PM
. . . .
                                                                                          6 P

ON THIS DAY IN 1970: NATIONAL PUBLIC RADIO WAS FOUNDED.

NOTES AND/OR LIMERICKS

| YEAR: | 57 DAYS DOWN, 308 DAYS LEFT (UNLESS IT'S A LEAP YEAR [57/309]) |

MONDAY	TUESDAY	WEDNESDAY	THURSDAY	FRIDAY	SATURDAY ☐
. . . . ☐ TODAY	. . . . ☐ TODAY	. . . . ☐ TODAY	. . . . ☐ TODAY	. . . . ☐ TODAY	☐ SUNDAY

WRITE IN THE DATES BELOW (AND SHADE IN TODAY)

IT'S NATIONAL RETRO DAY

EACH KOOSH BALL IS MADE FROM OVER 2,000 RUBBER STRANDS.

LIZABETH TAYLOR WAS BORN IN 1932   JOSH GROBAN WAS BORN IN 1981

7 AM

AM

9 AM

O AM

11 AM

OON

1 PM

PM

3 PM

PM

5 PM

PM

ON THIS DAY IN 1984: CARL LEWIS SET THE INDOOR LONG JUMP WORLD RECORD.

BRILLIANT AND/OR TERRIBLE IDEAS

58 DAYS DOWN, 307 DAYS LEFT (UNLESS IT'S A LEAP YEAR [58/308])

YEAR:

FEBRUARY 28

		WRITE IN THE DATES BELOW (AND SHADE IN TODAY)			
MONDAY	TUESDAY	WEDNESDAY	THURSDAY	FRIDAY	SATURDAY ☐
. . . .	. . . .	. . . .	. . . .	. . . .	
☐ TODAY	☐ TODAY	☐ TODAY	☐ TODAY	☐ TODAY	☐ SUNDAY

IT'S NATIONAL TOOTH FAIRY DAY
TOOTH ENAMEL IS THE HARDEST PART OF THE HUMAN BODY.

JOHN TURTURRO WAS BORN IN 1957   GILBERT GOTTFRIED WAS BORN IN 195

7 AM
. . . .
8 A
. . . .
9 AM
. . . .
10 A
. . . .
11 AM
. . . .
NOO
. . . .
1 PM
. . . .
2 P
. . . .
3 PM
. . . .
4 P
. . . .
5 PM
. . . .
6 P

ON THIS DAY IN 2016: LEONARDO DICAPRIO WON AN OSCAR. FINALLY.

NOTES AND/OR LIMERICKS

YEAR:	59 DAYS DOWN, 306 DAYS LEFT (UNLESS IT'S A LEAP YEAR [59/307])

FEBRUARY 29

WRITE IN THE DATES BELOW (AND SHADE IN TODAY)					
MONDAY	**TUESDAY**	**WEDNESDAY**	**THURSDAY**	**FRIDAY**	**SATURDAY** ☐
☐ TODAY	☐ TODAY	☐ TODAY	☐ TODAY	☐ TODAY	☐ **SUNDAY**

IT'S A LEAP DAY (DEPENDING ON THE YEAR)
OH, AND ALSO RARE DISEASE DAY. FUN.

JA RULE WAS BORN IN 1976   TONY ROBBINS WAS BORN IN 1960

7 AM

8 AM

9 AM

10 AM

11 AM

NOON

1 PM

2 PM

3 PM

4 PM

5 PM

6 PM

ON THIS DAY IN 1960: THE FIRST PLAYBOY CLUB OPENED IN CHICAGO.

BRILLIANT AND/OR TERRIBLE IDEAS

IT'S A LEAP YEAR, FINALLY—60 DAYS DOWN, 306 DAYS LEFT

YEAR:

IT'S OFFICIALLY

× MARCH ×

OF THE YEAR

☐ ☐ ☐ ☐

MONTH THREE

. . . .

. . . .

. . . .

MARCH AT A GLANCE

CONGRATULATIONS, YOU MADE IT
TO THE MONTH OF MARCH

✖

CELEBRATE, IT'S:

NATIONAL FROZEN FOOD MONTH

IRISH-AMERICAN HERITAGE MONTH

NATIONAL NOODLE MONTH

NATIONAL NUTRITION MONTH

NATIONAL CRAFT MONTH

OFFICIAL SYMBOLS:

BIRTHSTONE: AQUAMARINE

FLOWERS: DAFFODIL & JONQUIL

TREES: WEEPING WILLOW & OAK

PISCES (FEB 20 / MAR 20)

ARIES (MAR 21 / APR 20)

✖

A FEW DATES TO KNOW*
LIKE, IMPORTANT ONES.

✖

**DAYLIGHT
SAVING TIME**
FIRST SUNDAY OF MARCH

**INTERNATIONAL
WOMEN'S DAY**
MARCH 8TH

IDES OF MARCH
MARCH 15TH

ST. PATRICK'S DAY
MARCH 17TH

START OF SPRING
(SPRING EQUINOX)
MARCH 19TH (OR 20TH)

**INTL. DAY FOR THE
ELIMINATION OF RACIAL
DISCRIMINATION**
MARCH 21ST

HOLI
(HINDUISM)
ON THE FULL MOON DAY OF
PHALGUNA (OFTEN IN MARCH)

MARK YOUR CALENDAR ✖ IT'S RIGHT OVER THERE

---

*A DISCLAIMER OF SORTS

HEY THERE. WE HERE AT BRASS MONKEY LIKE TO JOKE AROUND...BUT WE ALSO WANT TO TAKE A MINUTE TO RECOGNIZE JUST A FEW OF THE MANY HOLIDAYS & EVENTS THAT ARE IMPORTANT TO OUR FRIENDS AROUND THE GLOBE (AND AT HOME). YOU MAY BE DIFFERENT THAN US. WE MAY HAVE NEVER MET. BUT WE LOVE YOU ALL THE SAME.

SO, WITH ALL OF THAT SAID, IF YOU HAVEN'T HEARD OF A DAY, PLEASE LOOK IT UP. LEARNING ABOUT AND APPRECIATING CULTURES DIFFERENT THAN YOURS IS REALLY IMPORTANT...WAY MORE SO THAN POSTING A FEW 'STRAWBERRY JAM DAY' VIDEOS ON TIKTOK. DON'T GET US WRONG, THERE IS PLENTY OF ROOM FOR BOTH. JUST PLEASE DO BOTH.

MARCH AT A GLANCE

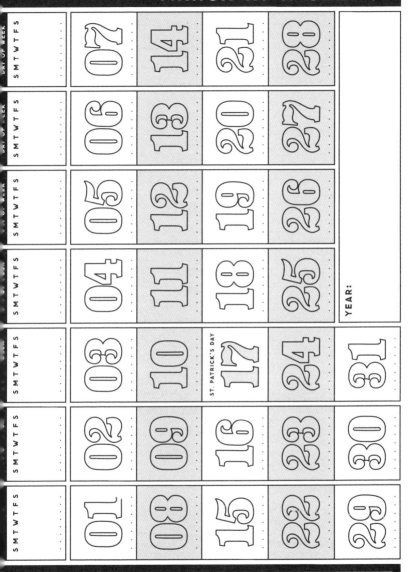

S M T W T F S	S M T W T F S	S M T W T F S	S M T W T F S	S M T W T F S	S M T W T F S	S M T W T F S
07	06	05	04	03	02	01
14	13	12	11	10	09	08
21	20	19	18	17 ST. PATRICK'S DAY	16	15
28	27	26	25	24	23	22
			YEAR:	31	30	29

WELL, WHAT ARE YOU WAITING FOR?

✕ START PLANNING. IN THE CALENDAR ABOVE, WE'VE MARKED THE MORE COMMON
U.S. HOLIDAYS ALREADY (THE ONES THAT ARE DATED, THAT IS). SO USE THE
LIST TO THE LEFT TO FILL IN THE REST...LIKE ALL OF THE ONES THAT CHANGE
DATES FROM YEAR TO YEAR, FOR EXAMPLE. ✕

LISTS, NOTES & MEMOIRS

MY DEGREES TO KEVIN BACON
OR SOME BORING TO-DO LIST

1
2
3
4
5
6
7
8
9
10
11
12
13
14

MY DEGREES TO ACTUAL BACON
OR A GROCERY LIST OR SOMETHING

1
2
3
4
5
6
7
8
9
10
11
12
13
14

THINGS I COULD COUNT TO FALL ASLEEP (BESIDES SHEEP)
USE FIGURE 1 FOR ANY NECESSARY VISUAL AIDS

FIG. 1

1   4
2   5
3   6

MARCH 1

MONDAY	TUESDAY	WEDNESDAY	THURSDAY	FRIDAY	SATURDAY ☐
☐ TODAY	☐ TODAY	☐ TODAY	☐ TODAY	☐ TODAY	☐ SUNDAY

WRITE IN THE DATES BELOW (AND SHADE IN TODAY)

IT'S NATIONAL PIG DAY
PIGS DON'T HAVE SWEAT GLANDS (HENCE THE MUD).

LUPITA NYONG'O WAS BORN IN 1983   TIM MCGRAW WAS BORN IN 1967

7 AM

8 AM

9 AM

10 AM

11 AM

NOON

1 PM

2 PM

3 PM

4 PM

5 PM

6 PM

ON THIS DAY IN 2020: MIKE AND MELANIE STARTED BRASS MONKEY.

BRILLIANT AND/OR TERRIBLE IDEAS

60 DAYS DOWN, 305 DAYS LEFT (UNLESS IT'S A LEAP YEAR [61/305])

YEAR:

MARCH 2

WRITE IN THE DATES BELOW (AND SHADE IN TODAY)

MONDAY	TUESDAY	WEDNESDAY	THURSDAY	FRIDAY	SATURDAY ☐
. . . .	. . . .	. . . .	. . . .	. . . .	☐
☐ TODAY	☐ TODAY	☐ TODAY	☐ TODAY	☐ TODAY	SUNDAY

IT'S OLD STUFF DAY
THAT UNIVERSAL 'THRIFT STORE SMELL' COMES FROM OUR BODY OILS.

REBEL WILSON WAS BORN IN 1980   REGGIE BUSH WAS BORN IN 1985

7 AM

8 AM

9 AM

10 AM

11 AM

NOON

1 PM

2 PM

3 PM

4 PM

5 PM

6 PM

ON THIS DAY IN 1933: 'KING KONG' PREMIERED IN NEW YORK CITY.

NOTES AND/OR LIMERICKS

YEAR: 61 DAYS DOWN, 304 DAYS LEFT (UNLESS IT'S A LEAP YEAR [62/304])

WRITE IN THE DATES BELOW (AND SHADE IN TODAY)					
MONDAY	**TUESDAY**	**WEDNESDAY**	**THURSDAY**	**FRIDAY**	**SATURDAY** ☐
☐ TODAY	☐ TODAY	☐ TODAY	☐ TODAY	☐ TODAY	☐ SUNDAY

IT'S NATIONAL COLD CUTS DAY
THE UNITED STATES EATS 300 MILLION SANDWICHES A DAY.

CAMILA CABELLO WAS BORN IN 1997   JESSICA BIEL WAS BORN IN 1982

7 AM

8 AM

9 AM

10 AM

11 AM

NOON

1 PM

2 PM

3 PM

4 PM

5 PM

6 PM

ON THIS DAY IN 1923: THE FIRST ISSUE OF 'TIME' MAGAZINE APPEARED ON NEWSSTANDS.

BRILLIANT AND/OR TERRIBLE IDEAS

62 DAYS DOWN, 303 DAYS LEFT (UNLESS IT'S A LEAP YEAR [63/303])   YEAR:

MARCH 4

WRITE IN THE DATES BELOW (AND SHADE IN TODAY)

MONDAY	TUESDAY	WEDNESDAY	THURSDAY	FRIDAY	SATURDAY ☐
. . . .	. . . .	. . . .	. . . .	. . . .	☐
☐ TODAY	☐ TODAY	☐ TODAY	☐ TODAY	☐ TODAY	☐ SUNDAY

IT'S NATIONAL GRAMMAR DAY
IT'S OK OXFORD COMMA, WE CARE.

CATHERINA O'HARA WAS BORN IN 1954   BROOKLYN BECKHAM WAS BORN IN 1999

7 AM

. . . .
8 AM

9 AM

. . . .
10 AM

11 AM

. . . .
NOON

1 PM

. . . .
2 PM

. . . .
3 PM

. . . .
4 PM

. . . .
5 PM

. . . .
6 PM

ON THIS DAY IN 1837: THE CITY OF CHICAGO WAS INCORPORATED.

NOTES AND/OR LIMERICKS

YEAR: | 63 DAYS DOWN, 302 DAYS LEFT (UNLESS IT'S A LEAP YEAR [64/302])

WRITE IN THE DATES BELOW (AND SHADE IN TODAY)					
MONDAY	**TUESDAY**	**WEDNESDAY**	**THURSDAY**	**FRIDAY**	**SATURDAY** ☐
☐ TODAY	☐ TODAY	☐ TODAY	☐ TODAY	☐ TODAY	☐ **SUNDAY**

IT'S NATIONAL ABSINTHE DAY
THE UNITED STATES RE-LEGALIZED ABSINTHE IN 2007.

EVA MENDES WAS BORN IN 1974   PENN JILLETTE WAS BORN IN 1955

7 AM

8 AM

9 AM

10 AM

11 AM

NOON

1 PM

2 PM

3 PM

4 PM

5 PM

6 PM

ON THIS DAY IN 2004: MARTHA STEWART WAS CONVICTED.

BRILLIANT AND/OR TERRIBLE IDEAS

64 DAYS DOWN, 301 DAYS LEFT (UNLESS IT'S A LEAP YEAR [65/301])   YEAR:

MARCH 6

IT'S NATIONAL FROZEN FOOD DAY
DESPITE THE MYTH, FREEZING FOOD DOESN'T REMOVE NUTRIENTS.

SHAQUILLE O'NEAL WAS BORN IN 1972   TYLER THE CREATOR WAS BORN IN 1991

7 AM

8 AM

9 AM

10 AM

11 AM

NOON

1 PM

2 PM

3 PM

4 PM

5 PM

6 PM

ON THIS DAY IN 2012: A 3-YEAR-OLD MCNUGGET SOLD FOR $8,100 ON EBAY.

NOTES AND/OR LIMERICKS

YEAR:	65 DAYS DOWN, 300 DAYS LEFT (UNLESS IT'S A LEAP YEAR [66/300])

WRITE IN THE DATES BELOW (AND SHADE IN TODAY)					
MONDAY	**TUESDAY**	**WEDNESDAY**	**THURSDAY**	**FRIDAY**	**SATURDAY** ☐
☐ TODAY	☐ TODAY	☐ TODAY	☐ TODAY	☐ TODAY	☐ **SUNDAY**

IT'S NATIONAL CEREAL DAY

ALL FROOT LOOPS ARE REALLY ONE FLAVOR KNOWN AS 'FROOT.'

RACHEL WEISZ WAS BORN IN 1970   BRYAN CRANSTON WAS BORN IN 1956

7 AM

8 AM

9 AM

10 AM

11 AM

NOON

1 PM

2 PM

3 PM

4 PM

5 PM

6 PM

ON THIS DAY IN 2016: PEYTON MANNING ANNOUNCED HIS RETIREMENT FROM THE NFL.

BRILLIANT AND/OR TERRIBLE IDEAS

66 DAYS DOWN, 299 DAYS LEFT (UNLESS IT'S A LEAP YEAR [67/299])

YEAR:

MARCH 8

IT'S NATIONAL PROOFREADING DAY
WHICH REMINDS US, WE REALLY TO HIRE ONE.

FREDDIE PRINZE JR. WAS BORN IN 1976   KAT VON D WAS BORN IN 1982

7 AM
. . . .
                                                                              8 AM
. . . .
9 AM
. . . .
                                                                              10 AM
. . . .
11 AM
. . . .
                                                                              NOON
. . . .
1 PM
. . . .
                                                                              2 PM
. . . .
3 PM
. . . .
                                                                              4 PM
. . . .
5 PM
. . . .
                                                                              6 PM

ON THIS DAY IN 1993: 'BEAVIS AND BUTT-HEAD' PREMIERED ON MTV.

NOTES AND/OR LIMERICKS

YEAR:	67 DAYS DOWN, 298 DAYS LEFT (UNLESS IT'S A LEAP YEAR [68/298])

MARCH 9

	WRITE IN THE DATES BELOW (AND SHADE IN TODAY)				
MONDAY	TUESDAY	WEDNESDAY	THURSDAY	FRIDAY	SATURDAY ☐
☐ TODAY	☐ TODAY	☐ TODAY	☐ TODAY	☐ TODAY	☐ SUNDAY

IT'S NATIONAL MEATBALL DAY
THE LARGEST MEATBALL EVER MADE WAS 1,707 POUNDS.

LIL' BOW WOW WAS BORN IN 1987   OSCAR ISAAC WAS BORN IN 1979

7 AM

8 AM

9 AM

10 AM

11 AM

NOON

1 PM

2 PM

3 PM

4 PM

5 PM

6 PM

ON THIS DAY IN 1997: THE NOTORIOUS B.I.G. WAS SHOT & KILLED AT A STOPLIGHT.

BRILLIANT AND/OR TERRIBLE IDEAS

68 DAYS DOWN, 297 DAYS LEFT (UNLESS IT'S A LEAP YEAR [69/297]) | YEAR:

MARCH 10

MONDAY	TUESDAY	WEDNESDAY	THURSDAY	FRIDAY	SATURDAY ☐
. . . .	. . . .	. . . .	. . . .	. . . .	☐
☐ TODAY	☐ TODAY	☐ TODAY	☐ TODAY	☐ TODAY	SUNDAY

IT'S INTERNATIONAL BAGPIPE DAY
BAGPIPES WERE ORIGINALLY USED TO SCARE ENEMIES DURING BATTLE.

CHUCK NORRIS WAS BORN IN 1940   JON HAMM WAS BORN IN 197

7 AM
. . . .
8 AM
. . . .
9 AM
. . . .
10 AM
. . . .
11 AM
. . . .
NOON
. . . .
1 PM
. . . .
2 PM
. . . .
3 PM
. . . .
4 PM
. . . .
5 PM
. . . .
6 P

ON THIS DAY IN 1977: ASTRONOMERS DISCOVERED THE RINGS OF URANUS.

NOTES AND/OR LIMERICKS

YEAR: 69 DAYS DOWN, 296 DAYS LEFT (UNLESS IT'S A LEAP YEAR [70/296])

MARCH 11

MONDAY	TUESDAY	WEDNESDAY	THURSDAY	FRIDAY	SATURDAY ☐
☐ TODAY	☐ TODAY	☐ TODAY	☐ TODAY	☐ TODAY	☐ SUNDAY

WRITE IN THE DATES BELOW (AND SHADE IN TODAY)

IT'S DEBUNKING DAY
WE'LL START: TWINKIES ONLY HAVE A SHELF LIFE OF 45 DAYS, SORRY.

HORA BIRCH WAS BORN IN 1982   JODIE COMER WAS BORN IN 1993

7 AM

AM

9 AM

10 AM

11 AM

NOON

1 PM

PM

3 PM

PM

5 PM

PM

ON THIS DAY IN 1997: PAUL MCCARTNEY WAS KNIGHTED BY QUEEN ELIZABETH II.

BRILLIANT AND/OR TERRIBLE IDEAS

70 DAYS DOWN, 295 DAYS LEFT (UNLESS IT'S A LEAP YEAR [71/295])   YEAR:

MARCH 12

MONDAY	TUESDAY	WEDNESDAY	THURSDAY	FRIDAY	SATURDAY
. . . .	. . . .	. . . .	. . . .	. . . .	
☐ TODAY	☐ TODAY	☐ TODAY	☐ TODAY	☐ TODAY	☐ SUNDAY

IT'S ALFRED HITCHCOCK DAY
MR. HITCHCOCK WAS AFRAID OF EGGS.

DAVE EGGERS WAS BORN IN 1970   AARON ECKHART WAS BORN IN 196

7 AM
. . . .
                                                                                          8 A
. . . .
9 AM
. . . .
                                                                                          10 A
. . . .
11 AM
. . . .
                                                                                          NOO
. . . .
1 PM
. . . .
                                                                                          2 P
. . . .
3 PM
. . . .
                                                                                          4 P
. . . .
5 PM
. . . .
                                                                                          6 P

ON THIS DAY IN 2023: BRENDAN FRASER AND KE HUY QUAN WON THEIR FIRST OSCARS.

NOTES AND/OR LIMERICKS

YEAR: _____   71 DAYS DOWN, 294 DAYS LEFT (UNLESS IT'S A LEAP YEAR [72/294])

MARCH 13

MONDAY	TUESDAY	WEDNESDAY	THURSDAY	FRIDAY	SATURDAY ☐
. . . . ☐ TODAY	. . . . ☐ TODAY	. . . . ☐ TODAY	. . . . ☐ TODAY	. . . . ☐ TODAY	☐ SUNDAY

IT'S NATIONAL EARMUFF DAY
CHESTER GREENWOOD WAS ONLY 15 WHEN HE INVENTED THEM.

WILLIAM H. MACY WAS BORN IN 1950   EMILE HIRSCH WAS BORN IN 1985

7 AM

AM

9 AM

0 AM

11 AM

OON

1 PM

PM

3 PM

PM

5 PM

PM

ON THIS DAY IN 2004: LUCIANO PAVAROTTI PERFORMED HIS LAST OPERA.

BRILLIANT AND/OR TERRIBLE IDEAS

72 DAYS DOWN, 293 DAYS LEFT (UNLESS IT'S A LEAP YEAR [73/293])

YEAR:

MARCH 14

MONDAY	TUESDAY	WEDNESDAY	THURSDAY	FRIDAY	SATURDAY
WRITE IN THE DATES BELOW (AND SHADE IN TODAY)

| ☐ TODAY | ☐ TODAY | ☐ TODAY | ☐ TODAY | ☐ TODAY | ☐ SUNDAY |

IT'S NATIONAL PI DAY
THE PERFECT DAY TO BE IRRATIONAL.

ALBERT EINSTEIN WAS BORN IN 1879   SIMONE BILES WAS BORN IN 199

7 AM

8 A

9 AM

10 A

11 AM

NOO

1 PM

2 P

3 PM

4 P

5 PM

6 P

ON THIS DAY IN 1972: MUDDY WATERS WON HIS FIRST GRAMMY.

NOTES AND/OR LIMERICKS

YEAR: 73 DAYS DOWN, 292 DAYS LEFT (UNLESS IT'S A LEAP YEAR [74/292])

WRITE IN THE DATES BELOW (AND SHADE IN TODAY)					
MONDAY	**TUESDAY**	**WEDNESDAY**	**THURSDAY**	**FRIDAY**	**SATURDAY** ☐
· · · · · · · · · · ☐ TODAY	· · · · · · · · · · ☐ TODAY	· · · · · · · · · · ☐ TODAY	· · · · · · · · · · ☐ TODAY	· · · · · · · · · · ☐ TODAY	☐ **SUNDAY**

IT'S THE IDES OF MARCH.
JULIUS CAESAR WAS ASSASSINATED IN 44 BC.

VA LONGORIA WAS BORN IN 1975   WILL.I.AM WAS BORN IN 1975

7 AM

AM

9 AM

0 AM

11 AM

OON

1 PM

PM

3 PM

PM

5 PM

PM

ON THIS DAY IN 1985: THE FIRST DOMAIN NAME WAS REGISTERED (SYMBOLICS.COM).

BRILLIANT AND/OR TERRIBLE IDEAS

74 DAYS DOWN, 291 DAYS LEFT (UNLESS IT'S A LEAP YEAR [75/291])

YEAR:

MARCH 16

WRITE IN THE DATES BELOW (AND SHADE IN TODAY)

MONDAY	TUESDAY	WEDNESDAY	THURSDAY	FRIDAY	SATURDAY ☐
. . . . ☐ TODAY	. . . . ☐ TODAY	. . . . ☐ TODAY	. . . . ☐ TODAY	. . . . ☐ TODAY	☐ SUNDAY

IT'S LIPS APPRECIATION DAY
HUMAN LIPS ARE 100 TIMES MORE SENSITIVE THAN FINGERTIPS.

ALAN TUDYK WAS BORN IN 1971   LAUREN GRAHAM WAS BORN IN 196

7 AM
. . . .
8 A
. . . .
9 AM
. . . .
10 A
. . . .
11 AM
. . . .
NOO
. . . .
1 PM
. . . .
2 P
. . . .
3 PM
. . . .
4 P
. . . .
5 PM
. . . .
6 P

ON THIS DAY IN 1994: TONYA HARDING PLEADED GUILTY TO THE ATTACK ON NANCY KERRIGAN.

NOTES AND/OR LIMERICKS

YEAR: 75 DAYS DOWN, 290 DAYS LEFT (UNLESS IT'S A LEAP YEAR [76/290])

MARCH 17

MONDAY	TUESDAY	WEDNESDAY	THURSDAY	FRIDAY	SATURDAY ☐
. . . . ☐ TODAY	. . . . ☐ TODAY	. . . . ☐ TODAY	. . . . ☐ TODAY	. . . . ☐ TODAY	☐ SUNDAY

IT'S ST. PATRICK'S DAY
CHICAGO WAS FIRST TO SUCCESSFULLY DYE A RIVER GREEN FOR THE HOLIDAY.

NAT KING COLE WAS BORN IN 1919   ROB LOWE WAS BORN IN 1964

7 AM

8 AM

9 AM

10 AM

11 AM

NOON

1 PM

2 PM

3 PM

4 PM

5 PM

6 PM

ON THIS DAY IN 1762: NYC HELD ITS FIRST ST. PATRICK'S DAY PARADE.

BRILLIANT AND/OR TERRIBLE IDEAS

76 DAYS DOWN, 289 DAYS LEFT (UNLESS IT'S A LEAP YEAR [77/289])   YEAR:

MARCH 18

WRITE IN THE DATES BELOW (AND SHADE IN TODAY)

MONDAY	TUESDAY	WEDNESDAY	THURSDAY	FRIDAY	SATURDAY ☐
. . . . ☐ TODAY	. . . . ☐ TODAY	. . . . ☐ TODAY	. . . . ☐ TODAY	. . . . ☐ TODAY	☐ SUNDAY

IT'S NATIONAL SLOPPY JOE DAY
'MANWICH' WAS INVENTED AS A MORE CONVENIENT WAY TO MAKE SLOPPY JOES.

QUEEN LATIFAH WAS BORN IN 1970   LILLY COLLINS WAS BORN IN 198

7 AM

. . . .

8 AM

. . . .

9 AM

. . . .

10 A

. . . .

11 AM

. . . .

NOO

. . . .

1 PM

. . . .

2 P

. . . .

3 PM

. . . .

4 P

. . . .

5 PM

. . . .

6 P

ON THIS DAY IN 1992: DONNA SUMMER RECEIVED A STAR ON HOLLYWOOD'S WALK OF FAME.

NOTES AND/OR LIMERICKS

YEAR: 77 DAYS DOWN, 288 DAYS LEFT (UNLESS IT'S A LEAP YEAR [78/288])

MARCH 19

MONDAY	TUESDAY	WEDNESDAY	THURSDAY	FRIDAY	SATURDAY ☐
. . . .	. . . .	. . . .	. . . .	. . . .	
☐ TODAY	☐ TODAY	☐ TODAY	☐ TODAY	☐ TODAY	☐ SUNDAY

IT'S NATIONAL POULTRY DAY
CHICKENS CAN REMEMBER UP TO 100 FACES.

BRUCE WILLIS WAS BORN IN 1955   GLENN CLOSE WAS BORN IN 1947

7 AM

8 AM

9 AM

10 AM

11 AM

NOON

1 PM

2 PM

3 PM

4 PM

5 PM

6 PM

ON THIS DAY IN 1918: CONGRESS APPROVED DAYLIGHT SAVING TIME. JERKS.

BRILLIANT AND/OR TERRIBLE IDEAS

78 DAYS DOWN, 287 DAYS LEFT (UNLESS IT'S A LEAP YEAR [79/287])   YEAR:

MARCH 20

IT'S ALIEN ABDUCTION DAY
THE MOVIE 'ALIEN' WAS ORIGINALLY TITLED 'STAR BEAST.'

FRED ROGERS WAS BORN IN 1928   SPIKE LEE WAS BORN IN 195

7 AM

8 AM

9 AM

10 AM

11 AM

NOON

1 PM

2 PM

3 PM

4 PM

5 PM

6 PM

ON THIS DAY IN 1969: JOHN LENNON MARRIED YOKO ONO.

NOTES AND/OR LIMERICKS

YEAR: 79 DAYS DOWN, 286 DAYS LEFT (UNLESS IT'S A LEAP YEAR [80/286])

MARCH 21

MONDAY	TUESDAY	WEDNESDAY	THURSDAY	FRIDAY	SATURDAY ☐
. . . .	. . . .	. . . .	. . . .	. . . .	
☐ TODAY	☐ TODAY	☐ TODAY	☐ TODAY	☐ TODAY	☐ SUNDAY

IT'S NATIONAL PUPPETEER DAY
SHARI LEWIS HAD A LIFE-SIZE PUPPET OF FRED ASTAIRE.

MATTHEW BRODERICK WAS BORN IN 1962   ROSIE O'DONNELL WAS BORN IN 1962

7 AM

8 AM

9 AM

10 AM

11 AM

NOON

1 PM

2 PM

3 PM

4 PM

5 PM

6 PM

ON THIS DAY IN 2006: TWITTER WAS FOUNDED.

BRILLIANT AND/OR TERRIBLE IDEAS

80 DAYS DOWN, 285 DAYS LEFT (UNLESS IT'S A LEAP YEAR [81/285])   YEAR:

MARCH 22

IT'S NATIONAL GOOF-OFF DAY
IF WE MADE AN OFF-BRAND 'GOO GONE,' WE'D CALL IT GOOF OFF.

CONSTANCE WU WAS BORN IN 1982   REESE WITHERSPOON WAS BORN IN 1976

7 AM

. . . .

8 AM

. . . .

9 AM

. . . .

10 AM

. . . .

11 AM

. . . .

NOON

. . . .

1 PM

. . . .

2 PM

. . . .

3 PM

. . . .

4 PM

. . . .

5 PM

. . . .

6 PM

ON THIS DAY IN 1894: THE FIRST STANLEY CUP CHAMPIONSHIP WAS PLAYED.

NOTES AND/OR LIMERICKS

YEAR: 81 DAYS DOWN, 284 DAYS LEFT (UNLESS IT'S A LEAP YEAR [82/284])

MONDAY	TUESDAY	WEDNESDAY	THURSDAY	FRIDAY	SATURDAY ☐
. . . . ☐ TODAY	. . . . ☐ TODAY	. . . . ☐ TODAY	. . . . ☐ TODAY	. . . . ☐ TODAY	☐ SUNDAY

WRITE IN THE DATES BELOW (AND SHADE IN TODAY)

IT'S NATIONAL PUPPY DAY
THEY CAN SPEND 15 TO 20 HOURS A DAY SLEEPING.

CHAKA KHAN WAS BORN IN 1953   RANDALL PARK WAS BORN IN 1974

7 AM

8 AM

9 AM

10 AM

11 AM

NOON

1 PM

2 PM

3 PM

4 PM

5 PM

6 PM

ON THIS DAY IN 1987: THE SOAP OPERA 'THE BOLD AND THE BEAUTIFUL' PREMIERED.

BRILLIANT AND/OR TERRIBLE IDEAS

82 DAYS DOWN, 283 DAYS LEFT (UNLESS IT'S A LEAP YEAR [83/283])

YEAR:

MARCH 24

WRITE IN THE DATES BELOW (AND SHADE IN TODAY)

MONDAY	TUESDAY	WEDNESDAY	THURSDAY	FRIDAY	SATURDAY ☐
. . . .	. . . .	. . . .	. . . .	. . . .	
☐ TODAY	☐ TODAY	☐ TODAY	☐ TODAY	☐ TODAY	☐ SUNDAY

IT'S NATIONAL COCKTAIL DAY
THE MOVIE 'COCKTAIL' WAS REWRITTEN 40 TIMES.

JIM PARSONS WAS BORN IN 1973   HARRY HOUDINI WAS BORN IN 187

7 AM
. . . .
8 AM
. . . .
9 AM
. . . .
10 AM
. . . .
11 AM
. . . .
NOO
. . . .
1 PM
. . . .
2 PM
. . . .
3 PM
. . . .
4 P
. . . .
5 PM
. . . .
6 P

ON THIS DAY IN 1958: ELVIS PRESLEY JOINED THE UNITED STATES ARMY.

NOTES AND/OR LIMERICKS

YEAR: 83 DAYS DOWN, 282 DAYS LEFT (UNLESS IT'S A LEAP YEAR [84/282])

MARCH 25

WRITE IN THE DATES BELOW (AND SHADE IN TODAY)

MONDAY	TUESDAY	WEDNESDAY	THURSDAY	FRIDAY	SATURDAY ☐
. . . . ☐ TODAY	. . . . ☐ TODAY	. . . . ☐ TODAY	. . . . ☐ TODAY	. . . . ☐ TODAY	☐ SUNDAY

IT'S INTERNATIONAL WAFFLE DAY
NIKE'S FIRST RUNNING SHOES WERE MADE IN A WAFFLE IRON.

RETHA FRANKLIN WAS BORN IN 1942   ELTON JOHN WAS BORN IN 1947

7 AM

. . . .

AM

. . . .

9 AM

. . . .

O AM

. . . .

11 AM

. . . .

OON

. . . .

1 PM

. . . .

PM

. . . .

3 PM

. . . .

PM

. . . .

5 PM

. . . .

PM

ON THIS DAY IN 2001: BJÖRK WORE A SWAN DRESS TO THE OSCARS.

BRILLIANT AND/OR TERRIBLE IDEAS

84 DAYS DOWN, 281 DAYS LEFT (UNLESS IT'S A LEAP YEAR [85/281])

YEAR:

MARCH 26

WRITE IN THE DATES BELOW (AND SHADE IN TODAY)

MONDAY	TUESDAY	WEDNESDAY	THURSDAY	FRIDAY	SATURDAY ☐
. . . . ☐ TODAY	. . . . ☐ TODAY	. . . . ☐ TODAY	. . . . ☐ TODAY	. . . . ☐ TODAY	☐ SUNDAY

IT'S NATIONAL MAKE UP YOUR OWN HOLIDAY DAY
AKA: 'GIVE MELANIE BRIDGES TONS OF COMPLIMENTS DAY.'

(MELANIE@BRASSMONKEYGOODS.COM)

DIANA ROSS WAS BORN IN 1944   KIERA KNIGHTLEY WAS BORN IN 198

7 AM
. . . .
                                                                                    8 A
. . . .
9 AM
. . . .
                                                                                   10 A
. . . .
11 AM
. . . .
                                                                                   NOO
. . . .
1 PM
. . . .
                                                                                    2 P
. . . .
3 PM
. . . .
                                                                                    4 P
. . . .
5 PM
. . . .
                                                                                    6 P

ON THIS DAY IN 1953: JONAS SALK ANNOUNCED THE POLIO VACCINE.

NOTES AND/OR LIMERICKS

YEAR: 85 DAYS DOWN, 280 DAYS LEFT (UNLESS IT'S A LEAP YEAR [86/280])

MARCH 27

|---|---|---|---|---|---|
| MONDAY | TUESDAY | WEDNESDAY | THURSDAY | FRIDAY | SATURDAY ☐ |

WRITE IN THE DATES BELOW (AND SHADE IN TODAY)

☐ TODAY ☐ TODAY ☐ TODAY ☐ TODAY ☐ TODAY ☐ SUNDAY

IT'S INTERNATIONAL SCRIBBLE DAY
IF ONLY YOU HAD A PLACE TO DO THAT.

MARIAH CAREY WAS BORN IN 1969   MANUEL NEUER WAS BORN IN 1986

7 AM

8 AM

9 AM

10 AM

11 AM

NOON

1 PM

2 PM

3 PM

4 PM

5 PM

6 PM

ON THIS DAY IN 1948: BILLIE HOLIDAY PERFORMED AT CARNEGIE HALL.

BRILLIANT AND/OR TERRIBLE IDEAS

86 DAYS DOWN, 279 DAYS LEFT (UNLESS IT'S A LEAP YEAR [87/279])

YEAR:

MARCH 28

MONDAY	TUESDAY	WEDNESDAY	THURSDAY	FRIDAY	SATURDAY ☐
. . . .	. . . .	. . . .	. . . .	. . . .	
☐ TODAY	☐ TODAY	☐ TODAY	☐ TODAY	☐ TODAY	☐ SUNDAY

IT'S NATIONAL SOMETHING ON A STICK DAY
EACH SUMMER, 50% OF ALL MARSHMALLOWS SOLD ARE ROASTED.

LADY GAGA WAS BORN IN 1986   REBA MCENTIRE WAS BORN IN 195

7 AM

8 A

9 AM

10 A

11 AM

NOO

1 PM

2 P

3 PM

4 P

5 PM

6 P

ON THIS DAY IN 1995: JULIA ROBERTS AND LYLE LOVETT SPLIT UP.

NOTES AND/OR LIMERICKS

YEAR: 87 DAYS DOWN, 278 DAYS LEFT (UNLESS IT'S A LEAP YEAR [88/278])

WRITE IN THE DATES BELOW (AND SHADE IN TODAY)

MONDAY	TUESDAY	WEDNESDAY	THURSDAY	FRIDAY	SATURDAY ☐
☐ TODAY	☐ TODAY	☐ TODAY	☐ TODAY	☐ TODAY	☐ SUNDAY

IT'S NATIONAL MARBLES DAY
IN NORTH ENGLAND, THEY'RE CALLED 'TAWS' AND 'BOTTLE WASHERS.'

AMY SEDARIS WAS BORN IN 1961   LUCY LAWLESS WAS BORN IN 1968

7 AM

8 AM

9 AM

10 AM

11 AM

NOON

1 PM

2 PM

3 PM

4 PM

5 PM

6 PM

ON THIS DAY IN 2007: RIHANNA RELEASED THE SONG 'UMBRELLA.'

BRILLIANT AND/OR TERRIBLE IDEAS

88 DAYS DOWN, 277 DAYS LEFT (UNLESS IT'S A LEAP YEAR [89/277])

YEAR:

MARCH 30

WRITE IN THE DATES BELOW (AND SHADE IN TODAY)

MONDAY	TUESDAY	WEDNESDAY	THURSDAY	FRIDAY	SATURDAY ☐
. . . .	. . . .	. . . .	. . . .	. . . .	
☐ TODAY	☐ TODAY	☐ TODAY	☐ TODAY	☐ TODAY	☐ SUNDAY

IT'S NATIONAL FOLDING LAUNDRY DAY
THE AVERAGE AMERICAN FAMILY WASHES 8 TO 10 LOADS EVERY WEEK.

VINCENT VAN GOGH WAS BORN IN 1853   CELINE DION WAS BORN IN 1968

7 AM

8 AM

9 AM

10 AM

11 AM

NOON

1 PM

2 PM

3 PM

4 PM

5 PM

6 PM

ON THIS DAY IN 1987: VAN GOGH'S 'SUNFLOWERS' PAINTING SOLD FOR $39.7M.

NOTES AND/OR LIMERICKS

YEAR: 89 DAYS DOWN, 276 DAYS LEFT (UNLESS IT'S A LEAP YEAR [90/276])

WRITE IN THE DATES BELOW (AND SHADE IN TODAY)					
MONDAY	**TUESDAY**	**WEDNESDAY**	**THURSDAY**	**FRIDAY**	**SATURDAY** ☐
· · · · · · · · ☐ TODAY	· · · · · · · · ☐ TODAY	· · · · · · · · ☐ TODAY	· · · · · · · · ☐ TODAY	· · · · · · · · ☐ TODAY	☐ **SUNDAY**

IT'S NATIONAL BUNSEN BURNER DAY

BOTH HOWIE MANDEL & DAVE COULIER HAVE VOICED THE MUPPET, BUNSEN.

RHEA PERLMAN WAS BORN IN 1948   CHRISTOPHER WALKEN WAS BORN IN 1943

7 AM

8 AM

9 AM

10 AM

11 AM

NOON

1 PM

2 PM

3 PM

4 PM

5 PM

6 PM

ON THIS DAY IN 1988: TONI MORRISON'S 'BELOVED' WON A PULITZER PRIZE.

BRILLIANT AND/OR TERRIBLE IDEAS

90 DAYS DOWN, 275 DAYS LEFT (UNLESS IT'S A LEAP YEAR [91/275])   YEAR:

DERIVED FROM THE LATIN WORD APERIRE, WHICH MEANS TO OPEN.

IT'S OFFICIALLY

× APRIL ×

OF THE YEAR

☐ ☐ ☐ ☐

MONTH FOUR

. . . .

. . . .

. . . .

NAMED AFTER THE GREEK GODDESS OF LOVE, APHRODITE.

CONGRATULATIONS, YOU MADE IT
TO THE MONTH OF APRIL

✖

CELEBRATE, IT'S:

NATIONAL WELDING MONTH

KEEP AMERICA BEAUTIFUL MONTH

NATIONAL SOFT PRETZEL MONTH

INTERNATIONAL GUITAR MONTH

NATIONAL HUMOR MONTH

OFFICIAL SYMBOLS:

BIRTHSTONE: DIAMOND

FLOWERS: DAISY & SWEET PEA

TREES: ROWAN, MAPLE, & WALNUT

ARIES (MAR 21 / APR 19)

TAURUS (APR 20 / MAY 20)

✖

A FEW DATES TO KNOW*
LIKE, IMPORTANT ONES.

✖

APRIL FOOLS' DAY
APRIL 1ST

NATIONAL TARTAN DAY
APRIL 6TH

PASSOVER BEGINS
(JUDAISM)
15TH DAY OF THE HEBREW MONTH
OF NISAN (MARCH OR APRIL)

HANUMAN JAYANTI
(HINDUISM)
15TH DAY OF SHUKLA PAKSHA
(WAXING MOON PHASE) DURING THE
MONTH OF CHITRA (OFTEN APRIL)

MARK YOUR CALENDAR

EASTER
FIRST SUNDAY AFTER
THE FULL MOON
(ON OR AFTER MARCH 21ST)

THERAVADA NEW YEAR
(BUDDHISM)
FIRST FULL MOON OF APRIL

PALM SUNDAY
THE SUNDAY BEFORE EASTER
(COULD FALL IN MARCH)

DAY OF SILENCE
SECOND FRIDAY OF APRIL
(WITH EXCEPTIONS)

IT'S RIGHT OVER THERE

✖

*A DISCLAIMER OF SORTS

HEY THERE. WE HERE AT BRASS MONKEY LIKE TO JOKE AROUND...BUT WE ALSO WANT TO TAKE A MINUTE TO RECOGNIZE JUST A FEW OF THE MANY HOLIDAYS & EVENTS THAT ARE IMPORTANT TO OUR FRIENDS AROUND THE GLOBE (AND AT HOME). YOU MAY BE DIFFERENT THAN US. WE MAY HAVE NEVER MET. BUT WE LOVE YOU ALL THE SAME.

SO, WITH ALL OF THAT SAID, IF YOU HAVEN'T HEARD OF A DAY, PLEASE LOOK IT UP. LEARNING ABOUT AND APPRECIATING CULTURES DIFFERENT THAN YOURS IS REALLY IMPORTANT...WAY MORE SO THAN POSTING A FEW 'STRAWBERRY JAM DAY' VIDEOS ON TIKTOK. DON'T GET US WRONG, THERE IS PLENTY OF ROOM FOR BOTH. JUST PLEASE DO BOTH.

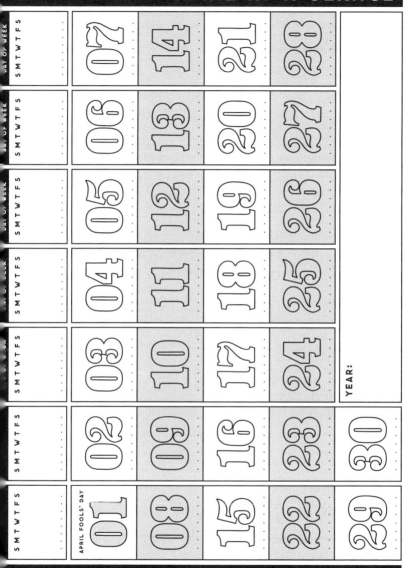

DAY OF WEEK S M T W T F S					YEAR:
APRIL FOOLS' DAY 01	02	03	04	05	06	07
08	09	10	11	12	13	14
15	16	17	18	19	20	21
22	23	24	25	26	27	28
29	30					

WELL, WHAT ARE YOU WAITING FOR?

✗ START PLANNING. IN THE CALENDAR ABOVE, WE'VE MARKED THE MORE COMMON U.S. HOLIDAYS ALREADY (THE ONES THAT ARE DATED, THAT IS). SO USE THE LIST TO THE LEFT TO FILL IN THE REST...LIKE ALL OF THE ONES THAT CHANGE DATES FROM YEAR TO YEAR, FOR EXAMPLE. ✗

LISTS, NOTES & MEMOIRS

KNOCK-OFF BRANDS
OR SOME BORING TO-DO LIST

1
2
3
4
5
6
7
8
9
10
11
12
13
14

KNOCK-OFF BANDS
OR A GROCERY LIST OR SOMETHING

1
2
3
4
5
6
7
8
9
10
11
12
13
14

TATTOO IDEAS THAT I'LL PROBABLY REGRET LATER
USE FIGURE 1 FOR ANY NECESSARY VISUAL AIDS

FIG. 1

1
2
3

4
5
6

APRIL 1

WRITE IN THE DATES BELOW (AND SHADE IN TODAY)					
MONDAY	TUESDAY	WEDNESDAY	THURSDAY	FRIDAY	SATURDAY ☐
. . . . ☐ TODAY	. . . . ☐ TODAY	. . . . ☐ TODAY	. . . . ☐ TODAY	. . . . ☐ TODAY	☐ SUNDAY

IT'S APRIL FOOLS' DAY
OH, AND ALSO NATIONAL TROMBONE PLAYERS DAY.

DEBBIE REYNOLDS WAS BORN IN 1932   DAVID OYELOWO WAS BORN IN 1976

7 AM

8 AM

9 AM

10 AM

11 AM

NOON

1 PM

2 PM

3 PM

4 PM

5 PM

PM

ON THIS DAY IN 2007: A PYTHON GOT LOOSE IN GOOGLE'S NYC OFFICE.

BRILLIANT AND/OR TERRIBLE IDEAS

91 DAYS DOWN, 274 DAYS LEFT (UNLESS IT'S A LEAP YEAR [92/274])   YEAR:

APRIL 2

WRITE IN THE DATES BELOW (AND SHADE IN TODAY)

MONDAY	TUESDAY	WEDNESDAY	THURSDAY	FRIDAY	SATURDAY ☐
. . . .	. . . .	. . . .	. . . .	. . . .	☐
☐ TODAY	☐ TODAY	☐ TODAY	☐ TODAY	☐ TODAY	☐ SUNDAY

IT'S NATIONAL FERRET DAY
A GROUP OF FERRET'S IS CALLED A BUSINESS.

MARVIN GAYE WAS BORN IN 1939 — MICHAEL FASSBENDER WAS BORN IN 1977

7 AM

8 AM

9 AM

10 AM

11 AM

NOON

1 PM

2 PM

3 PM

4 PM

5 PM

6 PM

ON THIS DAY IN 1986: ED KOCH SIGNED THE NYC GAY RIGHTS BILL INTO EFFECT.

NOTES AND/OR LIMERICKS

YEAR: | 92 DAYS DOWN, 273 DAYS LEFT (UNLESS IT'S A LEAP YEAR [93/273])

APRIL 3

WRITE IN THE DATES BELOW (AND SHADE IN TODAY)					
MONDAY	TUESDAY	WEDNESDAY	THURSDAY	FRIDAY	SATURDAY ☐
. . . .	. . . .	. . . .	. . . .	. . . .	
☐ TODAY	☐ TODAY	☐ TODAY	☐ TODAY	☐ TODAY	☐ SUNDAY

IT'S NATIONAL TWEED DAY
THE FABRIC USED TO BE CALLED 'TWEEL' AND WAS CHANGED BY ACCIDENT.

EDDIE MURPHY WAS BORN IN 1961   JANE GOODALL WAS BORN IN 1934

7 AM

8 AM

9 AM

10 AM

11 AM

NOON

1 PM

2 PM

3 PM

4 PM

5 PM

6 PM

ON THIS DAY IN 1953: THE FIRST CELL PHONE CALL WAS MADE.

BRILLIANT AND/OR TERRIBLE IDEAS

93 DAYS DOWN, 272 DAYS LEFT (UNLESS IT'S A LEAP YEAR [94/273])   YEAR:

APRIL 4

IT'S INTERNATIONAL CARROT DAY
CARROTS WERE FIRST GROWN AS MEDICINE, NOT FOOD.

MAYA ANGELOU WAS BORN IN 1928   HEATH LEDGER WAS BORN IN 1979

7 AM
. . . .
8 AM
. . . .
9 AM
. . . .
10 AM
. . . .
11 AM
. . . .
NOON
. . . .
1 PM
. . . .
2 PM
. . . .
3 PM
. . . .
4 PM
. . . .
5 PM
. . . .
6 PM

ON THIS DAY IN 1968: MARTIN LUTHER KING JR. WAS ASSASSINATED.

NOTES AND/OR LIMERICKS

YEAR: 94 DAYS DOWN, 271 DAYS LEFT (UNLESS IT'S A LEAP YEAR [95/271])

APRIL 5

MONDAY	TUESDAY	WEDNESDAY	THURSDAY	FRIDAY	SATURDAY ☐
☐ TODAY	☐ TODAY	☐ TODAY	☐ TODAY	☐ TODAY	☐ SUNDAY

WRITE IN THE DATES BELOW (AND SHADE IN TODAY)

IT'S BELL BOTTOMS DAY
SAILORS IN THE U.S. NAVY WORE THEM AS EARLY AS THE 19TH CENTURY.

LILY JAMES WAS BORN IN 1989   PHARREL WILLIAMS WAS BORN IN 1973

7 AM

8 AM

9 AM

10 AM

11 AM

NOON

1 PM

2 PM

3 PM

4 PM

5 PM

6 PM

ON THIS DAY IN 1994: KURT COBAIN COMMITTED SUICIDE.

BRILLIANT AND/OR TERRIBLE IDEAS

95 DAYS DOWN, 270 DAYS LEFT (UNLESS IT'S A LEAP YEAR [96/270])

YEAR:

APRIL 6

WRITE IN THE DATES BELOW (AND SHADE IN TODAY)

MONDAY	TUESDAY	WEDNESDAY	THURSDAY	FRIDAY	SATURDAY ☐
. . . . ☐ TODAY	. . . . ☐ TODAY	. . . . ☐ TODAY	. . . . ☐ TODAY	. . . . ☐ TODAY	☐ SUNDAY

IT'S NATIONAL SIAMESE CAT DAY
JAMES DEAN WAS GIVEN ONE BY ELIZABETH TAYLOR.

PAUL RUDD WAS BORN IN 1969   ZACH BRAFF WAS BORN IN 197

7 AM
. . . .
                                                                              8 AM
. . . .
9 AM
. . . .
                                                                             10 AM
. . . .
11 AM
. . . .
                                                                              NOO
. . . .
1 PM
. . . .
                                                                              2 PI
. . . .
3 PM
. . . .
                                                                              4 P
. . . .
5 PM
. . . .
                                                                              6 P

ON THIS DAY IN 1957: TROLLEY CARS STOPPED SERVICE IN NYC.

NOTES AND/OR LIMERICKS

YEAR: 96 DAYS DOWN, 269 DAYS LEFT (UNLESS IT'S A LEAP YEAR [97/269])

WRITE IN THE DATES BELOW (AND SHADE IN TODAY)					
MONDAY	**TUESDAY**	**WEDNESDAY**	**THURSDAY**	**FRIDAY**	**SATURDAY** ☐
. . . .	. . . .	. . . .	. . . .	. . . .	
☐ TODAY	☐ TODAY	☐ TODAY	☐ TODAY	☐ TODAY	☐ **SUNDAY**

IT'S NATIONAL BEER DAY

HUMANS CONSUME OVER 50 BILLION GALLONS OF BEER EVERY YEAR.

ILLIE HOLIDAY WAS BORN IN 1915   JACKIE CHAN WAS BORN IN 1954

7 AM

A M

9 AM

O AM

11 AM

OON

1 PM

PM

3 PM

PM

5 PM

PM

ON THIS DAY IN 1933: BEER COULD ONCE AGAIN BE PURCHASED IN THE UNITED STATES.

BRILLIANT AND/OR TERRIBLE IDEAS

97 DAYS DOWN, 268 DAYS LEFT (UNLESS IT'S A LEAP YEAR [98/268])   YEAR:

APRIL 8

WRITE IN THE DATES BELOW (AND SHADE IN TODAY)

MONDAY	TUESDAY	WEDNESDAY	THURSDAY	FRIDAY	SATURDAY
. . . .	. . . .	. . . .	. . . .	. . . .	. . . .
☐ TODAY	☐ TODAY	☐ TODAY	☐ TODAY	☐ TODAY	☐ SUNDAY

IT'S NATIONAL EMPANADA DAY
THE FIRST RECIPE WAS PUBLISHED IN A SPANISH COOKBOOK IN 1520.

ROBIN WRIGHT WAS BORN IN 1966   PATRICIA ARQUETTE WAS BORN IN 1968

7 AM

. . . .

8 AM

. . . .

9 AM

. . . .

10 AM

11 AM

. . . .

NOON

. . . .

1 PM

. . . .

2 PM

3 PM

. . . .

4 PM

. . . .

5 PM

. . . .

6 PM

ON THIS DAY IN 1879: MILK WAS SOLD IN GLASS BOTTLES FOR THE FIRST TIME.

NOTES AND/OR LIMERICKS

YEAR: 98 DAYS DOWN, 267 DAYS LEFT (UNLESS IT'S A LEAP YEAR [99/267])

APRIL 9

WRITE IN THE DATES BELOW (AND SHADE IN TODAY)

MONDAY	TUESDAY	WEDNESDAY	THURSDAY	FRIDAY	SATURDAY ☐
☐ TODAY	☐ TODAY	☐ TODAY	☐ TODAY	☐ TODAY	☐ SUNDAY

IT'S NATIONAL GIN AND TONIC DAY
SOME SAY IT WAS A MALARIA TREATMENT. WE SAY IT'S DELICIOUS.

IL NAS X WAS BORN IN 1999   KRISTEN STEWART WAS BORN IN 1990

7 AM

AM

9 AM

0 AM

11 AM

OON

1 PM

PM

3 PM

PM

5 PM

PM

ON THIS DAY IN 2009: THE SHOW 'PARKS AND RECREATION' DEBUTED ON NBC.

BRILLIANT AND/OR TERRIBLE IDEAS

99 DAYS DOWN, 266 DAYS LEFT (UNLESS IT'S A LEAP YEAR [100/266]) | YEAR:

APRIL 10

MONDAY	TUESDAY	WEDNESDAY	THURSDAY	FRIDAY	SATURDAY
. . . .	. . . .	. . . .	. . . .	. . . .	
☐ TODAY	☐ TODAY	☐ TODAY	☐ TODAY	☐ TODAY	☐ SUNDAY

IT'S INTERNATIONAL SAFETY PIN DAY
THE INVENTOR CREATED THEM IN 1849 TO HELP PAY OFF A DEBT OF $15.

MANDY MOORE WAS BORN IN 1984   STEVEN SEAGAL WAS BORN IN 195

7 AM

. . . .

8 A

9 AM

. . . .

10 A

11 AM

. . . .

NOC

1 PM

. . . .

2 P

3 PM

. . . .

4 P

5 PM

. . . .

6 P

ON THIS DAY IN 1970: PAUL MCCARTNEY ANNOUNCED THAT THE BEATLES HAD BROKEN UP.

NOTES AND/OR LIMERICKS

YEAR: | 100 DAYS DOWN, 265 DAYS LEFT (UNLESS IT'S A LEAP YEAR [101/265])

APRIL 11

WRITE IN THE DATES BELOW (AND SHADE IN TODAY)					
MONDAY	TUESDAY	WEDNESDAY	THURSDAY	FRIDAY	SATURDAY ☐
☐ TODAY	☐ TODAY	☐ TODAY	☐ TODAY	☐ TODAY	☐ SUNDAY

IT'S NATIONAL POUTINE DAY
JOEY CHESTNUT ONCE ATE 28 POUNDS OF IT IN 10 MINUTES.

ENNIFER ESPOSITO WAS BORN IN 1973   MICHELLE PHAN WAS BORN IN 1987

7 AM

AM

9 AM

) AM

11 AM

OON

1 PM

PM

3 PM

PM

5 PM

PM

ON THIS DAY IN 1921: IOWA BECAME THE FIRST STATE TO TAX CIGARETTES.

BRILLIANT AND/OR TERRIBLE IDEAS

101 DAYS DOWN, 264 DAYS LEFT (UNLESS IT'S A LEAP YEAR [102/264])   YEAR:

APRIL 12

MONDAY	TUESDAY	WEDNESDAY	THURSDAY	FRIDAY	SATURDAY
. . . .	. . . .	. . . .	. . . .	. . . .	. . . .
☐ TODAY	☐ TODAY	☐ TODAY	☐ TODAY	☐ TODAY	☐ SUNDAY

IT'S HAMSTER DAY
THERE ARE OVER 20 DIFFERENT SPECIES OF HAMSTERS.

SAOIRSE RONAN WAS BORN IN 1994   DAVID LETTERMAN WAS BORN IN 194

7 AM
. . . .
                                                                          8 A
. . . .
9 AM
. . . .
                                                                          10 A
11 AM
. . . .
                                                                          NOC
. . . .
1 PM
. . . .
                                                                          2 P
. . . .
3 PM
. . . .
                                                                          4 P
. . . .
5 PM
. . . .
                                                                          6 P

ON THIS DAY IN 1995: DREW BARRYMORE FLASHED DAVID LETTERMAN ON AIR.

YEAR: 102 DAYS DOWN, 263 DAYS LEFT (UNLESS IT'S A LEAP YEAR [103/263])

WRITE IN THE DATES BELOW (AND SHADE IN TODAY)					
MONDAY	TUESDAY	WEDNESDAY	THURSDAY	FRIDAY	SATURDAY ☐
. . . .	. . . .	. . . .	. . . .	. . . .	☐
☐ TODAY	☐ TODAY	☐ TODAY	☐ TODAY	☐ TODAY	☐ SUNDAY

IT'S SCRABBLE DAY

THE GAME WAS INVENTED IN 1931 BY AN UNEMPLOYED ARCHITECT.

ON PERLMAN WAS BORN IN 1950   LOU BEGA WAS BORN IN 1975

7 AM

AM

9 AM

O AM

11 AM

OON

1 PM

PM

3 PM

PM

5 PM

PM

ON THIS DAY IN 1979: THE LONGEST DOUBLES PING PONG GAME ENDED (101 HOURS).

BRILLIANT AND/OR TERRIBLE IDEAS

103 DAYS DOWN, 262 DAYS LEFT (UNLESS IT'S A LEAP YEAR [104/262])   YEAR:

APRIL 14

MONDAY	TUESDAY	WEDNESDAY	THURSDAY	FRIDAY	SATURDAY
. . . .	. . . .	. . . .	. . . .	. . . .	. . . .
☐ TODAY	☐ TODAY	☐ TODAY	☐ TODAY	☐ TODAY	☐ SUNDAY

IT'S NATIONAL PECAN DAY
PECANS AREN'T TECHNICALLY NUTS, THEY ARE A TYPE OF 'DRUPE.'

ADRIEN BRODY WAS BORN IN 1973   LORETTA LYNN WAS BORN IN 19

7 AM
. . . .
                                                                                  8 A
. . . .
9 AM
. . . .
                                                                                 10 A
. . . .
11 AM
. . . .
                                                                                  NOC
. . . .
1 PM
. . . .
                                                                                  2 P
. . . .
3 PM
. . . .
                                                                                  4 P
. . . .
5 PM
. . . .
                                                                                  6 P

ON THIS DAY IN 1912: THE TITANIC STRUCK AN ICEBERG AT 11:40 PM.

NOTES AND/OR LIMERICKS

YEAR: 104 DAYS DOWN, 261 DAYS LEFT (UNLESS IT'S A LEAP YEAR [105/261])

APRIL 15

WRITE IN THE DATES BELOW (AND SHADE IN TODAY)

MONDAY	TUESDAY	WEDNESDAY	THURSDAY	FRIDAY	SATURDAY ☐
☐ TODAY	☐ TODAY	☐ TODAY	☐ TODAY	☐ TODAY	☐ SUNDAY

IT'S NATIONAL AMERICAN SIGN LANGUAGE DAY
A.S.L. IS A COMBINATION OF SEVERAL PRE-EXISTING SIGN LANGUAGES.

ETH ROGEN WAS BORN IN 1982   EMMA WATSON WAS BORN IN 1990

7 AM

AM

9 AM

O AM

11 AM

OON

1 PM

PM

3 PM

PM

5 PM

PM

ON THIS DAY IN 1817: THE FIRST SCHOOL FOR THE DEAF IN THE UNITED STATES OPENED.

BRILLIANT AND/OR TERRIBLE IDEAS

105 DAYS DOWN, 260 DAYS LEFT (UNLESS IT'S A LEAP YEAR [106/260])

YEAR:

APRIL 16

MONDAY	TUESDAY	WEDNESDAY	THURSDAY	FRIDAY	SATURDAY ☐
. . . .	. . . .	. . . .	. . . .	. . . .	☐
☐ TODAY	☐ TODAY	☐ TODAY	☐ TODAY	☐ TODAY	SUNDAY

IT'S NATIONAL BEAN COUNTERS' DAY
SO HONOR YOUR ACCOUNTANT FRIENDS...BY DISPARAGING THEM?

ANYA TAYLOR JOY WAS BORN IN 1996   CHARLIE CHAPLIN WAS BORN IN 188

7 AM
. . . .
                                                                                          8 A
. . . .
9 AM
. . . .
                                                                                          10 A
. . . .
11 AM
. . . .
                                                                                          NOO
. . . .
1 PM
. . . .
                                                                                          2 P
. . . .
3 PM
. . . .
                                                                                          4 P
. . . .
5 PM
. . . .
                                                                                          6 P

ON THIS DAY IN 2017: KENDRICK LAMAR RECEIVED A PULITZER FOR 'DAMN.'

NOTES AND/OR LIMERICKS

YEAR: ___   106 DAYS DOWN, 259 DAYS LEFT (UNLESS IT'S A LEAP YEAR [107/259])

APRIL 17

MONDAY	TUESDAY	WEDNESDAY	THURSDAY	FRIDAY	SATURDAY ☐
. . . .	. . . .	. . . .	. . . .	. . . .	
☐ TODAY	☐ TODAY	☐ TODAY	☐ TODAY	☐ TODAY	☐ SUNDAY

WRITE IN THE DATES BELOW (AND SHADE IN TODAY)

IT'S NATIONAL KICKBALL DAY
WHEN IT WAS CREATED IN 1917, IT WAS KNOWN AS 'KICK BASEBALL.'

ROONEY MARA WAS BORN IN 1985   JENNIFER GARNER WAS BORN IN 1972

7 AM

8 AM

9 AM

10 AM

11 AM

NOON

1 PM

2 PM

3 PM

4 PM

5 PM

6 PM

ON THIS DAY IN 2011: 'GAME OF THRONES' PREMIERED ON HBO.

BRILLIANT AND/OR TERRIBLE IDEAS

107 DAYS DOWN, 258 DAYS LEFT (UNLESS IT'S A LEAP YEAR [108/258]) | YEAR:

APRIL 18

IT'S INTERNATIONAL JUGGLERS DAY
CHINESE WARRIORS JUGGLED SWORDS TO INTIMIDATE THEIR ENEMIES.

AMERICA FERRERA WAS BORN IN 1984   CONAN O'BRIEN WAS BORN IN 196

7 AM

8 A

9 AM

10 A

11 AM

NOO

1 PM

2 P

3 PM

4 P

5 PM

6 P

ON THIS DAY IN 1999: WAYNE GRETZKY PLAYED HIS LAST GAME IN THE NHL.

NOTES AND/OR LIMERICKS

YEAR: 108 DAYS DOWN, 257 DAYS LEFT (UNLESS IT'S A LEAP YEAR [109/257])

APRIL 19

MONDAY	TUESDAY	WEDNESDAY	THURSDAY	FRIDAY	SATURDAY ☐
. . . .	. . . .	. . . .	. . . .	. . . .	
☐ TODAY	☐ TODAY	☐ TODAY	☐ TODAY	☐ TODAY	☐ SUNDAY

IT'S BICYCLE DAY

JUST ANOTHER FUN DAY ABOUT BIKES? NOPE, IT'S ABOUT LSD. LOOK IT UP.

ALI WONG WAS BORN IN 1982   SIMU LIU WAS BORN IN 1989

7 AM

8 AM

9 AM

O AM

11 AM

NOON

1 PM

PM

3 PM

PM

5 PM

PM

ON THIS DAY IN 1897: THE FIRST BOSTON MARATHON WAS HELD.

BRILLIANT AND/OR TERRIBLE IDEAS

APRIL 20

MONDAY	TUESDAY	WEDNESDAY	THURSDAY	FRIDAY	SATURDAY
. . . .	. . . .	. . . .	. . . .	. . . .	
☐ TODAY	☐ TODAY	☐ TODAY	☐ TODAY	☐ TODAY	☐ SUNDAY

IT'S NATIONAL LOOK-ALIKE DAY
THE TWIN STRANGERS PROJECT CAN HELP LOCATE YOUR DOPPELGANGER.

GEORGE TAKEI WAS BORN IN 1937   JESSICA LANGE WAS BORN IN 194

7 AM
. . . .
                                                                                        8 A
. . . .
9 AM
. . . .
                                                                                        10 A
. . . .
11 AM
. . . .
                                                                                        NOO
. . . .
1 PM
. . . .
                                                                                        2 P
. . . .
3 PM
. . . .
                                                                                        4 P
. . . .
5 PM
. . . .
                                                                                        6 P

ON THIS DAY IN 2008: DANICA PATRICK BECAME THE FIRST WOMAN TO WIN AN INDY CAR RACE.

NOTES AND/OR LIMERICKS

YEAR: 110 DAYS DOWN, 255 DAYS LEFT (UNLESS IT'S A LEAP YEAR [111/255])

WRITE IN THE DATES BELOW (AND SHADE IN TODAY)					
MONDAY	**TUESDAY**	**WEDNESDAY**	**THURSDAY**	**FRIDAY**	**SATURDAY** ☐
☐ TODAY	☐ TODAY	☐ TODAY	☐ TODAY	☐ TODAY	☐ **SUNDAY**

IT'S KEEP OFF THE GRASS DAY

OVER 1,400 SPECIES OF GRASS EXIST IN THE UNITED STATES ALONE.

QUEEN ELIZABETH II WAS BORN IN 1926   ROB RIGGLE WAS BORN IN 1970

7 AM

8 AM

9 AM

10 AM

11 AM

NOON

1 PM

2 PM

3 PM

4 PM

5 PM

6 PM

ON THIS DAY IN 1984: 'AGAINST ALL ODDS' BY PHIL COLLINS HIT NUMBER ONE.

BRILLIANT AND/OR TERRIBLE IDEAS

111 DAYS DOWN, 254 DAYS LEFT (UNLESS IT'S A LEAP YEAR [112/254])   YEAR:

APRIL 22

MONDAY	TUESDAY	WEDNESDAY	THURSDAY	FRIDAY	SATURDAY ☐
. . . .	. . . .	. . . .	. . . .	. . . .	
☐ TODAY	☐ TODAY	☐ TODAY	☐ TODAY	☐ TODAY	☐ SUNDAY

IT'S EARTH DAY
THE EARTH TILTS AT ROUGHLY 66 DEGREES.

JACK NICHOLSON WAS BORN IN 1937   SHERRI SHEPHERD WAS BORN IN 1967

7 AM
. . . .
8 AM
. . . .
9 AM
. . . .
10 AM
11 AM
. . . .
NOON
. . . .
1 PM
. . . .
2 PM
3 PM
. . . .
4 PM
5 PM
. . . .
6 PM

ON THIS DAY IN 1970: THE FIRST EARTH DAY WAS OBSERVED.

YEAR: 112 DAYS DOWN, 253 DAYS LEFT (UNLESS IT'S A LEAP YEAR [113/253])

APRIL 23

IT'S NATIONAL PICNIC DAY
THE FIRST PICNIC TABLE WAS CREATED IN THE LATE 1800s.

SHIRLEY TEMPLE WAS BORN IN 1928   KAL PENN WAS BORN IN 1977

7 AM

8 AM

9 AM

10 AM

11 AM

NOON

1 PM

2 PM

3 PM

4 PM

5 PM

6 PM

ON THIS DAY IN 1985: COCA-COLA CHANGED FORMULAS AND RELEASED 'NEW COKE.'

BRILLIANT AND/OR TERRIBLE IDEAS

113 DAYS DOWN, 252 DAYS LEFT (UNLESS IT'S A LEAP YEAR [114/252])

YEAR:

APRIL 24

MONDAY	TUESDAY	WEDNESDAY	THURSDAY	FRIDAY	SATURDAY ☐
. . . .	. . . .	. . . .	. . . .	. . . .	☐
☐ TODAY	☐ TODAY	☐ TODAY	☐ TODAY	☐ TODAY	☐ SUNDAY

WRITE IN THE DATES BELOW (AND SHADE IN TODAY)

IT'S PIGS-IN-A-BLANKET DAY
'NAKKIPIILO' IS FINNISH FOR 'HIDDEN SAUSAGE.'

BARBARA STREISAND WAS BORN IN 1942   KELLY CLARKSON WAS BORN IN 1982

7 AM

8 AM

9 AM

10 AM

11 AM

NOON

1 PM

2 PM

3 PM

4 PM

5 PM

6 PM

ON THIS DAY IN 1800: THE LIBRARY OF CONGRESS WAS ESTABLISHED.

NOTES AND/OR LIMERICKS

YEAR: 114 DAYS DOWN, 251 DAYS LEFT (UNLESS IT'S A LEAP YEAR [115/251])

APRIL 25

MONDAY	TUESDAY	WEDNESDAY	THURSDAY	FRIDAY	SATURDAY ☐
. . . . ☐ TODAY	. . . . ☐ TODAY	. . . . ☐ TODAY	. . . . ☐ TODAY	. . . . ☐ TODAY	☐ SUNDAY

WRITE IN THE DATES BELOW (AND SHADE IN TODAY)

IT'S WORLD PENGUIN DAY
EXPLORERS ORIGINALLY CALLED THEM 'STRANGE-GEESE.'

ELLA FITZGERALD WAS BORN IN 1917   AL PACINO WAS BORN IN 1940

7 AM

8 AM

9 AM

10 AM

11 AM

NOON

1 PM

2 PM

3 PM

4 PM

5 PM

6 PM

ON THIS DAY IN 1992: THE FINAL EPISODE OF 'GROWING PAINS' AIRED.

BRILLIANT AND/OR TERRIBLE IDEAS

115 DAYS DOWN, 250 DAYS LEFT (UNLESS IT'S A LEAP YEAR [116/250])

YEAR:

APRIL 26

MONDAY	TUESDAY	WEDNESDAY	THURSDAY	FRIDAY	SATURDAY ☐
. . . . ☐ TODAY	. . . . ☐ TODAY	. . . . ☐ TODAY	. . . . ☐ TODAY	. . . . ☐ TODAY	☐ SUNDAY

IT'S NATIONAL PRETZEL DAY
IN 1993 THE PRETZEL MUSEUM WAS OPENED IN PHILADELPHIA.

CHANNING TATUM WAS BORN IN 1980   JET LI WAS BORN IN 196

7 AM
. . . .
8 AM
. . . .
9 AM
. . . .
10 AM
11 AM
. . . .
NOON
. . . .
1 PM
. . . .
2 PM
. . . .
3 PM
. . . .
4 PM
. . . .
5 PM
. . . .
6 PM

ON THIS DAY IN 1977: STUDIO 54 OPENED IN NEW YORK CITY.

NOTES AND/OR LIMERICKS

YEAR:	116 DAYS DOWN, 249 DAYS LEFT (UNLESS IT'S A LEAP YEAR [117/249])

APRIL 27

MONDAY	TUESDAY	WEDNESDAY	THURSDAY	FRIDAY	SATURDAY ☐
. . . . ☐ TODAY	. . . . ☐ TODAY	. . . . ☐ TODAY	. . . . ☐ TODAY	. . . . ☐ TODAY	☐ SUNDAY

IT'S NATIONAL PRIME RIB DAY
ALSO KNOWN AS A 'STANDING RIB ROAST,' AS IT'S ROASTED UPRIGHT.

CASEY KASEM WAS BORN IN 1932   LIZZO WAS BORN IN 1988

7 AM

8 AM

9 AM

10 AM

11 AM

NOON

1 PM

2 PM

3 PM

4 PM

5 PM

6 PM

ON THIS DAY IN 1981: PAUL MCCARTNEY'S BAND WINGS BROKE UP.

BRILLIANT AND/OR TERRIBLE IDEAS

117 DAYS DOWN, 248 DAYS LEFT (UNLESS IT'S A LEAP YEAR [118/248])   YEAR:

APRIL 28

IT'S NATIONAL BLUEBERRY PIE DAY
THE FIRST RECIPE FOR IT WAS PUBLISHED BY A WOMAN NAMED MRS. BLISS.

JESSICA ALBA WAS BORN IN 1981   PENÉLOPE CRUZ WAS BORN IN 1974

7 AM
. . . .
8 AM
. . . .
9 AM
. . . .
10 AM
11 AM
. . . .
NOON
. . . .
1 PM
. . . .
2 PM
. . . .
3 PM
. . . .
4 PM
. . . .
5 PM
. . . .
6 PM

ON THIS DAY IN 1954: THE 1ST ISSUE OF 'SPORTS ILLUSTRATED' WAS PUBLISHED.

NOTES AND/OR LIMERICKS

YEAR: 118 DAYS DOWN, 247 DAYS LEFT (UNLESS IT'S A LEAP YEAR [119/247])

WRITE IN THE DATES BELOW (AND SHADE IN TODAY)					
MONDAY	**TUESDAY**	**WEDNESDAY**	**THURSDAY**	**FRIDAY**	**SATURDAY** ☐
. . . .	. . . .	. . . .	. . . .	. . . .	☐
☐ TODAY	☐ TODAY	☐ TODAY	☐ TODAY	☐ TODAY	☐ **SUNDAY**

IT'S NATIONAL ZIPPER DAY
YKK STANDS FOR YOSHIDO KOGYO KABUSHIKIKAISHA.

JERRY SEINFELD WAS BORN IN 1954   UMA THURMAN WAS BORN IN 1970

7 AM

8 AM

9 AM

10 AM

11 AM

NOON

1 PM

2 PM

3 PM

4 PM

5 PM

6 PM

ON THIS DAY IN 2011: PRINCE WILLIAM MARRIED KATE MIDDLETON.

BRILLIANT AND/OR TERRIBLE IDEAS

119 DAYS DOWN, 246 DAYS LEFT (UNLESS IT'S A LEAP YEAR [120/246])   YEAR:

APRIL 30

MONDAY	TUESDAY	WEDNESDAY	THURSDAY	FRIDAY	SATURDAY ☐
☐ TODAY	☐ TODAY	☐ TODAY	☐ TODAY	☐ TODAY	☐ SUNDAY

IT'S NATIONAL BUBBLE TEA DAY
TAPIOCA PEARLS WERE ADDED TO SHAKEN MILK AND TEA DRINKS IN THE 1980s.

KIRSTEN DUNST WAS BORN IN 1982   GAL GADOT WAS BORN IN 1985

7 AM

8 AM

9 AM

10 AM

11 AM

NOON

1 PM

2 PM

3 PM

4 PM

5 PM

6 PM

ON THIS DAY IN 1997: BIG BEN STOPPED WORKING AT 12:11 PM (FOR 54 MINUTES).

NOTES AND/OR LIMERICKS

YEAR: | 120 DAYS DOWN, 245 DAYS LEFT (UNLESS IT'S A LEAP YEAR [121/245])

LISTS, NOTES & MEMOIRS

WAYS THIS MONTH WAS GREAT
'IT ENDED' IS A VALID ANSWER

1
2
3
4
5
6
7
8
9
10
11
12
13
14

WAYS THAT IT WASN'T
USE ADDITIONAL PAPER IF NEEDED

1
2
3
4
5
6
7
8
9
10
11
12
13
14

THINGS TO BUY NEXT TIME I'M DRUNK AT THE GROCERY STORE
USE FIGURE 1 FOR ANY NECESSARY VISUAL AIDS

FIG. 1

1
2
3

4
5
6

IT'S OFFICIALLY

OF THE YEAR

MONTH FIVE

. . . .

. . . .

. . . .

CONGRATULATIONS, YOU MADE IT
TO THE MONTH OF MAY

✖

CELEBRATE, IT'S:

NATIONAL BARBECUE MONTH

CORRECT YOUR POSTURE MONTH

NTL. CHAMBER MUSIC MONTH

AMERICAN CHEESE MONTH

NTL. WATER SAFETY MONTH

OFFICIAL SYMBOLS:

BIRTHSTONE: EMERALD

FLOWER: HAWTHORN

TREES: CHESTNUT & ASH

TAURUS (APR 20 / MAY 20)

GEMINI (MAY 21 / JUN 20)

✖

A FEW DATES TO KNOW*
LIKE, IMPORTANT ONES.

✖

MAY DAY
MAY 1ST

CINCO DE MAYO
MAY 5TH

RAMADAN
(ISLAMIC)
MOVES 11 DAYS EARLIER
(IN RELATION TO OUR CALENDAR)
EVERY YEAR. WE'D LOOK IT UP.

**AMNESTY
INTERNATIONAL DAY**
MAY 28TH

SHAVUOT
(JUDAISM)
6TH DAY OF THE HEBREW MONTH
OF SIVAN (MAY OR JUNE)

NATIONAL NURSES DAY
MAY 12TH

MEMORIAL DAY
THE LAST MONDAY IN MAY

PENTECOST
(CHRISTIANITY)
7TH SUNDAY AFTER EASTER
(USUALLY IN MAY)

MARK YOUR CALENDAR ✖ IT'S RIGHT OVER THERE

*A DISCLAIMER OF SORTS

HEY THERE. WE HERE AT BRASS MONKEY LIKE TO JOKE AROUND...BUT WE ALSO WANT TO TAKE A MINUTE TO RECOGNIZE JUST A FEW OF THE MANY HOLIDAYS & EVENTS THAT ARE IMPORTANT TO OUR FRIENDS AROUND THE GLOBE (AND AT HOME). YOU MAY BE DIFFERENT THAN US. WE MAY HAVE NEVER MET. BUT WE LOVE YOU ALL THE SAME.

SO, WITH ALL OF THAT SAID, IF YOU HAVEN'T HEARD OF A DAY, PLEASE LOOK IT UP. LEARNING ABOUT AND APPRECIATING CULTURES DIFFERENT THAN YOURS IS REALLY IMPORTANT...WAY MORE SO THAN POSTING A FEW 'STRAWBERRY JAM DAY' VIDEOS ON TIKTOK. DON'T GET US WRONG, THERE IS PLENTY OF ROOM FOR BOTH. JUST PLEASE DO BOTH.

MAY AT A GLANCE

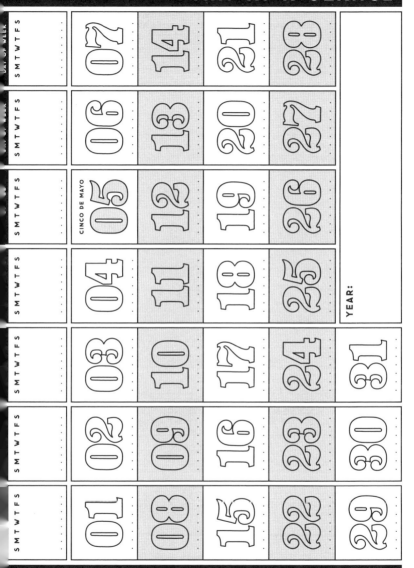

YEAR:

S M T W T F S	S M T W T F S	S M T W T F S	S M T W T F S	S M T W T F S	S M T W T F S	S M T W T F S
07	06	CINCO DE MAYO 05	04	03	02	01
14	13	12	11	10	09	08
21	20	19	18	17	16	15
28	27	26	25	24	23	22
				31	30	29

WELL, WHAT ARE YOU WAITING FOR?

✕ START PLANNING. IN THE CALENDAR ABOVE, WE'VE MARKED THE MORE COMMON
U.S. HOLIDAYS ALREADY (THE ONES THAT ARE DATED, THAT IS). SO USE THE
LIST TO THE LEFT TO FILL IN THE REST...LIKE ALL OF THE ONES THAT CHANGE
DATES FROM YEAR TO YEAR, FOR EXAMPLE. ✕

LISTS, NOTES & MEMOIRS

REASONS I'M STILL SINGLE
OR SOME BORING TO-DO LIST

1
2
3
4
5
6
7
8
9
10
11
12
13
14

REASONS I WISH I WERE
OR A GROCERY LIST OR SOMETHING

1
2
3
4
5
6
7
8
9
10
11
12
13
14

WHAT MY MILKSHAKE BRINGS TO THE YARD
USE FIGURE 1 FOR ANY NECESSARY VISUAL AIDS

FIG. 1

1
2
3

4
5
6

MAY 1

WRITE IN THE DATES BELOW (AND SHADE IN TODAY)

MONDAY	TUESDAY	WEDNESDAY	THURSDAY	FRIDAY	SATURDAY ☐
. . . . ☐ TODAY	. . . . ☐ TODAY	. . . . ☐ TODAY	. . . . ☐ TODAY	. . . . ☐ TODAY	☐ SUNDAY

IT'S PHONE IN SICK DAY
57% OF PEOPLE ADMIT TO FAKING SICKNESS.

WES ANDERSON WAS BORN IN 1969   JAMIE DORNAN WAS BORN IN 1982

7 AM

8 AM

9 AM

10 AM

11 AM

NOON

1 PM

2 PM

3 PM

4 PM

5 PM

6 PM

ON THIS DAY IN 1999: 'SPONGEBOB SQUAREPANTS' DEBUTED ON NICKELODEON.

BRILLIANT AND/OR TERRIBLE IDEAS

YEAR:

MAY 2

IT'S NATIONAL SCURVY AWARENESS DAY
PEOPLE USED TO THINK SCURVY WAS CAUSED BY LAZINESS.

DWAYNE JOHNSON WAS BORN IN 1972   LILY ALLEN WAS BORN IN 198

7 AM

8 AM

9 AM

10 AM

11 AM

NOON

1 PM

2 PM

3 PM

4 PM

5 PM

6 PM

ON THIS DAY IN 1956: THE WEATHER CHANNEL BEGAN BROADCASTING IN THE U.S.

NOTES AND/OR LIMERICKS

YEAR: 122 DAYS DOWN, 243 DAYS LEFT (UNLESS IT'S A LEAP YEAR [123/243])

MAY 3

WRITE IN THE DATES BELOW (AND SHADE IN TODAY)					
MONDAY	**TUESDAY**	**WEDNESDAY**	**THURSDAY**	**FRIDAY**	**SATURDAY** ☐
☐ TODAY	☐ TODAY	☐ TODAY	☐ TODAY	☐ TODAY	☐ **SUNDAY**

IT'S NATIONAL PARANORMAL DAY
ABOUT 80% OF AMERICANS BELIEVE IN GHOSTS.

SUGAR RAY ROBINSON WAS BORN IN 1921   JAMES BROWN WAS BORN IN 1933

7 AM

8 AM

9 AM

10 AM

11 AM

NOON

1 PM

2 PM

3 PM

4 PM

5 PM

6 PM

ON THIS DAY IN 1991: THE 356TH (AND FINAL) EPISODE OF 'DALLAS' AIRED.

BRILLIANT AND/OR TERRIBLE IDEAS

123 DAYS DOWN, 242 DAYS LEFT (UNLESS IT'S A LEAP YEAR [124/242])   YEAR:

MAY 4

IT'S STAR WARS DAY
MAY THE FOURTH BE WITH YOU.

AUDREY HEPBURN WAS BORN IN 1929   LANCE BASS WAS BORN IN 197

7 AM
. . . .

8 A
. . . .

9 AM
. . . .

10 A
. . . .

11 AM
. . . .

NOO
. . . .

1 PM
. . . .

2 P
. . . .

3 PM
. . . .

4 P
. . . .

5 PM
. . . .

6 P

ON THIS DAY IN 1959: THE FIRST ANNUAL GRAMMY AWARDS CEREMONY WAS HELD.

NOTES AND/OR LIMERICKS

YEAR: 124 DAYS DOWN, 241 DAYS LEFT (UNLESS IT'S A LEAP YEAR [125/241])

MAY 5

	WRITE IN THE DATES BELOW (AND SHADE IN TODAY)				
MONDAY	TUESDAY	WEDNESDAY	THURSDAY	FRIDAY	SATURDAY ☐
☐ TODAY	☐ TODAY	☐ TODAY	☐ TODAY	☐ TODAY	☐ SUNDAY

IT'S CINCO DE MAYO
IT'S ALSO HUG A SHED AND TAKE A SELFIE DAY.

HENRY CAVILL WAS BORN IN 1983   ADELE WAS BORN IN 1988

7 AM

8 AM

9 AM

10 AM

11 AM

NOON

1 PM

2 PM

3 PM

4 PM

5 PM

6 PM

ON THIS DAY IN 2017: ANNA WINTOUR WAS MADE A DAME BY QUEEN ELIZABETH II.

BRILLIANT AND/OR TERRIBLE IDEAS

125 DAYS DOWN, 240 DAYS LEFT (UNLESS IT'S A LEAP YEAR [126/240])   YEAR:

MAY 6

MONDAY	TUESDAY	WEDNESDAY	THURSDAY	FRIDAY	SATURDAY ☐
. . . .	. . . .	. . . .	. . . .	. . . .	
☐ TODAY	☐ TODAY	☐ TODAY	☐ TODAY	☐ TODAY	☐ SUNDAY

WRITE IN THE DATES BELOW (AND SHADE IN TODAY)

IT'S NATIONAL NURSES DAY
FLORENCE NIGHTINGALE HAD A PET OWL NAMED ATHENA.

GEORGE CLOONEY WAS BORN IN 1961   WILLIE MAYS WAS BORN IN 193⟩

7 AM

. . . .
8 AM

. . . .
9 AM

. . . .
10 A

11 AM

. . . .
NOO

. . . .
1 PM

. . . .
2 P

3 PM

. . . .
4 P

. . . .
5 PM

. . . .
6 P

ON THIS DAY IN 1994: BOBCAT GOLDTHWAIT SET FIRE TO THE 'TONIGHT SHOW' COUCH.

NOTES AND/OR LIMERICKS

YEAR: 126 DAYS DOWN, 239 DAYS LEFT (UNLESS IT'S A LEAP YEAR [127/239])

MAY 7

WRITE IN THE DATES BELOW (AND SHADE IN TODAY)

MONDAY	TUESDAY	WEDNESDAY	THURSDAY	FRIDAY	SATURDAY ☐
. . . . ☐ TODAY	. . . . ☐ TODAY	. . . . ☐ TODAY	. . . . ☐ TODAY	. . . . ☐ TODAY	☐ SUNDAY

IT'S NATIONAL COSMOPOLITAN DAY
BLAME 'SEX AND THE CITY.'

AIDY BRYANT WAS BORN IN 1987   EVA PERÓN WAS BORN IN 1919

7 AM

8 AM

9 AM

10 AM

11 AM

NOON

1 PM

2 PM

3 PM

4 PM

5 PM

6 PM

ON THIS DAY IN 1994: EDVARD MUNCH'S 'THE SCREAM' WAS RECOVERED UNDAMAGED.

BRILLIANT AND/OR TERRIBLE IDEAS

127 DAYS DOWN, 238 DAYS LEFT (UNLESS IT'S A LEAP YEAR [128/238])   YEAR:

MAY 8

MONDAY	TUESDAY	WEDNESDAY	THURSDAY	FRIDAY	SATURDAY ☐
. . . .	. . . .	. . . .	. . . .	. . . .	
☐ TODAY	☐ TODAY	☐ TODAY	☐ TODAY	☐ TODAY	☐ SUNDAY

IT'S NO SOCKS DAY
THE EARLIEST SOCKS WERE MADE FROM MATTED ANIMAL HAIR.

ENRIQUE IGLESIAS WAS BORN IN 1975   DAVID ATTENBOROUGH WAS BORN IN 192▮

7 AM
. . . .
8 A▮
. . . .
9 AM
. . . .
10 A▮
. . . .
11 AM
. . . .
NOO▮
. . . .
1 PM
. . . .
2 P▮
. . . .
3 PM
. . . .
4 P▮
. . . .
5 PM
. . . .
6 P▮

ON THIS DAY IN 2010: BETTY WHITE HOSTED 'SATURDAY NIGHT LIVE.'

NOTES AND/OR LIMERICKS

YEAR: 128 DAYS DOWN, 237 DAYS LEFT (UNLESS IT'S A LEAP YEAR [129/237])

MAY 9

IT'S NATIONAL MOSCATO DAY
THE SAME TYPE OF GRAPES USED FOR MOSCATO ARE USED FOR RAISINS.

ROSARIO DAWSON WAS BORN IN 1979   BILLY JOEL WAS BORN IN 1949

7 AM

8 AM

9 AM

10 AM

11 AM

NOON

1 PM

2 PM

3 PM

4 PM

5 PM

6 PM

ON THIS DAY IN 1992: 'THE GOLDEN GIRLS' SEASON FINALE AIRED.

BRILLIANT AND/OR TERRIBLE IDEAS

129 DAYS DOWN, 236 DAYS LEFT (UNLESS IT'S A LEAP YEAR [130/236])   YEAR:

MAY 10

IT'S NATIONAL SHRIMP DAY
THE PISTOL SHRIMP CAN PRODUCE SOUNDS LOUDER THAN A GUNSHOT.

FRED ASTAIRE WAS BORN IN 1899   KENAN THOMPSON WAS BORN IN 197?

7 AM
. . . .
8 AM
. . . .
9 AM
. . . .
10 AM
. . . .
11 AM
. . . .
NOON
. . . .
1 PM
. . . .
2 PM
. . . .
3 PM
. . . .
4 PM
. . . .
5 PM
. . . .
6 PM

ON THIS DAY IN 1877: THE FIRST TELEPHONE WAS INSTALLED IN THE WHITE HOUSE.

NOTES AND/OR LIMERICKS

YEAR: 130 DAYS DOWN, 235 DAYS LEFT (UNLESS IT'S A LEAP YEAR [131/235])

MAY 11

MONDAY	TUESDAY	WEDNESDAY	THURSDAY	FRIDAY	SATURDAY ☐
. . . .	. . . .	. . . .	. . . .	. . . .	☐
☐ TODAY	☐ TODAY	☐ TODAY	☐ TODAY	☐ TODAY	☐ SUNDAY

IT'S EAT WHAT YOU WANT TO DAY
IN NYC? CHECK OUT SHOPSIN'S ON THE LOWER EAST SIDE.

SALVADOR DALI WAS BORN IN 1904   LANA CONDOR WAS BORN IN 1997

7 AM

8 AM

9 AM

10 AM

11 AM

NOON

1 PM

2 PM

3 PM

4 PM

5 PM

6 PM

ON THIS DAY IN 1981: 'CATS' PREMIERED IN THE WEST END.

BRILLIANT AND/OR TERRIBLE IDEAS

131 DAYS DOWN, 234 DAYS LEFT (UNLESS IT'S A LEAP YEAR [132/234])   YEAR:

MAY 12

IT'S NATIONAL LIMERICK DAY
THE FIRST COLLECTION OF LIMERICKS DATES BACK TO THE 1820s.

RAMI MALEK WAS BORN IN 1981   EMILIO ESTEVEZ WAS BORN IN 196

7 AM
. . . .
                                                                                            8 AM
. . . .
9 AM
. . . .
                                                                                            10 AM
. . . .
11 AM
. . . .
                                                                                            NOON
. . . .
1 PM
. . . .
                                                                                            2 PM
. . . .
3 PM
. . . .
                                                                                            4 PM
. . . .
5 PM
. . . .
                                                                                            6 P

ON THIS DAY IN 1995: 'AS THE WORLD TURNS' AIRED THEIR 10,000TH EPISODE.

NOTES AND/OR LIMERICKS

YEAR: 132 DAYS DOWN, 233 DAYS LEFT (UNLESS IT'S A LEAP YEAR [133/233])

MAY 13

	WRITE IN THE DATES BELOW (AND SHADE IN TODAY)				
MONDAY	**TUESDAY**	**WEDNESDAY**	**THURSDAY**	**FRIDAY**	**SATURDAY** ☐
☐ TODAY	☐ TODAY	☐ TODAY	☐ TODAY	☐ TODAY	☐ **SUNDAY**

IT'S NATIONAL LEPRECHAUN DAY
THEY ARE A PROTECTED SPECIES UNDER EUROPEAN LAW.

STEVIE WONDER WAS BORN IN 1950   BEA ARTHUR WAS BORN IN 1922

7 AM

8 AM

9 AM

10 AM

11 AM

NOON

1 PM

2 PM

3 PM

4 PM

5 PM

6 PM

ON THIS DAY IN 1977: HOWARD STERN BEGAN BROADCASTING AT WRNW.

BRILLIANT AND/OR TERRIBLE IDEAS

133 DAYS DOWN, 232 DAYS LEFT (UNLESS IT'S A LEAP YEAR [134/232])   YEAR:

MAY 14

WRITE IN THE DATES BELOW (AND SHADE IN TODAY)

MONDAY	TUESDAY	WEDNESDAY	THURSDAY	FRIDAY	SATURDAY ☐
☐ TODAY	☐ TODAY	☐ TODAY	☐ TODAY	☐ TODAY	☐ SUNDAY

IT'S NATIONAL BUTTERMILK BISCUIT DAY
THE FIRST READY-BAKE BISCUITS WERE PATENTED IN 1931.

CATE BLANCHETT WAS BORN IN 1969   GEORGE LUCAS WAS BORN IN 1944

7 AM

. . . .
8 AM
. . . .
9 AM
. . . .
10 AM
. . . .
11 AM
. . . .
NOON
. . . .
1 PM
. . . .
2 PM
. . . .
3 PM
. . . .
4 PM
. . . .
5 PM
. . . .
6 PM

ON THIS DAY IN 1998: 7 MILLION PEOPLE WATCHED THE FINALE OF 'SEINFELD.'

NOTES AND/OR LIMERICKS

YEAR: 134 DAYS DOWN, 231 DAYS LEFT (UNLESS IT'S A LEAP YEAR [135/231])

MAY 15

MONDAY	TUESDAY	WEDNESDAY	THURSDAY	FRIDAY	SATURDAY ☐
☐ TODAY	☐ TODAY	☐ TODAY	☐ TODAY	☐ TODAY	☐ SUNDAY

WRITE IN THE DATES BELOW (AND SHADE IN TODAY)

IT'S NATIONAL NYLON STOCKING DAY
UPON RELEASE IN 1940, DUPONT SOLD 4 MILLION PAIRS IN 2 DAYS.

DAVID KRUMHOLTZ WAS BORN IN 1978   EMMITT SMITH WAS BORN IN 1969

7 AM

8 AM

9 AM

10 AM

11 AM

NOON

1 PM

2 PM

3 PM

4 PM

5 PM

6 PM

ON THIS DAY IN 2004: 'SHREK 2' PREMIERED AT THE CANNES FILM FESTIVAL.

BRILLIANT AND/OR TERRIBLE IDEAS

135 DAYS DOWN, 230 DAYS LEFT (UNLESS IT'S A LEAP YEAR [136/230])   YEAR:

MAY 16

WRITE IN THE DATES BELOW (AND SHADE IN TODAY)

MONDAY	TUESDAY	WEDNESDAY	THURSDAY	FRIDAY	SATURDAY ☐
. . . . ☐ TODAY	. . . . ☐ TODAY	. . . . ☐ TODAY	. . . . ☐ TODAY	. . . . ☐ TODAY	☐ SUNDAY

IT'S NATIONAL SEA MONKEY DAY
THEY AREN'T MONKEYS AND THEY DON'T LIVE IN THE SEA.

LIBERACE WAS BORN IN 1919   JANET JACKSON WAS BORN IN 1966

7 AM
. . . .
8 AM
. . . .
9 AM
. . . .
10 AM
. . . .
11 AM
. . . .
NOON
. . . .
1 PM
. . . .
2 PM
. . . .
3 PM
. . . .
4 PM
. . . .
5 PM
. . . .
6 PM

ON THIS DAY IN 1875: ROOT BEER WAS INVENTED BY CHARLES ELMER HIRES.

NOTES AND/OR LIMERICKS

YEAR: 136 DAYS DOWN, 229 DAYS LEFT (UNLESS IT'S A LEAP YEAR [137/229])

MAY 17

WRITE IN THE DATES BELOW (AND SHADE IN TODAY)					
MONDAY	TUESDAY	WEDNESDAY	THURSDAY	FRIDAY	SATURDAY ☐
☐ TODAY	☐ TODAY	☐ TODAY	☐ TODAY	☐ TODAY	☐ SUNDAY

IT'S NATIONAL HUNT FOR MUSHROOMS DAY
SOME MUSHROOMS MULTIPLY WHEN STRUCK BY LIGHTNING.

BOB SAGET WAS BORN IN 1956   TRENT REZNOR WAS BORN IN 1965

7 AM

8 AM

9 AM

10 AM

11 AM

NOON

1 PM

2 PM

3 PM

4 PM

5 PM

6 PM

ON THIS DAY IN 1792: THE NEW YORK STOCK EXCHANGE WAS FORMED.

BRILLIANT AND/OR TERRIBLE IDEAS

137 DAYS DOWN, 228 DAYS LEFT (UNLESS IT'S A LEAP YEAR [138/228])   YEAR:

MAY 18

IT'S INTERNATIONAL MUSEUM DAY
THERE'S A MUSEUM IN TOKYO DEDICATED TO PARASITES.

CHOW YUN-FAT WAS BORN IN 1955   TINA FEY WAS BORN IN 1970

7 AM

8 AM

9 AM

10 AM

11 AM

NOON

1 PM

2 PM

3 PM

4 PM

5 PM

6 PM

ON THIS DAY IN 1934: TRANS WORLD AIRLINES (TWA) BEGAN COMMERCIAL FLIGHTS.

NOTES AND/OR LIMERICKS

YEAR: 138 DAYS DOWN, 227 DAYS LEFT (UNLESS IT'S A LEAP YEAR [139/227])

MONDAY	TUESDAY	WEDNESDAY	THURSDAY	FRIDAY	SATURDAY ☐
. . . . ☐ TODAY	. . . . ☐ TODAY	. . . . ☐ TODAY	. . . . ☐ TODAY	. . . . ☐ TODAY	☐ SUNDAY

WRITE IN THE DATES BELOW (AND SHADE IN TODAY)

IT'S NATIONAL DEVIL'S FOOD CAKE DAY
THE EARLIEST RECIPE FOR THE TREAT WAS PUBLISHED IN 1898.

KENNY SHOPSIN WAS BORN IN 1942   MALCOLM X WAS BORN IN 1925

7 AM

8 AM

9 AM

10 AM

11 AM

NOON

1 PM

2 PM

3 PM

4 PM

5 PM

6 PM

ON THIS DAY IN 1962: MARILYN MONROE SANG 'HAPPY BIRTHDAY' TO JFK.

BRILLIANT AND/OR TERRIBLE IDEAS

139 DAYS DOWN, 226 DAYS LEFT (UNLESS IT'S A LEAP YEAR [140/226])   YEAR:

MAY 20

IT'S WORLD BEE DAY
THEY FLY 55,000 MILES TO PRODUCE 1 POUND OF HONEY.

CHER WAS BORN IN 1946   JIMMY STEWART WAS BORN IN 1908

7 AM

8 AM

9 AM

10 AM

11 AM

NOON

1 PM

2 PM

3 PM

4 PM

5 PM

6 PM

ON THIS DAY IN 2013: YAHOO! PURCHASED TUMBLR FOR $1.1 BILLION.

NOTES AND/OR LIMERICKS

YEAR: 140 DAYS DOWN, 225 DAYS LEFT (UNLESS IT'S A LEAP YEAR [141/225])

MAY 21

WRITE IN THE DATES BELOW (AND SHADE IN TODAY)

MONDAY	TUESDAY	WEDNESDAY	THURSDAY	FRIDAY	SATURDAY ☐
☐ TODAY	☐ TODAY	☐ TODAY	☐ TODAY	☐ TODAY	☐ SUNDAY

IT'S INTERNATIONAL TEA DAY
MORE THAN 2 BILLION CUPS OF TEA ARE DRUNK EVERY DAY.

NOTORIOUS B.I.G. WAS BORN IN 1972   MR. T WAS BORN IN 1952

7 AM

8 AM

9 AM

10 AM

11 AM

NOON

1 PM

2 PM

3 PM

4 PM

5 PM

6 PM

ON THIS DAY IN 1980: WILE E. COYOTE FINALLY CAUGHT THE ROAD RUNNER.

BRILLIANT AND/OR TERRIBLE IDEAS

141 DAYS DOWN, 224 DAYS LEFT (UNLESS IT'S A LEAP YEAR [142/224])   YEAR:

MAY 22

WRITE IN THE DATES BELOW (AND SHADE IN TODAY)					
MONDAY	TUESDAY	WEDNESDAY	THURSDAY	FRIDAY	SATURDAY ☐
. . . .	. . . .	. . . .	. . . .	. . . .	
☐ TODAY	☐ TODAY	☐ TODAY	☐ TODAY	☐ TODAY	☐ SUNDAY

IT'S NATIONAL SOLITAIRE DAY

AN INTERN DEVELOPED THE SOLITAIRE SOFTWARE FOR MICROSOFT IN 1989.

HARVEY MILK WAS BORN IN 1930   NAOMI CAMPBELL WAS BORN IN 1970

7 AM

. . . .
8 AM

. . . .
9 AM

. . . .
10 AM

11 AM

. . . .
NOON

. . . .
1 PM

. . . .
2 PM

. . . .
3 PM

. . . .
4 PM

5 PM

. . . .
6 PM

ON THIS DAY IN 1986: CHER CALLED DAVID LETTERMAN AN ASSHOLE ON TV.

NOTES AND/OR LIMERICKS

YEAR: 142 DAYS DOWN, 223 DAYS LEFT (UNLESS IT'S A LEAP YEAR [143/223])

MAY 23

WRITE IN THE DATES BELOW (AND SHADE IN TODAY)					
MONDAY	**TUESDAY**	**WEDNESDAY**	**THURSDAY**	**FRIDAY**	**SATURDAY** ☐
☐ TODAY	☐ TODAY	☐ TODAY	☐ TODAY	☐ TODAY	☐ **SUNDAY**

IT'S NATIONAL TAFFY DAY
LAFFY TAFFY WAS ORIGINALLY CALLED 'BEICH'S BANANA CARAMEL.'

DREW CAREY WAS BORN IN 1958   KEN JENNINGS WAS BORN IN 1974

7 AM

8 AM

9 AM

10 AM

11 AM

NOON

1 PM

2 PM

3 PM

4 PM

5 PM

6 PM

ON THIS DAY IN 2005: TOM CRUISE JUMPED AROUND ON OPRAH'S COUCH.

BRILLIANT AND/OR TERRIBLE IDEAS

143 DAYS DOWN, 222 DAYS LEFT (UNLESS IT'S A LEAP YEAR [144/222])   YEAR:

MAY 24

IT'S NATIONAL SCAVENGER HUNT DAY
TAKE A PICTURE OF A BRASS MONKEY AND TAG US.

JOHN C. REILLY WAS BORN IN 1965   TOMMY CHONG WAS BORN IN 1938

7 AM

                             8 AM

9 AM

                             10 AM

11 AM

                             NOON

1 PM

                             2 PM

3 PM

                             4 PM

5 PM

                             6 PM

ON THIS DAY IN 1883: THE BROOKLYN BRIDGE OPENED TO THE PUBLIC.

NOTES AND/OR LIMERICKS

YEAR: 144 DAYS DOWN, 221 DAYS LEFT (UNLESS IT'S A LEAP YEAR [145/221])

WRITE IN THE DATES BELOW (AND SHADE IN TODAY)					
MONDAY	**TUESDAY**	**WEDNESDAY**	**THURSDAY**	**FRIDAY**	**SATURDAY** ☐
☐ TODAY	☐ TODAY	☐ TODAY	☐ TODAY	☐ TODAY	☐ **SUNDAY**

IT'S GEEK PRIDE DAY

STEVE URKEL WAS ONLY SUPPOSED TO BE IN ONE EPISODE.

MIKE MYERS WAS BORN IN 1963   IAN MCKELLEN WAS BORN IN 1939

7 AM

8 AM

9 AM

10 AM

11 AM

NOON

1 PM

2 PM

3 PM

4 PM

5 PM

6 PM

ON THIS DAY IN 1977: THE ORIGINAL 'STAR WARS' PREMIERED.

BRILLIANT AND/OR TERRIBLE IDEAS

145 DAYS DOWN, 220 DAYS LEFT (UNLESS IT'S A LEAP YEAR [146/220])   YEAR:

MAY 26

WRITE IN THE DATES BELOW (AND SHADE IN TODAY)

MONDAY	TUESDAY	WEDNESDAY	THURSDAY	FRIDAY	SATURDAY ☐
. . . .	. . . .	. . . .	. . . .	. . . .	
☐ TODAY	☐ TODAY	☐ TODAY	☐ TODAY	☐ TODAY	☐ SUNDAY

IT'S NATIONAL PAPER AIRPLANE DAY
THE FURTHEST THAT ONE HAS EVER BEEN THROWN IS 226' 10".

MILES DAVIS WAS BORN IN 1926   JOHN WAYNE WAS BORN IN 1907

7 AM

8 AM

9 AM

10 AM

11 AM

NOON

1 PM

2 PM

3 PM

4 PM

5 PM

6 PM

ON THIS DAY IN 1978: THE FIRST LEGAL U.S. CASINO (OUTSIDE OF NY) OPENED.

NOTES AND/OR LIMERICKS

YEAR: 146 DAYS DOWN, 219 DAYS LEFT (UNLESS IT'S A LEAP YEAR [147/219])

MAY 27

IT'S NATIONAL GRAPE POPSICLE DAY
INVENTED BY FRANK EPPERSON IN 1905, WHEN HE WAS 11 YEARS OLD.

ANDRÉ 3000 WAS BORN IN 1975   JACK MCBRAYER WAS BORN IN 1973

7 AM

8 AM

9 AM

10 AM

11 AM

NOON

1 PM

2 PM

3 PM

4 PM

5 PM

6 PM

ON THIS DAY IN 1930: ADHESIVE TAPE WAS PATENTED.

BRILLIANT AND/OR TERRIBLE IDEAS

147 DAYS DOWN, 218 DAYS LEFT (UNLESS IT'S A LEAP YEAR [148/218])   YEAR:

MAY 28

WRITE IN THE DATES BELOW (AND SHADE IN TODAY)

MONDAY	TUESDAY	WEDNESDAY	THURSDAY	FRIDAY	SATURDAY ☐
. . . .	. . . .	. . . .	. . . .	. . . .	
☐ TODAY	☐ TODAY	☐ TODAY	☐ TODAY	☐ TODAY	☐ SUNDAY

IT'S NATIONAL BRISKET DAY
NO COW BREED IS ACTUALLY NATIVE TO AMERICA.

JAKE JOHNSON WAS BORN IN 1978   KYLIE MINOGUE WAS BORN IN 1968

7 AM
. . . .
8 AM
. . . .
9 AM
. . . .
10 AM
. . . .
11 AM
. . . .
NOON
. . . .
1 PM
. . . .
2 PM
. . . .
3 PM
. . . .
4 PM
. . . .
5 PM
. . . .
6 PM

ON THIS DAY IN 1897: JELL-O WAS FIRST INTRODUCED.

NOTES AND/OR LIMERICKS

YEAR: 148 DAYS DOWN, 217 DAYS LEFT (UNLESS IT'S A LEAP YEAR [149/217])

MAY 29

IT'S MOUNT EVEREST DAY
THE FIRST TIME IT WAS EVER SUCCESSFULLY CLIMBED WAS IN 1953.

LAVERNE COX WAS BORN IN 1972   JOHN F. KENNEDY WAS BORN IN 1917

7 AM

8 AM

9 AM

10 AM

11 AM

NOON

1 PM

2 PM

3 PM

4 PM

5 PM

6 PM

ON THIS DAY IN 1987: MICHAEL JACKSON TRIED TO BUY THE ELEPHANT MAN'S REMAINS.

BRILLIANT AND/OR TERRIBLE IDEAS

149 DAYS DOWN, 216 DAYS LEFT (UNLESS IT'S A LEAP YEAR [150/216])   YEAR:

MAY 30

MONDAY	TUESDAY	WEDNESDAY	THURSDAY	FRIDAY	SATURDAY ☐
☐ TODAY	☐ TODAY	☐ TODAY	☐ TODAY	☐ TODAY	☐ SUNDAY

IT'S NATIONAL MINT JULEP DAY
IN THE 1700s THE DRINK WAS USED TO TREAT STOMACH ACHES.

CEE LO GREEN WAS BORN IN 1975   IDINA MENZEL WAS BORN IN 197

7 AM

8 AM

9 AM

10 AM

11 AM

NOO

1 PM

2 P

3 PM

4 P

5 PM

6 P

ON THIS DAY IN 1996: WENDY GUEY SPELLED 'VIVISEPULTURE' TO WIN THE NSB.

NOTES AND/OR LIMERICKS

YEAR: 150 DAYS DOWN, 215 DAYS LEFT (UNLESS IT'S A LEAP YEAR [151/215])

MAY 31

WRITE IN THE DATES BELOW (AND SHADE IN TODAY)					
MONDAY	**TUESDAY**	**WEDNESDAY**	**THURSDAY**	**FRIDAY**	**SATURDAY** ☐
☐ TODAY	☐ TODAY	☐ TODAY	☐ TODAY	☐ TODAY	☐ SUNDAY

IT'S NATIONAL SMILING DAY
SMILING IS MORE CONTAGIOUS THAN THE FLU.

CLINT EASTWOOD WAS BORN IN 1930   BROOKE SHIELDS WAS BORN IN 1965

7 AM

8 AM

9 AM

10 AM

11 AM

NOON

1 PM

2 PM

3 PM

4 PM

5 PM

6 PM

ON THIS DAY IN 2021: NAOMI OSAKA PULLED OUT OF THE FRENCH OPEN.

BRILLIANT AND/OR TERRIBLE IDEAS

151 DAYS DOWN, 214 DAYS LEFT (UNLESS IT'S A LEAP YEAR [152/214])   YEAR:

NO OTHER MONTH IN THE YEAR BEGINS ON THE SAME DAY OF THE WEEK.

IT'S OFFICIALLY

OF THE YEAR

☐ ☐ ☐ ☐

MONTH SIX

. . . .

. . . .

. . . .

NAMED AFTER THE ROMAN GODDESS OF MARRIAGE, JUNO.

JUNE AT A GLANCE

CONGRATULATIONS, YOU MADE IT
TO THE MONTH OF JUNE

✖

CELEBRATE, IT'S:	OFFICIAL SYMBOLS:
LGBTQIA PRIDE MONTH	BIRTHSTONE: PEARL
NTL. HOMEOWNERSHIP MONTH	FLOWERS: ROSE & HONEYSUCKLE
NATIONAL ICED TEA MONTH	TREES: ASH, FIG, & APPLE
TURKEY LOVERS MONTH	GEMINI (MAY 21 / JUN 20)
NATIONAL SOUL FOOD MONTH	CANCER (JUN 21 / JUL 22)

✖

A FEW DATES TO KNOW*
LIKE, IMPORTANT ONES.

✖

WLD. ENVIRONMENT DAY JUNE 5TH	**NATIVE AMERICAN CITIZENSHIP DAY** JUNE 15TH
D-DAY (WWII) JUNE 6TH	**MARTYRDOM OF GURU ARJAN DEV (SIKHISM)** JUNE 16TH
FLAG DAY JUNE 14TH	
ST. VLADIMIR DAY (ROMAN CATHOLIC) JUNE 15TH	**START OF SUMMER (SUMMER SOLSTICE)** JUNE 20TH (OR 21ST)
JUNETEENTH JUNE 19TH	**FORGIVENESS DAY** JUNE 26TH

MARK YOUR CALENDAR ✖ IT'S RIGHT OVER THERE

---

*A DISCLAIMER OF SORTS

HEY THERE. WE HERE AT BRASS MONKEY LIKE TO JOKE AROUND...BUT WE ALSO WANT TO TAKE A MINUTE TO RECOGNIZE JUST A FEW OF THE MANY HOLIDAYS & EVENTS THAT ARE IMPORTANT TO OUR FRIENDS AROUND THE GLOBE (AND AT HOME). YOU MAY BE DIFFERENT THAN US. WE MAY HAVE NEVER MET. BUT WE LOVE YOU ALL THE SAME.

SO, WITH ALL OF THAT SAID, IF YOU HAVEN'T HEARD OF A DAY, PLEASE LOOK IT UP. LEARNING ABOUT AND APPRECIATING CULTURES DIFFERENT THAN YOURS IS REALLY IMPORTANT...WAY MORE SO THAN POSTING A FEW 'STRAWBERRY JAM DAY' VIDEOS ON TIKTOK. DON'T GET US WRONG, THERE IS PLENTY OF ROOM FOR BOTH. JUST PLEASE DO BOTH.

JUNE AT A GLANCE

S M T W T F S	S M T W T F S	S M T W T F S	S M T W T F S	S M T W T F S	S M T W T F S	S M T W T F S
01	02	03	04	05	06	07
08	09	10	11	12	13	14 FLAG DAY
15	16	17	18	19 JUNETEENTH	20	21
22	23	24	25	26	27	28
29	30					

YEAR:

WELL, WHAT ARE YOU WAITING FOR?

✕ START PLANNING. IN THE CALENDAR ABOVE, WE'VE MARKED THE MORE COMMON U.S. HOLIDAYS ALREADY (THE ONES THAT ARE DATED, THAT IS). SO USE THE LIST TO THE LEFT TO FILL IN THE REST...LIKE ALL OF THE ONES THAT CHANGE DATES FROM YEAR TO YEAR, FOR EXAMPLE. ✕

LISTS, NOTES & MEMOIRS

MY JAMS (SONGS)
OR SOME BORING TO-DO LIST

1
2
3
4
5
6
7
8
9
10
11
12
13
14

MY JAMS (PRESERVES)
OR A GROCERY LIST OR SOMETHING

1
2
3
4
5
6
7
8
9
10
11
12
13
14

REASONS THAT I CAN'T HAVE NICE THINGS
USE FIGURE 1 FOR ANY NECESSARY VISUAL AIDS

FIG. 1

1   4
2   5
3   6

JUNE 1

MONDAY	TUESDAY	WEDNESDAY	THURSDAY	FRIDAY	SATURDAY ☐
. . . .	. . . .	. . . .	. . . .	. . . .	☐
☐ TODAY	☐ TODAY	☐ TODAY	☐ TODAY	☐ TODAY	SUNDAY

IT'S NATIONAL OLIVE DAY

THE OLDEST OLIVE TREE IS OVER 4,000 YEARS OLD.

MARILYN MONROE WAS BORN IN 1926   MORGAN FREEMAN WAS BORN IN 1937

7 AM

AM

9 AM

10 AM

11 AM

NOON

1 PM

PM

3 PM

PM

5 PM

PM

ON THIS DAY IN 1974: THE HEIMLICH MANEUVER WAS FIRST PUBLISHED.

BRILLIANT AND/OR TERRIBLE IDEAS

152 DAYS DOWN, 213 DAYS LEFT (UNLESS IT'S A LEAP YEAR [153/213])   YEAR:

JUNE 2

MONDAY	TUESDAY	WEDNESDAY	THURSDAY	FRIDAY	SATURDAY ☐
. . . .	. . . .	. . . .	. . . .	. . . .	
☐ TODAY	☐ TODAY	☐ TODAY	☐ TODAY	☐ TODAY	☐ SUNDAY

IT'S NATIONAL ROTISSERIE CHICKEN DAY
THE FIRST DEPICTIONS OF THEM CAN BE FOUND IN PAINTINGS FROM THE 1300s.

AWKWAFINA WAS BORN IN 1988   WAYNE BRADY WAS BORN IN 197

7 AM
. . . .
                                                                                    8 A
. . . .
9 AM
. . . .
                                                                                    10 A
. . . .
11 AM
. . . .
                                                                                    NOO
. . . .
1 PM
. . . .
                                                                                    2 P
. . . .
3 PM
. . . .
                                                                                    4 P
. . . .
5 PM
. . . .
                                                                                    6 P

ON THIS DAY IN 1989: THE FILM 'DEAD POET'S SOCIETY' WAS RELEASED.

NOTES AND/OR LIMERICKS

YEAR: 153 DAYS DOWN, 212 DAYS LEFT (UNLESS IT'S A LEAP YEAR [154/212])

MONDAY	TUESDAY	WEDNESDAY	THURSDAY	FRIDAY	SATURDAY ☐

WRITE IN THE DATES BELOW (AND SHADE IN TODAY)

☐ TODAY | ☐ TODAY | ☐ TODAY | ☐ TODAY | ☐ TODAY | ☐ SUNDAY

IT'S NATIONAL EGG DAY
THE AVERAGE HEN LAYS 266 OF THEM PER YEAR.

OSEPHINE BAKER WAS BORN IN 1906   ANDERSON COOPER WAS BORN IN 1967

7 AM

AM

9 AM

O AM

11 AM

OON

1 PM

PM

3 PM

PM

5 PM

PM

ON THIS DAY IN 1992: BILL CLINTON PLAYED SAX ON THE 'ARSENIO HALL SHOW.'

BRILLIANT AND/OR TERRIBLE IDEAS

154 DAYS DOWN, 211 DAYS LEFT (UNLESS IT'S A LEAP YEAR [155/211])   YEAR:

JUNE 4

WRITE IN THE DATES BELOW (AND SHADE IN TODAY)

MONDAY	TUESDAY	WEDNESDAY	THURSDAY	FRIDAY	SATURDAY
. . . . ☐ TODAY	. . . . ☐ TODAY	. . . . ☐ TODAY	. . . . ☐ TODAY	. . . . ☐ TODAY	☐ ☐ SUNDAY

IT'S NATIONAL HUG YOUR CAT DAY
CATS SPEND ABOUT 70% OF THEIR LIVES ASLEEP.

ANGELINA JOLIE WAS BORN IN 1975   BRUCE DERN WAS BORN IN 193[ ]

7 AM

8 A[ ]

9 AM

10 A[ ]

11 AM

NOO[ ]

1 PM

2 P[ ]

3 PM

4 P[ ]

5 PM

6 P[ ]

ON THIS DAY IN 1984: BRUCE SPRINGSTEEN'S 'BORN IN THE USA' WAS RELEASED.

NOTES AND/OR LIMERICKS

YEAR: _____   155 DAYS DOWN, 210 DAYS LEFT (UNLESS IT'S A LEAP YEAR [156/210])

JUNE 5

WRITE IN THE DATES BELOW (AND SHADE IN TODAY)

MONDAY	TUESDAY	WEDNESDAY	THURSDAY	FRIDAY	SATURDAY ☐
. . . .	. . . .	. . . .	. . . .	. . . .	☐
☐ TODAY	☐ TODAY	☐ TODAY	☐ TODAY	☐ TODAY	☐ SUNDAY

IT'S NATIONAL GINGERBREAD DAY
THE FIRST KNOWN GINGERBREAD RECIPE IS FROM 2400 BC.

MARK WAHLBERG WAS BORN IN 1971   NICK KROLL WAS BORN IN 1978

7 AM

AM

9 AM

0 AM

11 AM

OON

1 PM

PM

3 PM

PM

5 PM

PM

ON THIS DAY IN 1985: FERRIS BUELLER TOOK HIS FICTIONAL DAY OFF.

BRILLIANT AND/OR TERRIBLE IDEAS

156 DAYS DOWN, 209 DAYS LEFT (UNLESS IT'S A LEAP YEAR [157/209])   YEAR:

JUNE 6

MONDAY	TUESDAY	WEDNESDAY	THURSDAY	FRIDAY	SATURDAY ☐
. . . . ☐ TODAY	. . . . ☐ TODAY	. . . . ☐ TODAY	. . . . ☐ TODAY	. . . . ☐ TODAY	☐ SUNDAY

IT'S NATIONAL DRIVE-IN MOVIE DAY
THE ORIGINAL COST TO SEE A DRIVE-IN MOVIE WAS 25 CENTS.

JASON ISAACS WAS BORN IN 1963   PAUL GIAMATTI WAS BORN IN 196

7 AM
. . . .
8 A
. . . .
9 AM
. . . .
10 A
. . . .
11 AM
. . . .
NOO
. . . .
1 PM
. . . .
2 P
. . . .
3 PM
. . . .
4 P
. . . .
5 PM
. . . .
6 P

ON THIS DAY IN 1983: 'READING RAINBOW' PREMIERED ON PBS.

NOTES AND/OR LIMERICKS

YEAR:	157 DAYS DOWN, 208 DAYS LEFT (UNLESS IT'S A LEAP YEAR [158/208])

WRITE IN THE DATES BELOW (AND SHADE IN TODAY)					
MONDAY	**TUESDAY**	**WEDNESDAY**	**THURSDAY**	**FRIDAY**	**SATURDAY** ☐
. . . . ☐ TODAY	. . . . ☐ TODAY	. . . . ☐ TODAY	. . . . ☐ TODAY	. . . . ☐ TODAY	☐ **SUNDAY**

IT'S NATIONAL VCR DAY
THE LAST ONE WAS MADE IN AUGUST 2016.

PRINCE WAS BORN IN 1958   BILL HADER WAS BORN IN 1978

7 AM

8 AM

9 AM

10 AM

11 AM

NOON

1 PM

2 PM

3 PM

4 PM

5 PM

6 PM

ON THIS DAY IN 1990: UNIVERSAL STUDIOS OPENED IN FLORIDA.

BRILLIANT AND/OR TERRIBLE IDEAS

158 DAYS DOWN, 207 DAYS LEFT (UNLESS IT'S A LEAP YEAR [159/207])   YEAR:

JUNE 8

MONDAY	TUESDAY	WEDNESDAY	THURSDAY	FRIDAY	SATURDAY ☐
. . . .	. . . .	. . . .	. . . .	. . . .	
☐ TODAY	☐ TODAY	☐ TODAY	☐ TODAY	☐ TODAY	☐ SUNDAY

IT'S NATIONAL BEST FRIENDS DAY
ONLY 1 OUT OF 2 FRIENDSHIPS LAST.

JOAN RIVERS WAS BORN IN 1933   JULIANA MARGULIES WAS BORN IN 196

7 AM
. . . .
8 AM
. . . .
9 AM
. . . .
10 AM
. . . .
11 AM
. . . .
NOON
. . . .
1 PM
. . . .
2 PM
. . . .
3 PM
. . . .
4 PM
. . . .
5 PM
. . . .
6 P

ON THIS DAY IN 1966: THE NFL AND AFL ANNOUNCED THEIR MERGER.

NOTES AND/OR LIMERICKS																								

YEAR:	159 DAYS DOWN, 206 DAYS LEFT (UNLESS IT'S A LEAP YEAR [160/206])

		WRITE IN THE DATES BELOW (AND SHADE IN TODAY)			
MONDAY	TUESDAY	WEDNESDAY	THURSDAY	FRIDAY	SATURDAY ☐
☐ TODAY	☐ TODAY	☐ TODAY	☐ TODAY	☐ TODAY	☐ SUNDAY

IT'S NATIONAL STRAWBERRY RHUBARB PIE DAY
THE LEAVES ON RHUBARB ARE POISONOUS TO BOTH HUMANS AND ANIMALS.

MICHAEL J. FOX WAS BORN IN 1961   NATALIE PORTMAN WAS BORN IN 1981

7 AM

8 AM

9 AM

10 AM

11 AM

NOON

1 PM

2 PM

3 PM

4 PM

5 PM

6 PM

ON THIS DAY IN 1984: CYNDI LAUPER'S 'TIME AFTER TIME' REACHED #1 ON THE U.S. CHARTS.

BRILLIANT AND/OR TERRIBLE IDEAS

160 DAYS DOWN, 205 DAYS LEFT (UNLESS IT'S A LEAP YEAR [161/205])   YEAR:

JUNE 10

MONDAY	TUESDAY	WEDNESDAY	THURSDAY	FRIDAY	SATURDAY [
. . . .	. . . .	. . . .	. . . .	. . . .	
☐ TODAY	☐ TODAY	☐ TODAY	☐ TODAY	☐ TODAY	☐ SUNDA

IT'S NATIONAL BALLPOINT PEN DAY
AN AVERAGE PEN CAN WRITE APPROXIMATELY 45,000 WORDS.

JUDY GARLAND WAS BORN IN 1922   BILL BURR WAS BORN IN 19

7 AM
. . . .
                                                                                        8 A
. . . .
9 AM
. . . .
                                                                                       10 A
. . . .
11 AM
. . . .
                                                                                       NOC
. . . .
1 PM
. . . .
                                                                                        2 P
. . . .
3 PM
. . . .
                                                                                        4 P
. . . .
5 PM
. . . .
                                                                                        6 P

ON THIS DAY IN 1949: SAAB REVEALED ITS FIRST AUTOMOBILE.

NOTES AND/OR LIMERICKS

YEAR: 161 DAYS DOWN, 204 DAYS LEFT (UNLESS IT'S A LEAP YEAR [162/204])

JUNE 11

MONDAY	TUESDAY	WEDNESDAY	THURSDAY	FRIDAY	SATURDAY ☐
. . . .	. . . .	. . . .	. . . .	. . . .	☐
☐ TODAY	☐ TODAY	☐ TODAY	☐ TODAY	☐ TODAY	SUNDAY

IT'S NATIONAL CORN ON THE COB DAY
THERE'S ONE STRAND OF SILK PER KERNEL OF CORN.

PETER DINKLAGE WAS BORN IN 1969   GENE WILDER WAS BORN IN 1933

7 AM

. . . .

8 AM

. . . .

9 AM

. . . .

10 AM

. . . .

11 AM

. . . .

NOON

. . . .

1 PM

. . . .

2 PM

. . . .

3 PM

. . . .

4 PM

. . . .

5 PM

. . . .

6 PM

ON THIS DAY IN 1949: HANK WILLIAMS SR. DEBUTED AT THE GRAND OLE OPRY.

BRILLIANT AND/OR TERRIBLE IDEAS

JUNE 12

MONDAY	TUESDAY	WEDNESDAY	THURSDAY	FRIDAY	SATURDAY ☐
. . . .	. . . .	. . . .	. . . .	. . . .	
☐ TODAY	☐ TODAY	☐ TODAY	☐ TODAY	☐ TODAY	☐ SUNDAY

IT'S NATIONAL RED ROSE DAY
PRESIDENT REAGAN DECLARED THEM THE NATIONAL FLOWER IN 1986.

ANNE FRANK WAS BORN IN 1929   ALLY SHEEDY WAS BORN IN 196

7 AM

8 AM

9 AM

10 AM

11 AM

NOON

1 PM

2 PM

3 PM

4 PM

5 PM

6 PM

ON THIS DAY IN 1942: ANNE FRANK RECEIVED A DIARY FOR HER 13TH BIRTHDAY.

NOTES, AND/OR LIMERICKS

YEAR: 163 DAYS DOWN, 202 DAYS LEFT (UNLESS IT'S A LEAP YEAR [164/202])

MONDAY	TUESDAY	WEDNESDAY	THURSDAY	FRIDAY	SATURDAY ☐
. . . .	. . . .	. . . .	. . . .	. . . .	
☐ TODAY	☐ TODAY	☐ TODAY	☐ TODAY	☐ TODAY	☐ SUNDAY

IT'S WORLD SOFTBALL DAY

IT WAS ORIGINALLY GOING TO BE CALLED 'KITTEN BALL.'

KAT DENNINGS WAS BORN IN 1986   CHRIS EVANS WAS BORN IN 1981

7 AM

8 AM

9 AM

10 AM

11 AM

NOON

1 PM

2 PM

3 PM

4 PM

5 PM

6 PM

ON THIS DAY IN 1920: THE USPS FORBID THE MAILING OF CHILDREN.

BRILLIANT AND/OR TERRIBLE IDEAS

164 DAYS DOWN, 201 DAYS LEFT (UNLESS IT'S A LEAP YEAR [165/201])

YEAR:

JUNE 14

MONDAY	TUESDAY	WEDNESDAY	THURSDAY	FRIDAY	SATURDAY ☐
. . . .	. . . .	. . . .	. . . .	. . . .	
☐ TODAY	☐ TODAY	☐ TODAY	☐ TODAY	☐ TODAY	☐ SUNDAY

IT'S NATIONAL BOURBON DAY
95% OF ALL BOURBON IS PRODUCED IN KENTUCKY.

BOY GEORGE WAS BORN IN 1961   LANG LANG WAS BORN IN 1982

7 AM
. . . .
8 AM
. . . .
9 AM
. . . .
10 AM
. . . .
11 AM
. . . .
NOON
. . . .
1 PM
. . . .
2 PM
. . . .
3 PM
. . . .
4 PM
. . . .
5 PM
. . . .
6 PM

ON THIS DAY IN 2022: BTS ANNOUNCED A HIATUS TO COMPLETE MANDATORY MILITARY SERVICE.

NOTES AND/OR LIMERICKS

YEAR: | 165 DAYS DOWN, 200 DAYS LEFT (UNLESS IT'S A LEAP YEAR [166/200])

JUNE 15

WRITE IN THE DATES BELOW (AND SHADE IN TODAY)					
MONDAY	**TUESDAY**	**WEDNESDAY**	**THURSDAY**	**FRIDAY**	**SATURDAY** ☐
. . . .	. . . .	. . . .	. . . .	. . . .	
☐ TODAY	☐ TODAY	☐ TODAY	☐ TODAY	☐ TODAY	☐ SUNDAY

IT'S NATIONAL LOBSTER DAY
LOBSTERS SQUIRT URINE AT ONE ANOTHER DURING COURTSHIP.

ICE CUBE WAS BORN IN 1969   COURTNEY COX WAS BORN IN 1964

7 AM

8 AM

9 AM

10 AM

11 AM

NOON

1 PM

2 PM

3 PM

4 PM

5 PM

6 PM

ON THIS DAY IN 1934: THE GREAT SMOKY MOUNTAIN NATIONAL PARK WAS FOUNDED.

BRILLIANT AND/OR TERRIBLE IDEAS

166 DAYS DOWN, 199 DAYS LEFT (UNLESS IT'S A LEAP YEAR [167/199])   YEAR:

JUNE 16

MONDAY	TUESDAY	WEDNESDAY	THURSDAY	FRIDAY	SATURDAY ☐
. . . . ☐ TODAY	. . . . ☐ TODAY	. . . . ☐ TODAY	. . . . ☐ TODAY	. . . . ☐ TODAY	☐ SUNDAY

IT'S WORLD JUGGLING DAY
JUGGLING BURNS 280 CALORIES PER HOUR.

TUPAC SHAKUR WAS BORN IN 1971   JOYCE CAROL OATES WAS BORN IN 1938

7 AM
. . . .
8 AM
. . . .
9 AM
. . . .
10 AM
. . . .
11 AM
. . . .
NOON
. . . .
1 PM
. . . .
2 PM
. . . .
3 PM
. . . .
4 PM
. . . .
5 PM
. . . .
6 PM

ON THIS DAY IN 1884: THE FIRST ROLLER COASTER OPENED ON CONEY ISLAND.

NOTES AND/OR LIMERICKS

YEAR: | 167 DAYS DOWN, 198 DAYS LEFT (UNLESS IT'S A LEAP YEAR [168/198])

JUNE 17

MONDAY	TUESDAY	WEDNESDAY	THURSDAY	FRIDAY	SATURDAY ☐
☐ TODAY	☐ TODAY	☐ TODAY	☐ TODAY	☐ TODAY	☐ SUNDAY

IT'S NATIONAL MASCOT DAY
SNOOPY HAS BEEN NASA'S MASCOT SINCE 1968.

WILL FORTE WAS BORN IN 1970   VENUS WILLIAMS WAS BORN IN 1980

7 AM

8 AM

9 AM

10 AM

11 AM

NOON

1 PM

2 PM

3 PM

4 PM

5 PM

6 PM

ON THIS DAY IN 1885: THE STATUE OF LIBERTY ARRIVED IN NEW YORK HARBOR.

BRILLIANT AND/OR TERRIBLE IDEAS

168 DAYS DOWN, 197 DAYS LEFT (UNLESS IT'S A LEAP YEAR [169/197])   YEAR:

JUNE 18

WRITE IN THE DATES BELOW (AND SHADE IN TODAY)

MONDAY	TUESDAY	WEDNESDAY	THURSDAY	FRIDAY	SATURDAY ☐
. . . . ☐ TODAY	. . . . ☐ TODAY	. . . . ☐ TODAY	. . . . ☐ TODAY	. . . . ☐ TODAY	☐　　SUNDAY

IT'S NATIONAL GO FISHING DAY
THE FIRST RODS AND REELS WERE INVENTED IN THE 1770s.

PAUL MCCARTNEY WAS BORN IN 1942   ROGER EBERT WAS BORN IN 1942

7 AM
. . . .
8 AM
. . . .
9 AM
. . . .
10 AM
. . . .
11 AM
. . . .
NOON
. . . .
1 PM
. . . .
2 PM
. . . .
3 PM
. . . .
4 PM
. . . .
5 PM
. . . .
6 PM

ON THIS DAY IN 1873: SUSAN B. ANTHONY WAS FINED $100 FOR TRYING TO VOTE.

NOTES AND/OR LIMERICKS

YEAR: 169 DAYS DOWN, 196 DAYS LEFT (UNLESS IT'S A LEAP YEAR [170/196])

JUNE 19

MONDAY	TUESDAY	WEDNESDAY	THURSDAY	FRIDAY	SATURDAY ☐
☐ TODAY	☐ TODAY	☐ TODAY	☐ TODAY	☐ TODAY	☐ SUNDAY

IT'S JUNETEENTH.
TEXAS WAS THE FIRST STATE TO DECLARE IT A HOLIDAY.

ZOE SALDANA WAS BORN IN 1978   PAUL DANO WAS BORN IN 1984

7 AM

8 AM

9 AM

10 AM

11 AM

NOON

1 PM

2 PM

3 PM

4 PM

5 PM

6 PM

ON THIS DAY IN 1941: CHEERIE OATS (RENAMED CHEERIOS) WERE INVENTED.

BRILLIANT AND/OR TERRIBLE IDEAS

170 DAYS DOWN, 195 DAYS LEFT (UNLESS IT'S A LEAP YEAR [171/195])   YEAR:

JUNE 20

MONDAY	TUESDAY	WEDNESDAY	THURSDAY	FRIDAY	SATURDAY ☐
. . . .	. . . .	. . . .	. . . .	. . . .	
☐ TODAY	☐ TODAY	☐ TODAY	☐ TODAY	☐ TODAY	☐ SUNDAY

IT'S NATIONAL AMERICAN EAGLE DAY
IT'S ILLEGAL TO PICK UP ONE OF THEIR FEATHER'S WITHOUT A PERMIT.

NICOLE KIDMAN WAS BORN IN 1967   LIONEL RICHIE WAS BORN IN 1949

7 AM
. . . .
                                                                                            8 AM
. . . .
9 AM
. . . .
                                                                                            10 AM
. . . .
11 AM
. . . .
                                                                                            NOON
. . . .
1 PM
. . . .
                                                                                            2 PM
. . . .
3 PM
. . . .
                                                                                            4 PM
. . . .
5 PM
. . . .
                                                                                            6 PM

ON THIS DAY IN 1975: THE MOVIE 'JAWS' OPENED IN THEATERS.

NOTES AND/OR LIMERICKS

| YEAR: | 171 DAYS DOWN, 194 DAYS LEFT (UNLESS IT'S A LEAP YEAR [172/194]) |

JUNE 21

MONDAY	TUESDAY	WEDNESDAY	THURSDAY	FRIDAY	SATURDAY ☐
☐ TODAY	☐ TODAY	☐ TODAY	☐ TODAY	☐ TODAY	☐ SUNDAY

IT'S NATIONAL DAY OF THE GONG

IN CHINA, CHAU GONGS WERE USED TO CLEAR THE WAY FOR OFFICIALS.

PRINCE WILLIAM WAS BORN IN 1982   LANA DEL REY WAS BORN IN 1985

7 AM

8 AM

9 AM

10 AM

11 AM

NOON

1 PM

2 PM

3 PM

4 PM

5 PM

6 PM

ON THIS DAY IN 1939: LOU GEHRIG RETIRED FROM BASEBALL DUE TO ALS.

BRILLIANT AND/OR TERRIBLE IDEAS

172 DAYS DOWN, 193 DAYS LEFT (UNLESS IT'S A LEAP YEAR [173/193])

YEAR:

JUNE 22

WRITE IN THE DATES BELOW (AND SHADE IN TODAY)

MONDAY	TUESDAY	WEDNESDAY	THURSDAY	FRIDAY	SATURDAY ☐
. . . . ☐ TODAY	. . . . ☐ TODAY	. . . . ☐ TODAY	. . . . ☐ TODAY	. . . . ☐ TODAY	☐ SUNDAY

IT'S NATIONAL ONION RINGS DAY
EATING PARSLEY HELPS ELIMINATE ONION BREATH.

CYNDI LAUPER WAS BORN IN 1953   DONALD FAISON WAS BORN IN 1974

7 AM
. . . .
8 AM
. . . .
9 AM
. . . .
10 AM
. . . .
11 AM
. . . .
NOON
. . . .
1 PM
. . . .
2 PM
. . . .
3 PM
. . . .
4 PM
. . . .
5 PM
. . . .
6 PM

ON THIS DAY IN 1990: ADAM SANDLER JOINED THE CAST OF 'SATURDAY NIGHT LIVE.'

NOTES AND/OR LIMERICKS

YEAR: 173 DAYS DOWN, 192 DAYS LEFT (UNLESS IT'S A LEAP YEAR [174/192])

JUNE 23

	WRITE IN THE DATES BELOW (AND SHADE IN TODAY)				
MONDAY	TUESDAY	WEDNESDAY	THURSDAY	FRIDAY	SATURDAY ☐
☐ TODAY	☐ TODAY	☐ TODAY	☐ TODAY	☐ TODAY	☐ SUNDAY

IT'S PINK FLAMINGO DAY
THE LAWN ORNAMENTS WERE DESIGNED IN 1957.

FRANCES MCDORMAND WAS BORN IN 1957   SELMA BLAIR WAS BORN IN 1972

7 AM

8 AM

9 AM

10 AM

11 AM

NOON

1 PM

2 PM

3 PM

4 PM

5 PM

6 PM

ON THIS DAY IN 2014: CLAUDE MONET'S 'WATER LILIES' SOLD FOR $54 MILLION.

BRILLIANT AND/OR TERRIBLE IDEAS

174 DAYS DOWN, 191 DAYS LEFT (UNLESS IT'S A LEAP YEAR [175/191])   YEAR:

JUNE 24

IT'S NATIONAL PRALINES DAY
FRENCH SETTLERS FIRST INTRODUCED THE RECIPE TO NEW ORLEANS IN 1727.

MINDY KALING WAS BORN IN 1979   SOLANGE WAS BORN IN 1986

7 AM

8 AM

9 AM

10 AM

11 AM

NOON

1 PM

2 PM

3 PM

4 PM

5 PM

6 PM

ON THIS DAY IN 1992: BILLY JOEL RECEIVED AN HONORARY HIGH SCHOOL DIPLOMA.

NOTES AND/OR LIMERICKS

YEAR: 175 DAYS DOWN, 190 DAYS LEFT (UNLESS IT'S A LEAP YEAR [176/190])

WRITE IN THE DATES BELOW (AND SHADE IN TODAY)					
MONDAY	**TUESDAY**	**WEDNESDAY**	**THURSDAY**	**FRIDAY**	**SATURDAY** ☐
. . . .	. . . .	. . . .	. . . .	. . . .	☐
☐ TODAY	☐ TODAY	☐ TODAY	☐ TODAY	☐ TODAY	☐ SUNDAY

IT'S NATIONAL CATFISH DAY
THEIR ENTIRE BODIES ARE COVERED WITH OVER 27,000 TASTE BUDS.

RICKY GERVAIS WAS BORN IN 1961   GEORGE ORWELL WAS BORN IN 1903

7 AM

8 AM

9 AM

10 AM

11 AM

NOON

1 PM

2 PM

3 PM

4 PM

5 PM

6 PM

ON THIS DAY IN 1993: THE LAST 'LATE NIGHT WITH DAVID LETTERMAN' AIRED.

BRILLIANT AND/OR TERRIBLE IDEAS

176 DAYS DOWN, 189 DAYS LEFT (UNLESS IT'S A LEAP YEAR [177/189])   YEAR:

JUNE 26

IT'S NATIONAL CANOE DAY
THE LONGEST CANOE TRIP WAS OVER 12,000 MILES.

AUBREY PLAZA WAS BORN IN 1984   NICK OFFERMAN WAS BORN IN 197

7 AM

. . . .

8 A

. . . .

9 AM

. . . .

10 A

. . . .

11 AM

. . . .

NOO

. . . .

1 PM

. . . .

2 P

. . . .

3 PM

. . . .

4 P

. . . .

5 PM

. . . .

6 P

ON THIS DAY IN 2018: THE HELLO KITTY BULLET TRAIN WAS UNVEILED IN JAPAN.

NOTES AND/OR LIMERICKS

YEAR: 177 DAYS DOWN, 188 DAYS LEFT (UNLESS IT'S A LEAP YEAR [178/188])

JUNE 27

MONDAY	TUESDAY	WEDNESDAY	THURSDAY	FRIDAY	SATURDAY ☐
. . . .	. . . .	. . . .	. . . .	. . . .	
☐ TODAY	☐ TODAY	☐ TODAY	☐ TODAY	☐ TODAY	☐ SUNDAY

IT'S NATIONAL BINGO DAY
RUSSEL CROWE'S FIRST JOB WAS AS A BINGO CALLER.

HELEN KELLER WAS BORN IN 1880   VERA WANG WAS BORN IN 1949

7 AM

. . . .

8 AM

. . . .

9 AM

. . . .

10 AM

. . . .

11 AM

. . . .

NOON

. . . .

1 PM

. . . .

2 PM

. . . .

3 PM

. . . .

4 PM

. . . .

5 PM

. . . .

6 PM

ON THIS DAY IN 1985: ROUTE 66 WAS REMOVED FROM THE U.S. HIGHWAY SYSTEM.

BRILLIANT AND/OR TERRIBLE IDEAS

JUNE 28

WRITE IN THE DATES BELOW (AND SHADE IN TODAY)

MONDAY	TUESDAY	WEDNESDAY	THURSDAY	FRIDAY	SATURDAY ☐
. . . .	. . . .	. . . .	. . . .	. . . .	
☐ TODAY	☐ TODAY	☐ TODAY	☐ TODAY	☐ TODAY	☐ SUNDAY

IT'S NATIONAL TAPIOCA DAY

IT'S PROCESSED FROM THE OTHERWISE POISONOUS CASSAVA ROOT.

KATHY BATES WAS BORN IN 1948   JOHN CUSACK WAS BORN IN 196

7 AM
. . . .
8 AM
. . . .
9 AM
. . . .
10 AM
11 AM
. . . .
NOO
. . . .
1 PM
. . . .
2 P
. . . .
3 PM
. . . .
4 P
. . . .
5 PM
. . . .
6 P

ON THIS DAY IN 1894: LABOR DAY BECAME AN OFFICIAL U.S. HOLIDAY.

NOTES AND/OR LIMERICKS

YEAR: 179 DAYS DOWN, 186 DAYS LEFT (UNLESS IT'S A LEAP YEAR [180/186])

JUNE 29

		WRITE IN THE DATES BELOW (AND SHADE IN TODAY)			
MONDAY	TUESDAY	WEDNESDAY	THURSDAY	FRIDAY	SATURDAY ☐
☐ TODAY	☐ TODAY	☐ TODAY	☐ TODAY	☐ TODAY	☐ SUNDAY

IT'S NATIONAL WAFFLE IRON DAY
IT WAS PATENTED IN 1869 BY CORNELIUS SWARTHOUT.

COLIN JOST WAS BORN IN 1982   LILY RABE WAS BORN IN 1982

7 AM

8 AM

9 AM

10 AM

11 AM

NOON

1 PM

2 PM

3 PM

4 PM

5 PM

6 PM

ON THIS DAY IN 1998: THE LIFETIME MOVIE NETWORK MADE ITS DEBUT.

BRILLIANT AND/OR TERRIBLE IDEAS

180 DAYS DOWN, 185 DAYS LEFT (UNLESS IT'S A LEAP YEAR [181/185])   YEAR:

JUNE 30

MONDAY	TUESDAY	WEDNESDAY	THURSDAY	FRIDAY	SATURDAY ☐
. . . .	. . . .	. . . .	. . . .	. . . .	☐
☐ TODAY	☐ TODAY	☐ TODAY	☐ TODAY	☐ TODAY	☐ SUNDAY

IT'S INTERNATIONAL ASTEROID DAY
THERE ARE CURRENTLY OVER 822,000 KNOWN ASTEROIDS.

LIZZY CAPLAN WAS BORN IN 1982   MIKE TYSON WAS BORN IN 1966

7 AM

8 AM

9 AM

10 AM

11 AM

NOON

1 PM

2 PM

3 PM

4 PM

5 PM

6 PM

ON THIS DAY IN 1936: THE BOOK 'GONE WITH THE WIND' WAS FIRST PUBLISHED.

NOTES AND/OR LIMERICKS

YEAR: 181 DAYS DOWN, 184 DAYS LEFT (UNLESS IT'S A LEAP YEAR [182/184])

LISTS, NOTES & MEMOIRS

WAYS THIS MONTH WAS GREAT
'IT ENDED' IS A VALID ANSWER

1
2
3
4
5
6
7
8
9
10
11
12
13
14

WAYS THAT IT WASN'T
USE ADDITIONAL PAPER IF NEEDED

1
2
3
4
5
6
7
8
9
10
11
12
13
14

POTENTIAL WAYS TO GET OUT OF FUTURE JURY DUTY
USE FIGURE 1 FOR ANY NECESSARY VISUAL AIDS

FIG. 1

1   4
2   5
3   6

IT'S OFFICIALLY

OF THE YEAR

☐ ☐ ☐ ☐

MONTH SEVEN

. . . .

. . . .

. . . .

JULY AT A GLANCE

CONGRATULATIONS, YOU MADE IT
TO THE MONTH OF JULY

✖

CELEBRATE, IT'S:

NATIONAL HEMP MONTH

WORLD WATERCOLOR MONTH

NATIONAL HORSERADISH MONTH

INDEPENDENT RETAILER MONTH

NATIONAL ICE CREAM MONTH

OFFICIAL SYMBOLS:

BIRTHSTONE: RUBY

FLOWERS: LARKSPUR & WATER LILY

TREES: APPLE, FIR, & CYPRESS

CANCER (JUN 21 / JUL 22)

LEO (JUL 23 / AUG 22)

✖

A FEW DATES TO KNOW*
LIKE, IMPORTANT ONES.

✖

CANADA DAY
JULY 1ST

INDEPENDENCE DAY
JULY 4TH

WLD. POPULATION DAY
JULY 11TH

BASTILLE DAY
JULY 14TH

PIONEER DAY
(MORMONISM)
JULY 24TH

NELSON MANDELA INTERNATIONAL DAY
JULY 18TH

ASALHA PUJA
(BUDDHISM)
ON THE FULL MOON DAY
OF THE 8TH LUNAR MONTH
(USUALLY IN JULY)

THE BIRTHDAY OF HAILE SELASSIE I
(RASTAFARIANISM)
JULY 23RD

MARK YOUR CALENDAR ✖ IT'S RIGHT OVER THERE

*A DISCLAIMER OF SORTS

HEY THERE. WE HERE AT BRASS MONKEY LIKE TO JOKE AROUND...BUT WE ALSO WANT TO TAKE A MINUTE TO RECOGNIZE JUST A FEW OF THE MANY HOLIDAYS & EVENTS THAT ARE IMPORTANT TO OUR FRIENDS AROUND THE GLOBE (AND AT HOME). YOU MAY BE DIFFERENT THAN US. WE MAY HAVE NEVER MET. BUT WE LOVE YOU ALL THE SAME.

SO, WITH ALL OF THAT SAID, IF YOU HAVEN'T HEARD OF A DAY, PLEASE LOOK IT UP. LEARNING ABOUT AND APPRECIATING CULTURES DIFFERENT THAN YOURS IS REALLY IMPORTANT...WAY MORE SO THAN POSTING A FEW 'STRAWBERRY JAM DAY' VIDEOS ON TIKTOK. DON'T GET US WRONG, THERE IS PLENTY OF ROOM FOR BOTH. JUST PLEASE DO BOTH.

JULY AT A GLANCE

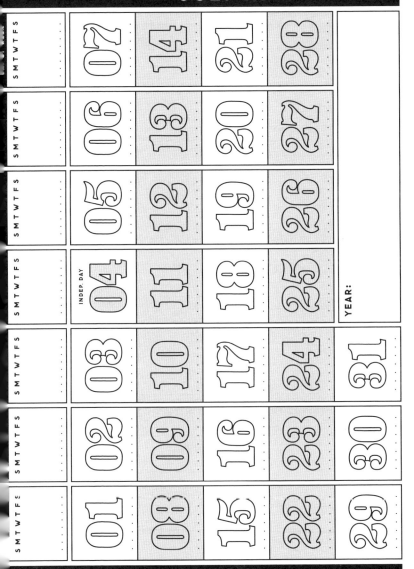

SMTWTFS | SMTWTFS | SMTWTFS | SMTWTFS | SMTWTFS | SMTWTFS | SMTWTFS

01 02 03 INDEP. DAY 04 05 06 07
08 09 10 11 12 13 14
15 16 17 18 19 20 21
22 23 24 25 26 27 28
29 30 31

YEAR:

WELL, WHAT ARE YOU WAITING FOR?

✗ START PLANNING. IN THE CALENDAR ABOVE, WE'VE MARKED THE MORE COMMON ✗
U.S. HOLIDAYS ALREADY (THE ONES THAT ARE DATED, THAT IS). SO USE THE
LIST TO THE LEFT TO FILL IN THE REST...LIKE ALL OF THE ONES THAT CHANGE
DATES FROM YEAR TO YEAR, FOR EXAMPLE.

LISTS, NOTES & MEMOIRS

WORST ADVICE I'VE RECEIVED
OR SOME BORING TO-DO LIST

1

2

3

4

5

6

7

8

9

10

11

12

13

14

BEST ADVICE I'VE IGNORED
OR A GROCERY LIST OR SOMETHING

1

2

3

4

5

6

7

8

9

10

11

12

13

14

THINGS THAT I HAVE DEFINITELY LOST FOREVER
USE FIGURE 1 FOR ANY NECESSARY VISUAL AIDS

FIG. 1

1

2

3

4

5

6

JULY 1

MONDAY	TUESDAY	WEDNESDAY	THURSDAY	FRIDAY	SATURDAY ☐
. . . . ☐ TODAY	. . . . ☐ TODAY	. . . . ☐ TODAY	. . . . ☐ TODAY	. . . . ☐ TODAY	☐ SUNDAY

IT'S INTERNATIONAL CHICKEN WING DAY
AMERICANS EAT APPROXIMATELY 30 BILLION WINGS A YEAR.

DIANA SPENCER WAS BORN IN 1961   MISSY ELLIOTT WAS BORN IN 1971

7 AM

AM

9 AM

O AM

11 AM

OON

1 PM

PM

3 PM

PM

5 PM

PM

ON THIS DAY IN 1941: THE FIRST TV COMMERCIAL AIRED. IT WAS FOR WATCHES.

BRILLIANT AND/OR TERRIBLE IDEAS

182 DAYS DOWN, 183 DAYS LEFT (UNLESS IT'S A LEAP YEAR [183/183])   YEAR:

JULY 2

MONDAY	TUESDAY	WEDNESDAY	THURSDAY	FRIDAY	SATURDAY ☐
. . . . ☐ TODAY	. . . . ☐ TODAY	. . . . ☐ TODAY	. . . . ☐ TODAY	. . . . ☐ TODAY	☐ ☐ SUNDAY

IT'S WORLD U.F.O. DAY
FORMER PRESIDENT JIMMY CARTER SAYS HE SAW ONE IN 1969.

MARGOT ROBBIE WAS BORN IN 1990   LINDSAY LOHAN WAS BORN IN 198

7 AM
. . . .
8 A
. . . .
9 AM
. . . .
10 A
. . . .
11 AM
. . . .
NOO
. . . .
1 PM
. . . .
2 P
. . . .
3 PM
. . . .
4 P
. . . .
5 PM
. . . .
6 P

ON THIS DAY IN 1962: THE FIRST WAL-MART OPENED IN ROGERS, ARKANSAS.

NOTES AND/OR LIMERICKS

YEAR: 183 DAYS DOWN, 182 DAYS LEFT (UNLESS IT'S A LEAP YEAR [184/182])

WRITE IN THE DATES BELOW (AND SHADE IN TODAY)					
MONDAY	TUESDAY	WEDNESDAY	THURSDAY	FRIDAY	SATURDAY ☐
☐ TODAY	☐ TODAY	☐ TODAY	☐ TODAY	☐ TODAY	☐ SUNDAY

IT'S DISOBEDIENCE DAY
BUT WE REFUSE TO PARTICIPATE.

TOM CRUISE WAS BORN IN 1962   AUDRA MCDONALD WAS BORN IN 1970

7 AM

8 AM

9 AM

10 AM

11 AM

NOON

1 PM

2 PM

3 PM

4 PM

5 PM

6 PM

ON THIS DAY IN 1985: 'BACK TO THE FUTURE' WAS RELEASED.

BRILLIANT AND/OR TERRIBLE IDEAS

184 DAYS DOWN, 181 DAYS LEFT (UNLESS IT'S A LEAP YEAR [185/181])   YEAR:

JULY 4

MONDAY	TUESDAY	WEDNESDAY	THURSDAY	FRIDAY	SATURDAY ☐
. . . .	. . . .	. . . .	. . . .	. . . .	
☐ TODAY	☐ TODAY	☐ TODAY	☐ TODAY	☐ TODAY	☐ SUNDAY

IT'S INDEPENDENCE DAY
IT'S ALSO NATIONAL BARBECUE DAY.

POST MALONE WAS BORN IN 1995   MALIA OBAMA WAS BORN IN 1998

7 AM
. . . .
8 AM
. . . .
9 AM
. . . .
10 AM
. . . .
11 AM
. . . .
NOON
. . . .
1 PM
. . . .
2 PM
. . . .
3 PM
. . . .
4 PM
. . . .
5 PM
. . . .
6 PM

ON THIS DAY IN 1971: KOKO THE GORILLA WAS BORN AT THE SAN FRANCISCO ZOO.

NOTES AND/OR LIMERICKS

YEAR: 185 DAYS DOWN, 180 DAYS LEFT (UNLESS IT'S A LEAP YEAR [186/180])

JULY 5

MONDAY	TUESDAY	WEDNESDAY	THURSDAY	FRIDAY	SATURDAY ☐

WRITE IN THE DATES BELOW (AND SHADE IN TODAY)

☐ TODAY	☐ TODAY	☐ TODAY	☐ TODAY	☐ TODAY	☐ SUNDAY

IT'S NATIONAL WORKAHOLICS DAY
THIS ONE IS HITTING A LITTLE TOO CLOSE TO HOME RIGHT NOW.

JEAN COCTEAU WAS BORN IN 1889   MEGAN RAPINOE WAS BORN IN 1985

7 AM

8 AM

9 AM

10 AM

11 AM

NOON

1 PM

2 PM

3 PM

4 PM

5 PM

6 PM

ON THIS DAY IN 1996: DOLLY THE SHEEP (THE FIRST CLONED MAMMAL) WAS BORN.

BRILLIANT AND/OR TERRIBLE IDEAS

186 DAYS DOWN, 179 DAYS LEFT (UNLESS IT'S A LEAP YEAR [187/179])   YEAR:

JULY 6

MONDAY	TUESDAY	WEDNESDAY	THURSDAY	FRIDAY	SATURDAY ☐
☐ TODAY	☐ TODAY	☐ TODAY	☐ TODAY	☐ TODAY	☐ SUNDAY

IT'S INTERNATIONAL KISSING DAY
TWO-THIRDS OF PEOPLE TILT THEIR HEAD TO THE RIGHT TO KISS.

FRIDA KAHLO WAS BORN IN 1907   KEVIN HART WAS BORN IN 1979

7 AM

8 AM

9 AM

10 AM

11 AM

NOON

1 PM

2 PM

3 PM

4 PM

5 PM

6 PM

ON THIS DAY IN 1957: PAUL MCCARTNEY AND JOHN LENNON MET FOR THE FIRST TIME.

NOTES AND/OR LIMERICKS

YEAR: 187 DAYS DOWN, 178 DAYS LEFT (UNLESS IT'S A LEAP YEAR [188/178])

JULY 7

MONDAY	TUESDAY	WEDNESDAY	THURSDAY	FRIDAY	SATURDAY ☐
. . . .	. . . .	. . . .	. . . .	. . . .	☐
☐ TODAY	☐ TODAY	☐ TODAY	☐ TODAY	☐ TODAY	☐ SUNDAY

IT'S NATIONAL MACARONI DAY
MACARONI NOODLES ARE THE MOST POPULAR NOODLE SHAPE IN THE U.S.

RINGO STARR WAS BORN IN 1940   MICHELLE KWAN WAS BORN IN 1980

7 AM

8 AM

9 AM

10 AM

11 AM

NOON

1 PM

2 PM

3 PM

4 PM

5 PM

6 PM

ON THIS DAY IN 1947: POSSIBLE U.F.O. DEBRIS WAS REPORTED IN ROSWELL, MN.

BRILLIANT AND/OR TERRIBLE IDEAS

188 DAYS DOWN, 177 DAYS LEFT (UNLESS IT'S A LEAP YEAR [189/177])   YEAR:

JULY 8

MONDAY	TUESDAY	WEDNESDAY	THURSDAY	FRIDAY	SATURDAY ☐
. . . .	. . . .	. . . .	. . . .	. . . .	
☐ TODAY	☐ TODAY	☐ TODAY	☐ TODAY	☐ TODAY	☐ SUNDAY

IT'S NATIONAL VIDEO GAME DAY
DONKEY KONG WAS INVENTED TO TRY AND COMPETE WITH PAC-MAN.

BECK WAS BORN IN 1970   KEVIN BACON WAS BORN IN 1958

7 AM
. . . .
                                                                                    8 AM
. . . .
9 AM
. . . .
                                                                                    10 AM
. . . .
11 AM
. . . .
                                                                                    NOON
. . . .
1 PM
. . . .
                                                                                    2 PM
. . . .
3 PM
. . . .
                                                                                    4 PM
. . . .
5 PM
. . . .
                                                                                    6 PM

ON THIS DAY IN 1889: THE FIRST ISSUE OF 'THE WALL STREET JOURNAL' WAS PUBLISHED.

NOTES AND/OR LIMERICKS

YEAR: 189 DAYS DOWN, 176 DAYS LEFT (UNLESS IT'S A LEAP YEAR [190/176])

JULY 9

WRITE IN THE DATES BELOW (AND SHADE IN TODAY)

MONDAY	TUESDAY	WEDNESDAY	THURSDAY	FRIDAY	SATURDAY ☐
☐ TODAY	☐ TODAY	☐ TODAY	☐ TODAY	☐ TODAY	☐ SUNDAY

IT'S NATIONAL SUGAR COOKIE DAY
SUGAR CAN BE JUST AS ADDICTIVE AS COCAINE.

TOM HANKS WAS BORN IN 1956   FRED SAVAGE WAS BORN IN 1976

7 AM

8 AM

9 AM

10 AM

11 AM

NOON

1 PM

2 PM

3 PM

4 PM

5 PM

6 PM

ON THIS DAY IN 1999: 'AMERICAN PIE' WAS RELEASED.

BRILLIANT AND/OR TERRIBLE IDEAS

190 DAYS DOWN, 175 DAYS LEFT (UNLESS IT'S A LEAP YEAR [191/175])

YEAR:

JULY 10

WRITE IN THE DATES BELOW (AND SHADE IN TODAY)

MONDAY	TUESDAY	WEDNESDAY	THURSDAY	FRIDAY	SATURDAY ☐
· · · · · · · · ·	· · · · · · · · ·	· · · · · · · · ·	· · · · · · · · ·	· · · · · · · · ·	☐
☐ TODAY	☐ TODAY	☐ TODAY	☐ TODAY	☐ TODAY	SUNDAY

IT'S NATIONAL PIÑA COLADA DAY
IT'S BEEN THE OFFICIAL DRINK OF PUERTO RICO SINCE 1978.

SOFÍA VERGARA WAS BORN IN 1972   JESSICA SIMPSON WAS BORN IN 1980

7 AM
· ·
8 AM
· ·
9 AM
· ·
10 AM
· ·
11 AM
· ·
NOON
· ·
1 PM
· ·
2 PM
· ·
3 PM
· ·
4 PM
· ·
5 PM
· ·
6 PM

ON THIS DAY IN 1999: THE U.S. WOMEN'S SOCCER TEAM WON THE WORLD CUP.

NOTES AND/OR LIMERICKS

YEAR:

191 DAYS DOWN, 174 DAYS LEFT (UNLESS IT'S A LEAP YEAR [192/174])

WRITE IN THE DATES BELOW (AND SHADE IN TODAY)					
MONDAY	TUESDAY	WEDNESDAY	THURSDAY	FRIDAY	SATURDAY ☐
☐ TODAY	☐ TODAY	☐ TODAY	☐ TODAY	☐ TODAY	☐ SUNDAY

IT'S NATIONAL MOJITO DAY
A FAVORITE DRINK (AMONG MANY) OF ERNEST HEMINGWAY.

LISA RINNA WAS BORN IN 1963   ANDREW BIRD WAS BORN IN 1973

7 AM

8 AM

9 AM

10 AM

11 AM

NOON

1 PM

2 PM

3 PM

4 PM

5 PM

6 PM

ON THIS DAY IN 1960: 'TO KILL A MOCKINGBIRD' WAS FIRST PUBLISHED.

BRILLIANT AND/OR TERRIBLE IDEAS

192 DAYS DOWN, 173 DAYS LEFT (UNLESS IT'S A LEAP YEAR [193/173])   YEAR:

JULY 12

MONDAY	TUESDAY	WEDNESDAY	THURSDAY	FRIDAY	SATURDAY ☐
. . . .	. . . .	. . . .	. . . .	. . . .	
☐ TODAY	☐ TODAY	☐ TODAY	☐ TODAY	☐ TODAY	☐ SUNDAY

IT'S ETCH-A-SKETCH DAY
THE FIRST PROTOTYPE HAD A JOYSTICK.

MALALA YOUSAFZAI WAS BORN IN 1997　　　　　　　RICHARD SIMMONS WAS BORN IN 1948

7 AM

8 AM

9 AM

10 AM

11 AM

NOON

1 PM

2 PM

3 PM

4 PM

5 PM

6 PM

ON THIS DAY IN 1962: THE ROLLING STONES PERFORMED THEIR FIRST CONCERT.

NOTES AND/OR LIMERICKS

YEAR:　　　　193 DAYS DOWN, 172 DAYS LEFT (UNLESS IT'S A LEAP YEAR [194/172])

JULY 13

		WRITE IN THE DATES BELOW (AND SHADE IN TODAY)			
MONDAY	**TUESDAY**	**WEDNESDAY**	**THURSDAY**	**FRIDAY**	**SATURDAY** ☐
☐ TODAY	☐ TODAY	☐ TODAY	☐ TODAY	☐ TODAY	☐ SUNDAY

IT'S NATIONAL FRENCH FRY DAY
THE AVERAGE AMERICAN CONSUMES ABOUT 30 POUNDS OF THEM EACH YEAR.

KEN JEONG WAS BORN IN 1969 · · · · · · · · · · · · · · · · HARRISON FORD WAS BORN IN 1942

7 AM

8 AM

9 AM

10 AM

11 AM

NOON

1 PM

2 PM

3 PM

4 PM

5 PM

6 PM

ON THIS DAY IN 2014: GERMANY WON THEIR FOURTH WORLD CUP.

BRILLIANT AND/OR TERRIBLE IDEAS

194 DAYS DOWN, 171 DAYS LEFT (UNLESS IT'S A LEAP YEAR [195/171])

YEAR:

JULY 14

MONDAY	TUESDAY	WEDNESDAY	THURSDAY	FRIDAY	SATURDAY ☐
☐ TODAY	☐ TODAY	☐ TODAY	☐ TODAY	☐ TODAY	☐ SUNDAY

IT'S NATIONAL MAC AND CHEESE DAY
KRAFT FIRST INTRODUCED BOXED MAC AND CHEESE IN 1937.

JANE LYNCH WAS BORN IN 1960   INGMAR BERGMAN WAS BORN IN 1918

7 AM

8 AM

9 AM

10 AM

11 AM

NOON

1 PM

2 PM

3 PM

4 PM

5 PM

6 PM

ON THIS DAY IN 1938: HOWARD HUGHES COMPLETED A FLIGHT AROUND THE WORLD.

NOTES AND/OR LIMERICKS

YEAR: | 195 DAYS DOWN, 170 DAYS LEFT (UNLESS IT'S A LEAP YEAR [196/170])

JULY 15

MONDAY	TUESDAY	WEDNESDAY	THURSDAY	FRIDAY	SATURDAY ☐
. . . .	. . . .	. . . .	. . . .	. . . .	. . . .
☐ TODAY	☐ TODAY	☐ TODAY	☐ TODAY	☐ TODAY	☐ SUNDAY

IT'S NATIONAL GUMMI WORM DAY
YOU CAN BUY GIANT ONES THAT WEIGH ALMOST 3 POUNDS.

FOREST WHITAKER WAS BORN IN 1961   DIANE KRUGER WAS BORN IN 1976

7 AM

8 AM

9 AM

10 AM

11 AM

NOON

1 PM

2 PM

3 PM

4 PM

5 PM

6 PM

ON THIS DAY IN 1997: GIANNI VERSACE WAS MURDERED.

BRILLIANT AND/OR TERRIBLE IDEAS

196 DAYS DOWN, 169 DAYS LEFT (UNLESS IT'S A LEAP YEAR [197/169])

YEAR:

JULY 16

<table>
<tr><th>MONDAY</th><th>TUESDAY</th><th>WEDNESDAY</th><th>THURSDAY</th><th>FRIDAY</th><th>SATURDAY ☐</th></tr>
<tr><td>☐ TODAY</td><td>☐ TODAY</td><td>☐ TODAY</td><td>☐ TODAY</td><td>☐ TODAY</td><td>☐ SUNDAY</td></tr>
</table>

WRITE IN THE DATES BELOW (AND SHADE IN TODAY)

IT'S WORLD SNAKE DAY

SNAKES DON'T HAVE EYELIDS AND SLEEP WITH THEIR EYES OPEN.

WILL FERRELL WAS BORN IN 1967   IDA B. WELLS WAS BORN IN 1862

7 AM

8 AM

9 AM

10 AM

11 AM

NOON

1 PM

2 PM

3 PM

4 PM

5 PM

6 PM

ON THIS DAY IN 1969: APOLLO 11 LAUNCHED FROM CAPE KENNEDY.

NOTES AND/OR LIMERICKS

YEAR: 197 DAYS DOWN, 168 DAYS LEFT (UNLESS IT'S A LEAP YEAR [198/168])

JULY 17

WRITE IN THE DATES BELOW (AND SHADE IN TODAY)					SATURDAY ☐
MONDAY	**TUESDAY**	**WEDNESDAY**	**THURSDAY**	**FRIDAY**	
☐ TODAY	☐ TODAY	☐ TODAY	☐ TODAY	☐ TODAY	☐ SUNDAY

IT'S NATIONAL TATTOO DAY
TATTOOING WAS BANNED IN NEW YORK CITY FROM 1961 TO 1997.

WONG KAR-WAI WAS BORN IN 1958   DONALD SUTHERLAND WAS BORN IN 1935

7 AM

8 AM

9 AM

10 AM

11 AM

NOON

1 PM

2 PM

3 PM

4 PM

5 PM

6 PM

ON THIS DAY IN 1984: THE LEGAL U.S. DRINKING AGE WAS RAISED TO 21.

BRILLIANT AND/OR TERRIBLE IDEAS

198 DAYS DOWN, 167 DAYS LEFT (UNLESS IT'S A LEAP YEAR [199/167])

YEAR:

JULY 18

WRITE IN THE DATES BELOW (AND SHADE IN TODAY)

MONDAY	TUESDAY	WEDNESDAY	THURSDAY	FRIDAY	SATURDAY ☐
. . . . ☐ TODAY	. . . . ☐ TODAY	. . . . ☐ TODAY	. . . . ☐ TODAY	. . . . ☐ TODAY	☐ SUNDAY

IT'S NATIONAL CAVIAR DAY
IT SHOULD ONLY BE EATEN WITH A MOTHER OF PEARL SPOON.

KRISTEN BELL WAS BORN IN 1980   NELSON MANDELA WAS BORN IN 1918

7 AM

8 AM

9 AM

10 AM

11 AM

NOON

1 PM

2 PM

3 PM

4 PM

5 PM

6 PM

ON THIS DAY IN 1992: THE FIRST PHOTO WAS PUBLISHED TO THE WORLD WIDE WEB.

NOTES AND/OR LIMERICKS

YEAR: 199 DAYS DOWN, 166 DAYS LEFT (UNLESS IT'S A LEAP YEAR [200/166])

WRITE IN THE DATES BELOW (AND SHADE IN TODAY)					
MONDAY	**TUESDAY**	**WEDNESDAY**	**THURSDAY**	**FRIDAY**	**SATURDAY** ☐
☐ TODAY	☐ TODAY	☐ TODAY	☐ TODAY	☐ TODAY	☐ **SUNDAY**

IT'S NATIONAL HOT DOG DAY
THE AVERAGE PERSON IN AMERICA EATS ABOUT 70 A YEAR.

BENEDICT CUMBERBATCH WAS BORN IN 1976   LIZZIE BORDEN WAS BORN IN 1860

7 AM

8 AM

9 AM

10 AM

11 AM

NOON

1 PM

2 PM

3 PM

4 PM

5 PM

PM

ON THIS DAY IN 2007: THE SHOW 'MAD MEN' PREMIERED ON AMC.

BRILLIANT AND/OR TERRIBLE IDEAS

200 DAYS DOWN, 165 DAYS LEFT (UNLESS IT'S A LEAP YEAR [201/165])   YEAR:

JULY 20

WRITE IN THE DATES BELOW (AND SHADE IN TODAY)

MONDAY	TUESDAY	WEDNESDAY	THURSDAY	FRIDAY	SATURDAY ☐
. . . . ☐ TODAY	. . . . ☐ TODAY	. . . . ☐ TODAY	. . . . ☐ TODAY	. . . . ☐ TODAY	☐ SUNDAY

IT'S NATIONAL MOON DAY
OVER 600 MILLION PEOPLE WATCHED THE MOON LANDING LIVE.

SANDRA OH WAS BORN IN 1971   CARLOS SANTANA WAS BORN IN 1947

7 AM

8 AM

9 AM

10 AM

11 AM

NOON

1 PM

2 PM

3 PM

4 PM

5 PM

6 PM

ON THIS DAY IN 1969: NEIL ARMSTRONG FIRST WALKED ON THE MOON.

NOTES AND/OR LIMERICKS

YEAR: 201 DAYS DOWN, 164 DAYS LEFT (UNLESS IT'S A LEAP YEAR [202/164])

JULY 21

MONDAY	TUESDAY	WEDNESDAY	THURSDAY	FRIDAY	SATURDAY ☐
. . . .	. . . .	. . . .	. . . .	. . . .	☐
☐ TODAY	☐ TODAY	☐ TODAY	☐ TODAY	☐ TODAY	SUNDAY

IT'S NATIONAL JUNK FOOD DAY
THE FIRST WHITE CASTLES OPENED IN 1921 IN WICHITA, KANSAS.

ERNEST HEMINGWAY WAS BORN IN 1899   ROBIN WILLIAMS WAS BORN IN 1951

7 AM

8 AM

9 AM

10 AM

11 AM

NOON

1 PM

2 PM

3 PM

4 PM

5 PM

6 PM

ON THIS DAY IN 1853: CENTRAL PARK WAS CREATED BY THE STATE OF NEW YORK.

BRILLIANT AND/OR TERRIBLE IDEAS

202 DAYS DOWN, 163 DAYS LEFT (UNLESS IT'S A LEAP YEAR [203/163])   YEAR:

JULY 22

WRITE IN THE DATES BELOW (AND SHADE IN TODAY)

MONDAY	TUESDAY	WEDNESDAY	THURSDAY	FRIDAY	SATURDAY ☐
. . . .	. . . .	. . . .	. . . .	. . . .	☐
☐ TODAY	☐ TODAY	☐ TODAY	☐ TODAY	☐ TODAY	SUNDAY

IT'S NATIONAL HAMMOCK DAY
THE BRITISH ROYAL NAVY MADE THEM THE OFFICIAL BED FOR SAILORS IN 1597.

WILLEM DAFOE WAS BORN IN 1955   ALEX TREBEK WAS BORN IN 1940

7 AM
. . . .
8 AM
. . . .
9 AM
. . . .
10 AM
. . . .
11 AM
. . . .
NOON
. . . .
1 PM
. . . .
2 PM
. . . .
3 PM
. . . .
4 PM
. . . .
5 PM
. . . .
6 PM

ON THIS DAY IN 1991: JEFFERY DAHMER WAS ARRESTED IN MILWAUKEE.

NOTES AND/OR LIMERICKS

YEAR: 203 DAYS DOWN, 162 DAYS LEFT (UNLESS IT'S A LEAP YEAR [204/162])

JULY 23

MONDAY	TUESDAY	WEDNESDAY	THURSDAY	FRIDAY	SATURDAY ☐
. . . . ☐ TODAY	. . . . ☐ TODAY	. . . . ☐ TODAY	. . . . ☐ TODAY	. . . . ☐ TODAY	☐ SUNDAY

IT'S SPRINKLES DAY
THEY WERE ORIGINALLY CALLED JIMMIES.

WOODY HARRELSON WAS BORN IN 1961   DANIEL RADCLIFFE WAS BORN IN 1989

7 AM

8 AM

9 AM

10 AM

11 AM

NOON

1 PM

2 PM

3 PM

4 PM

5 PM

6 PM

ON THIS DAY IN 2011: AMY WINEHOUSE WAS FOUND DEAD IN HER APARTMENT.

BRILLIANT AND/OR TERRIBLE IDEAS

204 DAYS DOWN, 161 DAYS LEFT (UNLESS IT'S A LEAP YEAR [205/161])   YEAR:

JULY 24

MONDAY	TUESDAY	WEDNESDAY	THURSDAY	FRIDAY	SATURDAY ☐
. . . .	. . . .	. . . .	. . . .	. . . .	
☐ TODAY	☐ TODAY	☐ TODAY	☐ TODAY	☐ TODAY	☐ SUNDAY

IT'S NATIONAL TEQUILA DAY
A TRUE TEQUILA DOESN'T HAVE A WORM. IT'S ONLY IN MEZCAL.

JENNIFER LOPEZ WAS BORN IN 1969   AMELIA EARHART WAS BORN IN 1897

7 AM
. . . .
                                                                                            8 AM
. . . .
9 AM
. . . .
                                                                                           10 AM
11 AM
. . . .
                                                                                            NOON
. . . .
1 PM
. . . .
                                                                                            2 PM
3 PM
. . . .
                                                                                            4 PM
. . . .
5 PM
. . . .
                                                                                            6 PM

ON THIS DAY IN 1969: APOLLO 11 SAFELY RETURNED TO EARTH.

NOTES AND/OR LIMERICKS

YEAR:	205 DAYS DOWN, 160 DAYS LEFT (UNLESS IT'S A LEAP YEAR [206/160])

JULY 25

MONDAY	TUESDAY	WEDNESDAY	THURSDAY	FRIDAY	SATURDAY ☐
. . . . ☐ TODAY	. . . . ☐ TODAY	. . . . ☐ TODAY	. . . . ☐ TODAY	. . . . ☐ TODAY	☐ SUNDAY

IT'S NATIONAL WINE AND CHEESE DAY
TRY PAIRING A RIESLING WITH MAC AND CHEESE—TRUST US.

MATT LEBLANC WAS BORN IN 1967   IMAN WAS BORN IN 1955

7 AM

8 AM

9 AM

10 AM

11 AM

NOON

1 PM

2 PM

3 PM

4 PM

5 PM

6 PM

ON THIS DAY IN 1948: LOUISE BROWN (THE WORLD'S FIRST IVF BABY) WAS BORN.

BRILLIANT AND/OR TERRIBLE IDEAS

206 DAYS DOWN, 159 DAYS LEFT (UNLESS IT'S A LEAP YEAR [207/159])   YEAR:

JULY 26

WRITE IN THE DATES BELOW (AND SHADE IN TODAY)

MONDAY	TUESDAY	WEDNESDAY	THURSDAY	FRIDAY	SATURDAY
. . . .	. . . .	. . . .	. . . .	. . . .	
☐ TODAY	☐ TODAY	☐ TODAY	☐ TODAY	☐ TODAY	☐ SUNDA

IT'S NATIONAL AUNT AND UNCLE DAY
SUSANNAH JONES HAD OVER 100 NIECES & NEPHEWS AT THE TIME OF HER DEATH.

SANDRA BULLOCK WAS BORN IN 1964   MICK JAGGER WAS BORN IN 19

7 AM
. . . .
8 A
. . . .
9 AM
. . . .
10 A
. . . .
11 AM
. . . .
NOC
. . . .
1 PM
. . . .
2
3 PM
. . . .
4
5 PM
. . . .
6

ON THIS DAY IN 1991: PAUL REUBENS WAS ARRESTED FOR EXPOSING HIMSELF.

NOTES AND/OR LIMERICKS

YEAR: 207 DAYS DOWN, 158 DAYS LEFT (UNLESS IT'S A LEAP YEAR [208/158])

JULY 27

		WRITE IN THE DATES BELOW (AND SHADE IN TODAY)			
MONDAY	TUESDAY	WEDNESDAY	THURSDAY	FRIDAY	SATURDAY ☐
. . . . ☐ TODAY	. . . . ☐ TODAY	. . . . ☐ TODAY	. . . . ☐ TODAY	. . . . ☐ TODAY	☐ SUNDAY

IT'S WALK ON STILTS DAY
BELGIUM HAS HELD STILT JOUSTING TOURNAMENTS FOR 600+ YEARS.

ONNIE YEN WAS BORN IN 1963   MAYA RUDOLPH WAS BORN IN 1972

7 AM

AM

9 AM

O AM

11 AM

OON

1 PM

PM

3 PM

PM

5 PM

PM

ON THIS DAY IN 2012: QUEEN ELIZABETH II OPENED THE LONDON OLYMPICS.

BRILLIANT AND/OR TERRIBLE IDEAS

208 DAYS DOWN, 157 DAYS LEFT (UNLESS IT'S A LEAP YEAR [209/157])   YEAR:

JULY 28

MONDAY	TUESDAY	WEDNESDAY	THURSDAY	FRIDAY	SATURDAY ☐
. . . . ☐ TODAY	. . . . ☐ TODAY	. . . . ☐ TODAY	. . . . ☐ TODAY	. . . . ☐ TODAY	☐ SUNDAY

IT'S NATIONAL WATER PARK DAY
THERE'S AN ABANDONED WATER PARK HIDDEN INSIDE OF DISNEY WORLD.

JACKIE KENNEDY WAS BORN IN 1929   LORI LOUGHLIN WAS BORN IN 196

7 AM
. . . .
8 A
. . . .
9 AM
. . . .
10 A
. . . .
11 AM
. . . .
NOO
. . . .
1 PM
. . . .
2 P
. . . .
3 PM
. . . .
4 P
. . . .
5 PM
. . . .
6 P

ON THIS DAY IN 1933: THE FIRST SINGING TELEGRAM WAS DELIVERED.

NOTES AND/OR LIMERICKS

YEAR: | 209 DAYS DOWN, 156 DAYS LEFT (UNLESS IT'S A LEAP YEAR [210/156])

JULY 29

MONDAY	TUESDAY	WEDNESDAY	THURSDAY	FRIDAY	SATURDAY ☐
. . . . ☐ TODAY	. . . . ☐ TODAY	. . . . ☐ TODAY	. . . . ☐ TODAY	. . . . ☐ TODAY	☐ SUNDAY

IT'S INTERNATIONAL TIGER DAY
THEIR ROARS CAN BE HEARD FROM OVER TWO MILES AWAY.

TIM GUNN WAS BORN IN 1953   MARTINA MCBRIDE WAS BORN IN 1966

7 AM

8 AM

9 AM

10 AM

11 AM

NOON

1 PM

2 PM

3 PM

4 PM

5 PM

6 PM

ON THIS DAY IN 1981: PRINCE (NOW KING) CHARLES MARRIED DIANA SPENCER.

BRILLIANT AND/OR TERRIBLE IDEAS

210 DAYS DOWN, 155 DAYS LEFT (UNLESS IT'S A LEAP YEAR [211/155])

YEAR:

JULY 30

		WRITE IN THE DATES BELOW (AND SHADE IN TODAY)			
MONDAY	**TUESDAY**	**WEDNESDAY**	**THURSDAY**	**FRIDAY**	**SATURDAY** ☐
. . . . ☐ TODAY	. . . . ☐ TODAY	. . . . ☐ TODAY	. . . . ☐ TODAY	. . . . ☐ TODAY	☐ **SUNDAY**

IT'S NATIONAL CHILI DOG DAY

MICKEY MOUSE'S FIRST WORDS ON SCREEN WERE 'HOT DOGS.'

TERRY CREWS WAS BORN IN 1968   LISA KUDROW WAS BORN IN 196

7 AM

. . . .

8 A

. . . .

9 AM

. . . .

10 A

. . . .

11 AM

. . . .

NOO

. . . .

1 PM

. . . .

2 P

. . . .

3 PM

. . . .

4 P

. . . .

5 PM

. . . .

6 P

ON THIS DAY IN 1991: METALLICA'S 'ENTER SANDMAN' WAS RELEASED.

NOTES AND/OR LIMERICKS

YEAR: 211 DAYS DOWN, 154 DAYS LEFT (UNLESS IT'S A LEAP YEAR [212/154])

JULY 31

MONDAY	TUESDAY	WEDNESDAY	THURSDAY	FRIDAY	SATURDAY ☐
. . . . ☐ TODAY	. . . . ☐ TODAY	. . . . ☐ TODAY	. . . . ☐ TODAY	. . . . ☐ TODAY	☐ SUNDAY

IT'S NATIONAL AVOCADO DAY
BOTH TOM SELLECK AND JAMIE FOXX OWN AVOCADO FARMS.

MARK CUBAN WAS BORN IN 1958   B.J. NOVAK WAS BORN IN 1979

7 AM

8 AM

9 AM

10 AM

11 AM

NOON

1 PM

2 PM

3 PM

4 PM

5 PM

6 PM

ON THIS DAY IN 1989: THE NINTENDO GAME BOY WAS RELEASED IN THE U.S.

BRILLIANT AND/OR TERRIBLE IDEAS

212 DAYS DOWN, 153 DAYS LEFT (UNLESS IT'S A LEAP YEAR [213/153])   YEAR:

IT'S OFFICIALLY

× **AUGUST** ×

OF THE YEAR

☐ ☐ ☐ ☐

MONTH EIGHT

. . . .

. . . .

. . . .

AUGUST AT A GLANCE

CONGRATULATIONS, YOU MADE IT
TO THE MONTH OF AUGUST

✖

CELEBRATE, IT'S

BLACK BUSINESS MONTH

NTL. BACK TO SCHOOL MONTH

NATIONAL EYE EXAM MONTH

INTERNATIONAL PEACE MONTH

NATIONAL CATFISH MONTH

OFFICIAL SYMBOLS

BIRTHSTONE: PERIDOT

FLOWERS: GLADIOLUS & POPPY

TREES: POPLAR, CEDAR, & PINE

LEO (JUL 23 / AUG 22)

VIRGO (AUG 23 / SEP 22)

✖

A FEW DATES TO KNOW*
LIKE, IMPORTANT ONES.

✖

LAMMAS
(PAGAN)
AUGUST 1ST

OBON
(BUDDHISM)
COMMONLY HELD BETWEEN
AUGUST 13TH AND 16TH

NTL. AVIATION DAY
AUGUST 19TH

ADMISSION DAY
(STATE OF HAWAII)
3RD FRIDAY OF AUGUST

RAKSHA BANDHAN
(HINDUISM)
THE LAST DAY OF THE HINDU
LUNAR MONTH OF SHRAAVANA
(OFTEN IN AUGUST)

WOMEN'S EQUALITY DAY
AUGUST 26TH

GANESH CHATURTHI
(HINDUISM)
STARTS ON THE FOURTH DAY
OF THE HINDU LUNAR MONTH OF
BHĀDRA (COULD FALL IN AUGUST
OR SEPTEMBER)

MARK YOUR CALENDAR   ✖   IT'S RIGHT OVER THERE

AUGUST AT A GLANCE

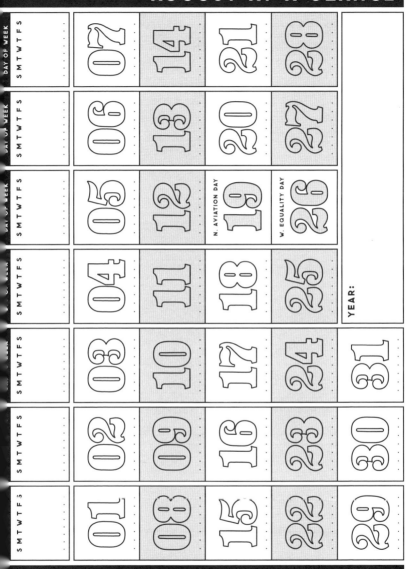

DAY OF WEEK
S M T W T F S

01
02
03
04
05
06
07
08
09
10
11
12
13
14
15
16
17
18
19 N. AVIATION DAY
20
21
22
23
24
25
26 W. EQUALITY DAY
27
28
29
30
31

YEAR:

WELL, WHAT ARE YOU WAITING FOR?

✖ START PLANNING. IN THE CALENDAR ABOVE, WE'VE MARKED THE MORE COMMON U.S. HOLIDAYS ALREADY (THE ONES THAT ARE DATED, THAT IS). SO USE THE LIST TO THE LEFT TO FILL IN THE REST...LIKE ALL OF THE ONES THAT CHANGE DATES FROM YEAR TO YEAR, FOR EXAMPLE. ✖

LISTS, NOTES & MEMOIRS

BEST FOODS FOR A FOOD FIGHT
OR SOME BORING TO-DO LIST

1
2
3
4
5
6
7
8
9
10
11
12
13
14

BEST FOODS FOR A KNIFE FIGHT
OR A GROCERY LIST OR SOMETHING

1
2
3
4
5
6
7
8
9
10
11
12
13
14

THINGS THAT I WAS WORRIED ABOUT AT AGE EIGHT
USE FIGURE 1 FOR ANY NECESSARY VISUAL AIDS

FIG. 1

1
2
3

4
5
6

		WRITE IN THE DATES BELOW (AND SHADE IN TODAY)			
MONDAY	TUESDAY	WEDNESDAY	THURSDAY	FRIDAY	SATURDAY ☐
☐ TODAY	☐ TODAY	☐ TODAY	☐ TODAY	☐ TODAY	☐ SUNDAY

IT'S NATIONAL PLANNER DAY
YOU SHOULD CELEBRATE BY POSTING YOUR FAVORITE ONE ONLINE.

SAM MENDES WAS BORN IN 1965   JASON MOMOA WAS BORN IN 1979

7 AM

8 AM

9 AM

10 AM

11 AM

NOON

1 PM

2 PM

3 PM

4 PM

5 PM

6 PM

ON THIS DAY IN 1944: ANNE FRANK MADE THE LAST ENTRY IN HER DIARY.

BRILLIANT AND/OR TERRIBLE IDEAS

213 DAYS DOWN, 152 DAYS LEFT (UNLESS IT'S A LEAP YEAR 214/252]) | YEAR:

AUGUST 2

WRITE IN THE DATES BELOW (AND SHADE IN TODAY)

MONDAY	TUESDAY	WEDNESDAY	THURSDAY	FRIDAY	SATURDAY ☐
☐ TODAY	☐ TODAY	☐ TODAY	☐ TODAY	☐ TODAY	☐ SUNDAY

IT'S NATIONAL ICE CREAM SANDWICH DAY
THE EARLIEST KNOWN RECIPE USED SPONGE CAKE INSTEAD OF COOKIES.

WES CRAVEN WAS BORN IN 1939   MARY-LOUISE PARKER WAS BORN IN 1964

7 AM

8 AM

9 AM

10 AM

11 AM

NOON

1 PM

2 PM

3 PM

4 PM

5 PM

6 PM

ON THIS DAY IN 1937: MARIJUANA WAS MADE ILLEGAL IN THE UNITED STATES.

NOTES AND/OR LIMERICKS

YEAR: 214 DAYS DOWN, 151 DAYS LEFT (UNLESS IT'S A LEAP YEAR [215/151])

AUGUST 3

MONDAY	TUESDAY	WEDNESDAY	THURSDAY	FRIDAY	SATURDAY ☐
☐ TODAY	☐ TODAY	☐ TODAY	☐ TODAY	☐ TODAY	☐ SUNDAY

IT'S NATIONAL WATERMELON DAY
SEEDLESS WATERMELONS WERE DEVELOPED IN 1939.

MARTHA STEWART WAS BORN IN 1941   TONY BENNETT WAS BORN IN 1926

7 AM

8 AM

9 AM

10 AM

11 AM

NOON

1 PM

2 PM

3 PM

4 PM

5 PM

6 PM

ON THIS DAY IN 2012: MICHAEL PHELPS WON HIS 17TH GOLD MEDAL.

BRILLIANT AND/OR TERRIBLE IDEAS

215 DAYS DOWN, 150 DAYS LEFT (UNLESS IT'S A LEAP YEAR [216/150])

YEAR:

AUGUST 4

IT'S NATIONAL CHOCOLATE CHIP COOKIE DAY
THEY'RE THE OFFICIAL STATE COOKIE OF MASSACHUSETTS.

LOUIS ARMSTRONG WAS BORN IN 1901   MEGHAN MARKLE WAS BORN IN 198'

7 AM
· ·
8 AM
· ·
9 AM
· ·
10 AM
· ·
11 AM
· ·
NOON
· ·
1 PM
· ·
2 PM
· ·
3 PM
· ·
4 PM
· ·
5 PM
· ·
6 PM

ON THIS DAY IN 2015: MISS PIGGY AND KERMIT ANNOUNCED THEIR BREAK-UP ON TWITTER.

NOTES AND/OR LIMERICKS

YEAR: 216 DAYS DOWN, 149 DAYS LEFT (UNLESS IT'S A LEAP YEAR [217/149])

AUGUST 5

MONDAY	TUESDAY	WEDNESDAY	THURSDAY	FRIDAY	SATURDAY ☐
. . . .	. . . .	. . . .	. . . .	. . . .	☐
☐ TODAY	☐ TODAY	☐ TODAY	☐ TODAY	☐ TODAY	☐ SUNDAY

IT'S NATIONAL OYSTER DAY
A SINGLE OYSTER CAN FILTER 50 GALLONS OF WATER A DAY.

NEIL ARMSTRONG WAS BORN IN 1930   LONI ANDERSON WAS BORN IN 1945

7 AM

8 AM

9 AM

10 AM

11 AM

NOON

1 PM

2 PM

3 PM

4 PM

5 PM

6 PM

ON THIS DAY IN 1914: THE FIRST ELECTRIC TRAFFIC LIGHT WAS INSTALLED.

BRILLIANT AND/OR TERRIBLE IDEAS

217 DAYS DOWN, 148 DAYS LEFT (UNLESS IT'S A LEAP YEAR [218/148])

YEAR:

AUGUST 6

MONDAY	TUESDAY	WEDNESDAY	THURSDAY	FRIDAY	SATURDAY ☐
· · · · · · ·	· · · · · · ·	· · · · · · ·	· · · · · · ·	· · · · · · ·	
☐ TODAY	☐ TODAY	☐ TODAY	☐ TODAY	☐ TODAY	☐ SUNDAY

IT'S NATIONAL ROOT BEER FLOAT DAY

ROOT BEER ACCOUNTS FOR 3 PERCENT OF THE U.S. SOFT DRINK MARKET.

ANDY WARHOL WAS BORN IN 1928   LUCILLE BALL WAS BORN IN 191

7 AM
· ·
                                                                          8 AM
· ·
9 AM
· ·
                                                                          10 AM
· ·
11 AM
· ·
                                                                          NOON
· ·
1 PM
· ·
                                                                          2 PM
· ·
3 PM
· ·
                                                                          4 PM
· ·
5 PM
· ·
                                                                          6 PM

ON THIS DAY IN 2012: NASA'S CURIOSITY ROVER LANDED ON MARS.

NOTES AND/OR LIMERICKS

YEAR: 218 DAYS DOWN, 147 DAYS LEFT (UNLESS IT'S A LEAP YEAR [219/147])

AUGUST 7

MONDAY	TUESDAY	WEDNESDAY	THURSDAY	FRIDAY	SATURDAY ☐
. . . .	. . . .	. . . .	. . . .	. . . .	
☐ TODAY	☐ TODAY	☐ TODAY	☐ TODAY	☐ TODAY	☐ SUNDAY

IT'S NATIONAL LIGHTHOUSE DAY
LIGHTHOUSES STARTED USING ELECTRIC LAMPS IN 1875.

CHARLIZE THERON WAS BORN IN 1975   MICHAEL SHANNON WAS BORN IN 1974

7 AM

8 AM

9 AM

10 AM

11 AM

NOON

1 PM

2 PM

3 PM

4 PM

5 PM

6 PM

ON THIS DAY IN 2009: KE$HA RELEASED THE SONG 'TIK TOK.'

BRILLIANT AND/OR TERRIBLE IDEAS

219 DAYS DOWN. 146 DAYS LEFT (UNLESS IT'S A LEAP YEAR [220/146])   YEAR:

AUGUST 8

MONDAY	TUESDAY	WEDNESDAY	THURSDAY	FRIDAY	SATURDAY ☐
. . . .	. . . .	. . . .	. . . .	. . . .	
☐ TODAY	☐ TODAY	☐ TODAY	☐ TODAY	☐ TODAY	☐ SUNDAY

IT'S INTERNATIONAL CAT DAY
A CAT WAS THE MAYOR OF TALKEETNA, ALASKA FOR 20 YEARS.

DUSTIN HOFFMAN WAS BORN IN 1937   SHAWN MENDES WAS BORN IN 1998

7 AM
. . . .
                                                                              8 AM
. . . .
9 AM
. . . .
                                                                              10 AM
. . . .
11 AM
. . . .
                                                                              NOON
. . . .
1 PM
. . . .
                                                                              2 PM
. . . .
3 PM
. . . .
                                                                              4 PM
. . . .
5 PM
. . . .
                                                                              6 PM

ON THIS DAY IN 1992: THE U.S. 'DREAM TEAM' WON GOLD AT THE OLYMPICS.

NOTES AND/OR LIMERICKS

YEAR: 220 DAYS DOWN, 145 DAYS LEFT (UNLESS IT'S A LEAP YEAR [221/145])

AUGUST 9

MONDAY	TUESDAY	WEDNESDAY	THURSDAY	FRIDAY	SATURDAY ☐
. . . .	. . . .	. . . .	. . . .	. . . .	
☐ TODAY	☐ TODAY	☐ TODAY	☐ TODAY	☐ TODAY	☐ SUNDAY

IT'S NATIONAL BOOK LOVERS DAY
THERE IS A WORD FOR LOVING THE SMELL OF OLD BOOKS—BIBLIOSMIA.

WHITNEY HOUSTON WAS BORN IN 1963   AUDREY TAUTOU WAS BORN IN 1976

7 AM

8 AM

9 AM

10 AM

11 AM

NOON

1 PM

2 PM

3 PM

4 PM

5 PM

6 PM

ON THIS DAY IN 2022: SERENA WILLIAMS ANNOUNCED HER PLAN TO RETIRE.

BRILLIANT AND/OR TERRIBLE IDEAS

221 DAYS DOWN, 144 DAYS LEFT (UNLESS IT'S A LEAP YEAR [222/144])

YEAR:

AUGUST 10

MONDAY	TUESDAY	WEDNESDAY	THURSDAY	FRIDAY	SATURDAY ☐
☐ TODAY	☐ TODAY	☐ TODAY	☐ TODAY	☐ TODAY	☐ SUNDAY

IT'S NATIONAL LAZY DAY
THE FIRST LA-Z-BOY RECLINER WAS A FOLDING WOOD-SLAT CHAIR.

ANTONIO BANDERAS WAS BORN IN 1960   KYLIE JENNER WAS BORN IN 1997

7 AM

8 AM

9 AM

10 AM

11 AM

NOON

1 PM

2 PM

3 PM

4 PM

5 PM

6 PM

ON THIS DAY IN 1993: RUTH BADER GINSBURG JOINED THE U.S. SUPREME COURT.

NOTES AND/OR LIMERICKS

YEAR: 222 DAYS DOWN, 143 DAYS LEFT (UNLESS IT'S A LEAP YEAR [223/143])

AUGUST 11

MONDAY	TUESDAY	WEDNESDAY	THURSDAY	FRIDAY	SATURDAY ☐
☐ TODAY	☐ TODAY	☐ TODAY	☐ TODAY	☐ TODAY	☐ SUNDAY

IT'S MOUNTAIN DAY
IT'S ONE OF JAPAN'S 16 PUBLIC HOLIDAYS.

VIOLA DAVIS WAS BORN IN 1965   CHRIS HEMSWORTH WAS BORN IN 1983

7 AM

8 AM

9 AM

10 AM

11 AM

NOON

1 PM

2 PM

3 PM

4 PM

5 PM

6 PM

ON THIS DAY IN 1951: THE FIRST MLB GAME WAS TELEVISED IN COLOR.

BRILLIANT AND/OR TERRIBLE IDEAS

223 DAYS DOWN, 142 DAYS LEFT (UNLESS IT'S A LEAP YEAR [224/142])   YEAR:

AUGUST 12

MONDAY	TUESDAY	WEDNESDAY	THURSDAY	FRIDAY	SATURDAY ☐
. . . .	. . . .	. . . .	. . . .	. . . .	☐
☐ TODAY	☐ TODAY	☐ TODAY	☐ TODAY	☐ TODAY	SUNDAY

IT'S NATIONAL VINYL RECORD DAY
IN 2020, RECORD SALES SURPASSED CD SALES FOR THE FIRST TIME SINCE THE 1980s.

CARA DELEVINGNE WAS BORN IN 1992   PETE SAMPRAS WAS BORN IN 1971

7 AM
. . . .
                                                                              8 AM
. . . .
9 AM
. . . .
                                                                              10 AM
. . . .
11 AM
. . . .
                                                                              NOON
. . . .
1 PM
. . . .
                                                                              2 PM
. . . .
3 PM
. . . .
                                                                              4 PM
. . . .
5 PM
. . . .
                                                                              6 PM

ON THIS DAY IN 1981: THE IBM PERSONAL COMPUTER WAS RELEASED.

NOTES AND/OR LIMERICKS

YEAR: 224 DAYS DOWN, 141 DAYS LEFT (UNLESS IT'S A LEAP YEAR [225/141]

AUGUST 13

IT'S INTERNATIONAL LEFT HANDERS DAY

NEARLY HALF OF ALL DOMESTICATED CATS ARE LEFT-HANDED (OR PAWED, IN THIS CASE).

ALFRED HITCHCOCK WAS BORN IN 1899   SRIDEVI KAPOOR WAS BORN IN 1963

7 AM

8 AM

9 AM

10 AM

11 AM

NOON

1 PM

2 PM

3 PM

4 PM

5 PM

6 PM

ON THIS DAY IN 1997: THE FIRST EPISODE OF 'SOUTH PARK' AIRED.

BRILLIANT AND/OR TERRIBLE IDEAS

225 DAYS DOWN, 140 DAYS LEFT (UNLESS IT'S A LEAP YEAR [226/140])   YEAR:

AUGUST 14

MONDAY	TUESDAY	WEDNESDAY	THURSDAY	FRIDAY	SATURDAY ☐
. . . .	. . . .	. . . .	. . . .	. . . .	☐
☐ TODAY	☐ TODAY	☐ TODAY	☐ TODAY	☐ TODAY	SUNDAY

IT'S WORLD LIZARD DAY

SHORT-HORNED LIZARD'S SQUIRT BLOOD FROM THEIR EYES AS A DEFENSE MECHANISM.

STEVE MARTIN WAS BORN IN 1945   HALLE BERRY WAS BORN IN 1966

7 AM
. . . .
                                                                          8 AM
. . . .
9 AM
. . . .
                                                                         10 AM
. . . .
11 AM
. . . .
                                                                          NOON
. . . .
1 PM
. . . .
                                                                          2 PM
. . . .
3 PM
. . . .
                                                                          4 PM
. . . .
5 PM
. . . .
                                                                          6 PM

ON THIS DAY IN 2000: 'DORA THE EXPLORER' PREMIERED ON NICK JR.

NOTES AND/OR LIMERICKS

YEAR:	226 DAYS DOWN, 139 DAYS LEFT (UNLESS IT'S A LEAP YEAR [227/139])

AUGUST 15

MONDAY	TUESDAY	WEDNESDAY	THURSDAY	FRIDAY	SATURDAY ☐
· · · · · · · · ☐ TODAY	· · · · · · · · ☐ TODAY	· · · · · · · · ☐ TODAY	· · · · · · · · ☐ TODAY	· · · · · · · · ☐ TODAY	☐ SUNDAY

IT'S NATIONAL FAILURES DAY
CRYSTAL PEPSI HAS ENTERED THE CHAT

JENNIFER LAWRENCE WAS BORN IN 1990   JULIA CHILD WAS BORN IN 1912

7 AM

8 AM

9 AM

10 AM

11 AM

NOON

1 PM

2 PM

3 PM

4 PM

5 PM

6 PM

ON THIS DAY IN 1969: THE WOODSTOCK MUSIC FESTIVAL OPENED IN UPSTATE NEW YORK.

BRILLIANT AND/OR TERRIBLE IDEAS

227 DAYS DOWN, 138 DAYS LEFT (UNLESS IT'S A LEAP YEAR [228/138])   YEAR:

AUGUST 16

MONDAY	TUESDAY	WEDNESDAY	THURSDAY	FRIDAY	SATURDAY ☐
. . . .	. . . .	. . . .	. . . .	. . . .	
☐ TODAY	☐ TODAY	☐ TODAY	☐ TODAY	☐ TODAY	☐ SUNDAY

IT'S NATIONAL ROLLER COASTER DAY
CEDAR POINT IN SANDUSKY, OHIO, IS THE COASTER CAPITAL OF THE WORLD.

MADONNA WAS BORN IN 1958   STEVE CARELL WAS BORN IN 1962

7 AM

. . . .
8 AM

. . . .
9 AM

. . . .
10 AM

. . . .
11 AM

. . . .
NOON

. . . .
1 PM

. . . .
2 PM

. . . .
3 PM

. . . .
4 PM

. . . .
5 PM

. . . .
6 PM

ON THIS DAY IN 1954: THE 1ST ISSUE OF 'SPORTS ILLUSTRATED' WAS PUBLISHED.

NOTES AND/OR LIMERICKS

YEAR: 228 DAYS DOWN, 137 DAYS LEFT (UNLESS IT'S A LEAP YEAR [229/137])

WRITE IN THE DATES BELOW (AND SHADE IN TODAY)					
MONDAY	TUESDAY	WEDNESDAY	THURSDAY	FRIDAY	SATURDAY ☐
. . . .	. . . .	. . . .	. . . .	. . . .	
☐ TODAY	☐ TODAY	☐ TODAY	☐ TODAY	☐ TODAY	☐ SUNDAY

IT'S NATIONAL NUMBER 2 PENCIL DAY
BREAD CRUMBS WERE USED BEFORE ERASERS WERE INVENTED.

ROBERT DE NIRO WAS BORN IN 1943   HELEN MCCRORY WAS BORN IN 1968

7 AM

8 AM

9 AM

10 AM

11 AM

NOON

1 PM

2 PM

3 PM

4 PM

5 PM

PM

ON THIS DAY IN 1907: THE PIKE PLACE MARKET OPENED IN SEATTLE.

BRILLIANT AND/OR TERRIBLE IDEAS

229 DAYS DOWN, 136 DAYS LEFT (UNLESS IT'S A LEAP YEAR [230/136])   YEAR:

AUGUST 18

MONDAY	TUESDAY	WEDNESDAY	THURSDAY	FRIDAY	SATURDAY ☐
. . . . ☐ TODAY	. . . . ☐ TODAY	. . . . ☐ TODAY	. . . . ☐ TODAY	. . . . ☐ TODAY	☐ SUNDAY

IT'S PINOT NOIR DAY
THE 2004 FILM 'SIDEWAYS' MADE IT TRENDY AGAIN.

JOHANNAH MILLER WAS BORN IN 1994   PATRICK SWAYZE WAS BORN IN 1952

7 AM
. . . .
                                                                              8 AM
. . . .
9 AM
. . . .
                                                                              10 AM
. . . .
11 AM
. . . .
                                                                              NOON
. . . .
1 PM
. . . .
                                                                              2 PM
. . . .
3 PM
. . . .
                                                                              4 PM
. . . .
5 PM
. . . .
                                                                              6 PM

ON THIS DAY IN 2012: USAIN BOLT WON HIS THIRD GOLD MEDAL AT THE BRAZIL OLYMPICS.

NOTES AND/OR LIMERICKS

YEAR:	230 DAYS DOWN, 135 DAYS LEFT (UNLESS IT'S A LEAP YEAR [231/135])

AUGUST 19

MONDAY	TUESDAY	WEDNESDAY	THURSDAY	FRIDAY	SATURDAY ☐
. . . . ☐ TODAY	. . . . ☐ TODAY	. . . . ☐ TODAY	. . . . ☐ TODAY	. . . . ☐ TODAY	☐ SUNDAY

IT'S INTERNATIONAL ORANGUTAN DAY
HUMANS SHARE NEARLY 97 PERCENT OF THE SAME DNA.

JOHN STAMOS WAS BORN IN 1963   MATTHEW PERRY WAS BORN IN 1969

7 AM

8 AM

9 AM

10 AM

11 AM

NOON

1 PM

2 PM

3 PM

4 PM

5 PM

6 PM

ON THIS DAY IN 1934: THE FIRST SOAP BOX DERBY WAS HELD IN DAYTON, OHIO.

BRILLIANT AND/OR TERRIBLE IDEAS

231 DAYS DOWN, 134 DAYS LEFT (UNLESS IT'S A LEAP YEAR [232/134])   YEAR:

AUGUST 20

MONDAY	TUESDAY	WEDNESDAY	THURSDAY	FRIDAY	SATURDAY ☐
. . . . ☐ TODAY	. . . . ☐ TODAY	. . . . ☐ TODAY	. . . . ☐ TODAY	. . . . ☐ TODAY	☐ SUNDAY

IT'S NATIONAL BACON LOVERS DAY
THE UNITED CHURCH OF BACON HAS OVER 25,000 MEMBERS.

DEMI LOVATO WAS BORN IN 1992   AMY ADAMS WAS BORN IN 1974

7 AM

8 AM

9 AM

10 AM

11 AM

NOON

1 PM

2 PM

3 PM

4 PM

5 PM

6 PM

ON THIS DAY IN 2016: SOUTH KOREAN GOLFER INBEE PARK WON AN OLYMPIC GOLD MEDAL.

NOTES AND/OR LIMERICKS

YEAR: 232 DAYS DOWN, 133 DAYS LEFT (UNLESS IT'S A LEAP YEAR [233/133])

AUGUST 21

MONDAY	TUESDAY	WEDNESDAY	THURSDAY	FRIDAY	SATURDAY ☐
. . . .	. . . .	. . . .	. . . .	. . . .	
☐ TODAY	☐ TODAY	☐ TODAY	☐ TODAY	☐ TODAY	☐ SUNDAY

WRITE IN THE DATES BELOW (AND SHADE IN TODAY)

IT'S NATIONAL SPUMONI DAY
A FROZEN ITALIAN DESSERT THAT YOU SHOULD PROBABLY JUST LOOK UP.

KASEY MUSGRAVES WAS BORN IN 1988 — USAIN BOLT WAS BORN IN 1986

7 AM

8 AM

9 AM

10 AM

11 AM

NOON

1 PM

2 PM

3 PM

4 PM

5 PM

6 PM

ON THIS DAY IN 1911: THE MONA LISA WAS STOLEN BY A LOUVRE EMPLOYEE.

BRILLIANT AND/OR TERRIBLE IDEAS

233 DAYS DOWN, 132 DAYS LEFT (UNLESS IT'S A LEAP YEAR [234/132])

YEAR:

AUGUST 22

MONDAY	TUESDAY	WEDNESDAY	THURSDAY	FRIDAY	SATURDAY ☐
. . . . ☐ TODAY	. . . . ☐ TODAY	. . . . ☐ TODAY	. . . . ☐ TODAY	. . . . ☐ TODAY	☐ SUNDAY

IT'S NATIONAL TOOTH FAIRY DAY

THE TOOTH FAIRY COLLECTS 300,000 TEETH EACH NIGHT ON AVERAGE.

KRISTEN WIIG WAS BORN IN 1973   DUA LIPA WAS BORN IN 199

7 AM

. . . .

8 AM

. . . .

9 AM

. . . .

10 AM

. . . .

11 AM

. . . .

NOON

. . . .

1 PM

. . . .

2 PM

. . . .

3 PM

. . . .

4 PM

. . . .

5 PM

. . . .

6 PM

ON THIS DAY IN 1902: THE CADILLAC MOTOR COMPANY WAS FOUNDED.

NOTES AND/OR LIMERICKS

YEAR: 234 DAYS DOWN, 131 DAYS LEFT (UNLESS IT'S A LEAP YEAR [235/131])

AUGUST 23

MONDAY	TUESDAY	WEDNESDAY	THURSDAY	FRIDAY	SATURDAY ☐
. . . .	. . . .	. . . .	. . . .	. . . .	
☐ TODAY	☐ TODAY	☐ TODAY	☐ TODAY	☐ TODAY	☐ SUNDAY

IT'S NATIONAL SPONGE CAKE DAY
THE EARLIEST KNOWN RECIPE WAS PUBLISHED IN 1615.

RIVER PHOENIX WAS BORN IN 1970   KOBE BRYANT WAS BORN IN 1978

7 AM
. . . .
AM
. . . .
9 AM
. . . .
O AM
. . . .
11 AM
. . . .
OON
. . . .
1 PM
. . . .
PM
. . . .
3 PM
. . . .
PM
. . . .
5 PM
. . . .
PM

ON THIS DAY IN 2007: THE HASHTAG WAS FIRST USED ON TWITTER.

BRILLIANT AND/OR TERRIBLE IDEAS

285 DAYS DOWN, 130 DAYS LEFT (UNLESS IT'S A LEAP YEAR [236/130])   YEAR:

AUGUST 24

MONDAY	TUESDAY	WEDNESDAY	THURSDAY	FRIDAY	SATURDAY ☐
· · · · · · · · ·	· · · · · · · · ·	· · · · · · · · ·	· · · · · · · · ·	· · · · · · · ·	
☐ TODAY	☐ TODAY	☐ TODAY	☐ TODAY	☐ TODAY	☐ SUNDAY

IT'S PLUTO DEMOTED DAY

IT WAS NAMED BY VENETIA BURNEY, AN 11-YEAR-OLD FROM ENGLAND.

RUPERT GRINT WAS BORN IN 1988   CHAD MICHAEL MURRAY WAS BORN IN 198

7 AM
· ·
8 A
· ·
9 AM
· ·
10 A
· ·
11 AM
· ·
NOO
· ·
1 PM
· ·
2 P
· ·
3 PM
· ·
4 P
· ·
5 PM
· ·
6 P

ON THIS DAY IN 1989: PETE ROSE WAS BANNED FROM BASEBALL FOR LIFE.

NOTES AND/OR LIMERICKS

YEAR: 236 DAYS DOWN, 129 DAYS LEFT (UNLESS IT'S A LEAP YEAR [237/129])

AUGUST 25

MONDAY	TUESDAY	WEDNESDAY	THURSDAY	FRIDAY	SATURDAY ☐
. . . . ☐ TODAY	. . . . ☐ TODAY	. . . . ☐ TODAY	. . . . ☐ TODAY	. . . . ☐ TODAY	☐ SUNDAY

IT'S NATIONAL BANANA SPLIT DAY
THE FIRST BANANA SPLITS COST 10 CENTS EACH.

EAN CONNERY WAS BORN IN 1930   BLAKE LIVELY WAS BORN IN 1987

7 AM

AM

9 AM

O AM

11 AM

OON

1 PM

PM

3 PM

PM

5 PM

PM

ON THIS DAY IN 1916: THE NATIONAL PARK SERVICE WAS CREATED.

BRILLIANT AND/OR TERRIBLE IDEAS

237 DAYS DOWN, 128 DAYS LEFT (UNLESS IT'S A LEAP YEAR [238/128])   YEAR:

AUGUST 26

MONDAY	TUESDAY	WEDNESDAY	THURSDAY	FRIDAY	SATURDAY ☐
. . . . ☐ TODAY	. . . . ☐ TODAY	. . . . ☐ TODAY	. . . . ☐ TODAY	. . . . ☐ TODAY	☐ SUNDAY

IT'S NATIONAL WOMEN'S EQUALITY DAY
NEW ZEALAND WAS THE FIRST COUNTRY TO GIVE WOMEN VOTING RIGHTS.

MELISSA MCCARTHY WAS BORN IN 1970   MACAULAY CULKIN WAS BORN IN 198

7 AM

. . . .

8 A

. . . .

9 AM

. . . .

10 A

. . . .

11 AM

. . . .

NOO

. . . .

1 PM

. . . .

2 P

. . . .

3 PM

. . . .

4 P

. . . .

5 PM

. . . .

6 P

ON THIS DAY IN 1990: BO JACKSON HIT HIS FOURTH CONSECUTIVE HOME RUN.

NOTES AND/OR LIMERICKS

YEAR: 238 DAYS DOWN, 127 DAYS LEFT (UNLESS IT'S A LEAP YEAR [239/127])

AUGUST 27

	WRITE IN THE DATES BELOW (AND SHADE IN TODAY)				
MONDAY	**TUESDAY**	**WEDNESDAY**	**THURSDAY**	**FRIDAY**	**SATURDAY** ☐
. . . . ☐ TODAY	. . . . ☐ TODAY	. . . . ☐ TODAY	. . . . ☐ TODAY	. . . . ☐ TODAY	☐ **SUNDAY**

IT'S WORLD ROCK PAPER SCISSORS DAY
MEN MOST COMMONLY CHOOSE ROCK ON THEIR FIRST THROW.

ARON PAUL WAS BORN IN 1979   CÉSAR MILAN WAS BORN IN 1969

7 AM

. . . .

AM

. . . .

9 AM

. . . .

O AM

. . . .

11 AM

. . . .

OON

. . . .

1 PM

. . . .

PM

. . . .

3 PM

. . . .

PM

. . . .

5 PM

. . . .

PM

ON THIS DAY IN 1955: THE FIRST 'GUINNESS BOOK OF RECORDS' WAS RELEASED.

BRILLIANT AND/OR TERRIBLE IDEAS

239 DAYS DOWN, 126 DAYS LEFT (UNLESS IT'S A LEAP YEAR [240/126])   YEAR:

AUGUST 28

MONDAY	TUESDAY	WEDNESDAY	THURSDAY	FRIDAY	SATURDAY ☐
. . . . ☐ TODAY	. . . . ☐ TODAY	. . . . ☐ TODAY	. . . . ☐ TODAY	. . . . ☐ TODAY	☐ SUNDAY

IT'S NATIONAL BOW TIE DAY

A PERSON WHO COLLECTS THEM IS CALLED A GRABATOLOGIST.

JACK BLACK WAS BORN IN 1969   SHANIA TWAIN WAS BORN IN 196

7 AM
. . . .
8 A
. . . .
9 AM
. . . .
10 A
. . . .
11 AM
. . . .
NOO
. . . .
1 PM
. . . .
2 P
. . . .
3 PM
. . . .
4 P
. . . .
5 PM
. . . .
6 P

ON THIS DAY IN 1996: PRINCE (NOW KING) CHARLES AND PRINCESS DIANA DIVORCED.

NOTES AND/OR LIMERICKS

YEAR: 240 DAYS DOWN, 125 DAYS LEFT (UNLESS IT'S A LEAP YEAR [241/125])

AUGUST 29

MONDAY	TUESDAY	WEDNESDAY	THURSDAY	FRIDAY	SATURDAY ☐
. . . .	. . . .	. . . .	. . . .	. . . .	
☐ TODAY	☐ TODAY	☐ TODAY	☐ TODAY	☐ TODAY	☐ SUNDAY

IT'S NATIONAL LEMON JUICE DAY
LEMON TREES CAN PRODUCE UP TO 600 POUNDS OF FRUIT EACH YEAR.

TEMPLE GRANDIN WAS BORN IN 1947   LIAM PAYNE WAS BORN IN 1993

7 AM

AM

9 AM

O AM

11 AM

OON

1 PM

PM

3 PM

PM

5 PM

PM

ON THIS DAY IN 1898: THE GOODYEAR TIRE COMPANY WAS FOUNDED.

BRILLIANT AND/OR TERRIBLE IDEAS

241 DAYS DOWN, 124 DAYS LEFT (UNLESS IT'S A LEAP YEAR [242/124])   YEAR:

AUGUST 30

MONDAY	TUESDAY	WEDNESDAY	THURSDAY	FRIDAY	SATURDAY ☐
. . . .	. . . .	. . . .	. . . .	. . . .	
☐ TODAY	☐ TODAY	☐ TODAY	☐ TODAY	☐ TODAY	☐ SUNDAY

IT'S NATIONAL BEACH DAY
OVER 22 STATES IN THE U.S. OFFER NUDE BEACHES.

CAMERON DIAZ WAS BORN IN 1972   PEGGY LIPTON WAS BORN IN 194

7 AM
. . . .
                                                                                    8 A

. . . .
9 AM
. . . .
                                                                                    10 A

. . . .
11 AM
. . . .
                                                                                    NOO

. . . .
1 PM
. . . .
                                                                                    2 P

. . . .
3 PM
. . . .
                                                                                    4 P

. . . .
5 PM
. . . .
                                                                                    6 P

ON THIS DAY IN 1993: 'THE LATE SHOW WITH DAVID LETTERMAN' DEBUTED ON CBS.

NOTES AND/OR LIMERICKS

YEAR: 242 DAYS DOWN, 123 DAYS LEFT (UNLESS IT'S A LEAP YEAR [243/123])

AUGUST 31

MONDAY	TUESDAY	WEDNESDAY	THURSDAY	FRIDAY	SATURDAY ☐
. . . .	. . . .	. . . .	. . . .	. . . .	
☐ TODAY	☐ TODAY	☐ TODAY	☐ TODAY	☐ TODAY	☐ SUNDAY

IT'S NATIONAL TRAIL MIX DAY
ALSO KNOWN AS 'SCROGGIN' TO NEW ZEALANDERS.

RICHARD GERE WAS BORN IN 1949   CHRIS TUCKER WAS BORN IN 1971

7 AM

8 AM

9 AM

10 AM

11 AM

NOON

1 PM

2 PM

3 PM

4 PM

5 PM

6 PM

ON THIS DAY IN 1997: PRINCESS DIANA WAS KILLED IN A CAR CRASH.

BRILLIANT AND/OR TERRIBLE IDEAS

243 DAYS DOWN, 122 DAYS LEFT (UNLESS IT'S A LEAP YEAR [244/122])   YEAR:

IT'S OFFICIALLY

× SEPTEMBER ×

OF THE YEAR

☐☐☐☐

MONTH NINE

. . . .

. . . .

. . . .

SEPTEMBER AT A GLANCE

CONGRATULATIONS, YOU MADE IT
TO THE MONTH OF SEPTEMBER

✖

CELEBRATE, IT'S:

NATIONAL MUSHROOM MONTH

CLASSICAL MUSIC MONTH

NTL. SQUARE DANCE MONTH

SELF IMPROVEMENT MONTH

NATIONAL COURTESY MONTH

OFFICIAL SYMBOLS:

BIRTHSTONE: SAPPHIRE

FLOWERS: ASTER & MORNING GLORY

TREES: LIME, OLIVE, & HAZELNUT

VIRGO (AUG 23 / SEP 22)

LIBRA (SEP 23 / OCT 22)

✖

A FEW DATES TO KNOW*
LIKE, IMPORTANT ONES.

✖

LABOR DAY
FIRST MONDAY IN SEPTEMBER

ENKUTATASH
(ETHIOPIA)
SEPTEMBER 11TH

YOM KIPPUR
(JUDAISM)
9 DAYS AFTER THE FIRST
DAY OF ROSH HASHANAH

MESKEL
(ETHIOPIAN ORTHODOX)
SEPTEMBER 27TH (OR 28TH)

PATRIOT DAY
SEPTEMBER 11TH

NATIVE AMERICAN DAY
FOURTH FRIDAY OF SEPTEMBER
(CALIFORNIA & NEVADA)

ROSH HASHANAH
(JUDAISM)
163 DAYS AFTER THE FIRST DAY OF
PASSOVER (USUALLY SEPTEMBER)

START OF FALL
(AUTUMNAL EQUINOX)
SEPTEMBER 22ND (OR 23RD)

MARK YOUR CALENDAR ✖ IT'S RIGHT OVER THERE

---

*A DISCLAIMER OF SORTS

HEY THERE. WE HERE AT BRASS MONKEY LIKE TO JOKE AROUND...BUT WE ALSO WANT TO TAKE A MINUTE TO RECOGNIZE JUST A FEW OF THE MANY HOLIDAYS & EVENTS THAT ARE IMPORTANT TO OUR FRIENDS AROUND THE GLOBE (AND AT HOME). YOU MAY BE DIFFERENT THAN US. WE MAY HAVE NEVER MET. BUT WE LOVE YOU ALL THE SAME.

SO, WITH ALL OF THAT SAID, IF YOU HAVEN'T HEARD OF A DAY, PLEASE LOOK IT UP. LEARNING ABOUT AND APPRECIATING CULTURES DIFFERENT THAN YOURS IS REALLY IMPORTANT...WAY MORE SO THAN POSTING A FEW 'STRAWBERRY JAM DAY' VIDEOS ON TIKTOK. DON'T GET US WRONG, THERE IS PLENTY OF ROOM FOR BOTH. JUST PLEASE DO BOTH.

SEPTEMBER AT A GLANCE

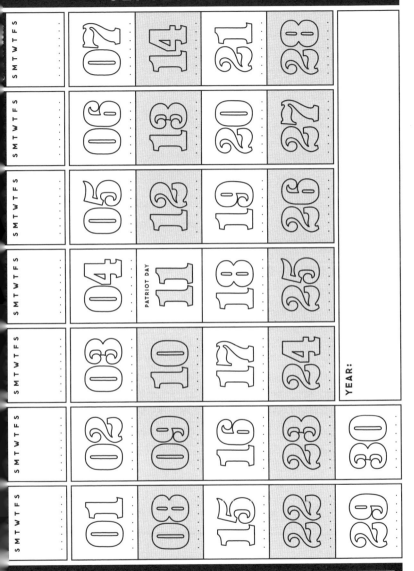

S M T W T F S	S M T W T F S	S M T W T F S	S M T W T F S	S M T W T F S	S M T W T F S	S M T W T F S
07	06	05	04	03	02	01
14	13	12	PATRIOT DAY 11	10	09	08
21	20	19	18	17	16	15
28	27	26	25	24	23	22
				YEAR:	30	29

WELL, WHAT ARE YOU WAITING FOR?

✗ START PLANNING. IN THE CALENDAR ABOVE, WE'VE MARKED THE MORE COMMON U.S. HOLIDAYS ALREADY (THE ONES THAT ARE DATED, THAT IS). SO USE THE LIST TO THE LEFT TO FILL IN THE REST...LIKE ALL OF THE ONES THAT CHANGE DATES FROM YEAR TO YEAR, FOR EXAMPLE. ✗

LISTS, NOTES & MEMOIRS

PEOPLE I'D LIKE TO BE FOR A DAY
OR SOME BORING TO-DO LIST

1
2
3
4
5
6
7
8
9
10
11
12
13
14

PEOPLE I'D LIKE TO BE FOREVER
OR A GROCERY LIST OR SOMETHING

1
2
3
4
5
6
7
8
9
10
11
12
13
14

TOTALLY RAD WORDS THAT NO ONE USES ANYMORE
USE FIGURE 1 FOR ANY NECESSARY VISUAL AIDS

FIG. 1

1
2
3

4
5
6

SEPTEMBER 1

MONDAY	TUESDAY	WEDNESDAY	THURSDAY	FRIDAY	SATURDAY ☐
. . . . ☐ TODAY	. . . . ☐ TODAY	. . . . ☐ TODAY	. . . . ☐ TODAY	. . . . ☐ TODAY	☐ SUNDAY

IT'S NATIONAL CHERRY POPOVER DAY
THE WORLD RECORD FOR SPITTING A CHERRY PIT IS 93 FEET 6.5 INCHES.

PADMA LAKSHMI WAS BORN IN 1970   ZENDAYA WAS BORN IN 1996

7 AM

8 AM

9 AM

10 AM

11 AM

NOON

1 PM

2 PM

3 PM

4 PM

5 PM

6 PM

ON THIS DAY IN 1878: EMMA NUTT BECAME THE FIRST FEMALE TELEPHONE OPERATOR.

BRILLIANT AND/OR TERRIBLE IDEAS

244 DAYS DOWN, 121 DAYS LEFT (UNLESS IT'S A LEAP YEAR [245/121])   YEAR:

SEPTEMBER 2

MONDAY	TUESDAY	WEDNESDAY	THURSDAY	FRIDAY	SATURDAY ☐
. . . .	. . . .	. . . .	. . . .	. . . .	☐
☐ TODAY	☐ TODAY	☐ TODAY	☐ TODAY	☐ TODAY	SUNDAY

IT'S WORLD COCONUT DAY
FALLING COCONUTS KILL ABOUT 150 PEOPLE EACH YEAR.

KEANU REEVES WAS BORN IN 1964   SALMA HAYEK WAS BORN IN 1966

7 AM
. . . .
                                                                              8 AM
. . . .
9 AM
. . . .
                                                                              10 AM
. . . .
11 AM
. . . .
                                                                              NOON
. . . .
1 PM
. . . .
                                                                              2 PM
. . . .
3 PM
. . . .
                                                                              4 PM
. . . .
5 PM
. . . .
                                                                              6 PM

ON THIS DAY IN 1666: THE GREAT FIRE OF LONDON DESTROYED EIGHTY PERCENT OF THE CITY.

NOTES AND/OR LIMERICKS

YEAR: | 245 DAYS DOWN, 120 DAYS LEFT (UNLESS IT'S A LEAP YEAR [246/120])

SEPTEMBER 3

MONDAY	TUESDAY	WEDNESDAY	THURSDAY	FRIDAY	SATURDAY ☐
. . . .	. . . .	. . . .	. . . .	. . . .	
☐ TODAY	☐ TODAY	☐ TODAY	☐ TODAY	☐ TODAY	☐ SUNDAY

IT'S NATIONAL SKYSCRAPER DAY
THE BURJ KHALIFA IN DUBAI IS THE WORLD'S TALLEST AT 2,717 FEET.

SHAUN WHITE WAS BORN IN 1986   KAIA GERBER WAS BORN IN 2001

7 AM

8 AM

9 AM

10 AM

11 AM

NOON

1 PM

2 PM

3 PM

4 PM

5 PM

6 PM

ON THIS DAY IN 1995: EBAY (THEN CALLED AUCTIONWEB) WAS FOUNDED.

BRILLIANT AND/OR TERRIBLE IDEAS

   YEAR:

SEPTEMBER 4

MONDAY	TUESDAY	WEDNESDAY	THURSDAY	FRIDAY	SATURDAY ☐
. . . .	. . . .	. . . .	. . . .	. . . .	
☐ TODAY	☐ TODAY	☐ TODAY	☐ TODAY	☐ TODAY	☐ SUNDAY

IT'S NATIONAL MACADAMIA NUT DAY
IT TAKES 300 LBS. OF PRESSURE PER SQUARE INCH TO BREAK IT'S SHELL.

BEYONCÉ WAS BORN IN 1981   WES BENTLEY WAS BORN IN 1978

7 AM

. . . .
8 AM

9 AM

. . . .
10 AM

11 AM

. . . .
NOON

. . . .
1 PM

. . . .
2 PM

3 PM

. . . .
4 PM

5 PM

. . . .
6 PM

ON THIS DAY IN 2002: KELLY CLARKSON WON THE FIRST SEASON OF 'AMERICAN IDOL.'

NOTES AND/OR LIMERICKS

YEAR:	247 DAYS DOWN, 118 DAYS LEFT (UNLESS IT'S A LEAP YEAR [248/118])

SEPTEMBER 5

WRITE IN THE DATES BELOW (AND SHADE IN TODAY)					SATURDAY ☐
MONDAY	**TUESDAY**	**WEDNESDAY**	**THURSDAY**	**FRIDAY**	
. . . .	. . . .	. . . .	. . . .	. . . .	
☐ TODAY	☐ TODAY	☐ TODAY	☐ TODAY	☐ TODAY	☐ SUNDAY

IT'S NATIONAL CHEESE PIZZA DAY
93% OF AMERICANS EAT PIZZA AT LEAST ONCE A MONTH.

MICHAEL KEATON WAS BORN IN 1951   FREDDIE MERCURY WAS BORN IN 1946

7 AM

8 AM

9 AM

10 AM

11 AM

NOON

1 PM

2 PM

3 PM

4 PM

5 PM

6 PM

ON THIS DAY IN 1882: THE FIRST LABOR DAY PARADE WAS HELD IN NEW YORK CITY.

BRILLIANT AND/OR TERRIBLE IDEAS

248 DAYS DOWN, 117 DAYS LEFT (UNLESS IT'S A LEAP YEAR [249/117])   YEAR:

SEPTEMBER 6

MONDAY	TUESDAY	WEDNESDAY	THURSDAY	FRIDAY	SATURDAY ☐
. . . .	. . . .	. . . .	. . . .	. . . .	
☐ TODAY	☐ TODAY	☐ TODAY	☐ TODAY	☐ TODAY	☐ SUNDAY

IT'S NATIONAL READ A BOOK DAY
WORLD RECORD HOLDER HOWARD BERG CAN READ 25,000 WORDS PER MINUTE.

IDRIS ELBA WAS BORN IN 1972   LAUREN LAPKUS WAS BORN IN 1985

7 AM

. . . .
8 AM
. . . .
9 AM

. . . .
10 AM
. . . .
11 AM

. . . .
NOON
. . . .
1 PM

. . . .
2 PM
. . . .
3 PM

. . . .
4 PM
. . . .
5 PM

. . . .
6 PM

ON THIS DAY IN 1995: CAL RIPKEN JR. PLAYED HIS 2,131ST CONSECUTIVE GAME.

NOTES AND/OR LIMERICKS

YEAR: 249 DAYS DOWN, 116 DAYS LEFT (UNLESS IT'S A LEAP YEAR [250/116])

SEPTEMBER 7

MONDAY	TUESDAY	WEDNESDAY	THURSDAY	FRIDAY	SATURDAY ☐
. . . .	. . . .	. . . .	. . . .	. . . .	
☐ TODAY	☐ TODAY	☐ TODAY	☐ TODAY	☐ TODAY	☐ SUNDAY

IT'S NATIONAL BEER LOVERS DAY
PEOPLE WORKING ON THE GREAT PYRAMIDS WERE PAID IN BEER.

BUDDY HOLLY WAS BORN IN 1936   QUEEN ELIZABETH I WAS BORN IN 1533

7 AM

8 AM

9 AM

10 AM

11 AM

NOON

1 PM

2 PM

3 PM

4 PM

5 PM

6 PM

ON THIS DAY IN 1993: 'THE CHEVY CHASE SHOW' DEBUTED. IT LASTED 6 WEEKS.

BRILLIANT AND/OR TERRIBLE IDEAS

250 DAYS DOWN, 115 DAYS LEFT (UNLESS IT'S A LEAP YEAR [251/115])

YEAR:

SEPTEMBER 8

MONDAY	TUESDAY	WEDNESDAY	THURSDAY	FRIDAY	SATURDAY ☐
☐ TODAY	☐ TODAY	☐ TODAY	☐ TODAY	☐ TODAY	☐ SUNDAY

IT'S IGUANA AWARENESS DAY
AND NOW YOU'RE AWARE, OUR JOB IS DONE.

PINK WAS BORN IN 1979   AIMEE MANN WAS BORN IN 1960

7 AM

. . . .
                                                                    8 AM
. . . .
9 AM

. . . .
                                                                    10 AM
. . . .
11 AM

. . . .
                                                                    NOON
. . . .
1 PM

. . . .
                                                                    2 PM
. . . .
3 PM

. . . .
                                                                    4 PM
. . . .
5 PM

. . . .
                                                                    6 PM

ON THIS DAY IN 2022: QUEEN ELIZABETH II PASSED AT THE AGE OF 96.

NOTES AND/OR LIMERICKS

YEAR:	251 DAYS DOWN, 114 DAYS LEFT (UNLESS IT'S A LEAP YEAR [252/114])

SEPTEMBER 9

IT'S INTERNATIONAL SUDOKU DAY
THERE ARE 5,472,730,538 POSSIBLE SOLUTIONS TO A 9X9 GRID.

ADAM SANDLER WAS BORN IN 1966   MICHELLE WILLIAMS WAS BORN IN 1980

7 AM

8 AM

9 AM

10 AM

11 AM

NOON

1 PM

2 PM

3 PM

4 PM

5 PM

6 PM

ON THIS DAY IN 1956: ELVIS PRESLEY FIRST APPEARED ON 'THE ED SULLIVAN SHOW.'

BRILLIANT AND/OR TERRIBLE IDEAS

252 DAYS DOWN, 113 DAYS LEFT (UNLESS IT'S A LEAP YEAR [253/113])   YEAR:

SEPTEMBER 10

IT'S WORLD SUICIDE PREVENTION DAY

IF YOU'RE WORRIED ABOUT SOMEONE YOU KNOW, REACH OUT TO THEM.

(GET 24/7, FREE & CONFIDENTIAL SUPPORT: 1-800-273-8225)

MISTY COPELAND WAS BORN IN 1982   COLIN FIRTH WAS BORN IN 1960

7 AM

8 AM

9 AM

10 AM

11 AM

NOON

1 PM

2 PM

3 PM

4 PM

5 PM

6 PM

ON THIS DAY IN 1991: NIRVANA RELEASED 'SMELLS LIKE TEEN SPIRIT.'

NOTES AND/OR LIMERICKS

YEAR: 253 DAYS DOWN, 112 DAYS LEFT (UNLESS IT'S A LEAP YEAR [254/112])

SEPTEMBER 11

MONDAY	TUESDAY	WEDNESDAY	THURSDAY	FRIDAY	SATURDAY ☐
. . . .	. . . .	. . . .	. . . .	. . . .	☐ SUNDAY
☐ TODAY	☐ TODAY	☐ TODAY	☐ TODAY	☐ TODAY	☐

IT'S PATRIOT DAY
THE FIRST PLANE STRUCK THE NORTH WTC TOWER AT 8:45 A.M.

TARAJI P. HENSON WAS BORN IN 1970   TED LEO WAS BORN IN 1970

7 AM

8 AM

9 AM

10 AM

11 AM

NOON

1 PM

2 PM

3 PM

4 PM

5 PM

6 PM

ON THIS DAY IN 2001: THINGS WOULD NEVER BE THE SAME AGAIN.

BRILLIANT AND/OR TERRIBLE IDEAS

254 DAYS DOWN, 111 DAYS LEFT (UNLESS IT'S A LEAP YEAR [255/111])   YEAR:

SEPTEMBER 12

WRITE IN THE DATES BELOW (AND SHADE IN TODAY)

MONDAY	TUESDAY	WEDNESDAY	THURSDAY	FRIDAY	SATURDAY ☐
. . . .	. . . .	. . . .	. . . .	. . . .	
☐ TODAY	☐ TODAY	☐ TODAY	☐ TODAY	☐ TODAY	☐ SUNDAY

IT'S NATIONAL CHOCOLATE MILKSHAKE DAY
THE FIRST KNOWN RECIPE FOR A MILKSHAKE INCLUDED ONE PART WHISKEY.

JENNIFER HUDSON WAS BORN IN 1981   PAUL F. TOMPKINS WAS BORN IN 1968

7 AM

8 AM

9 AM

10 AM

11 AM

NOON

1 PM

2 PM

3 PM

4 PM

5 PM

6 PM

ON THIS DAY IN 1978: 'TAXI' PREMIERED ON ABC.

NOTES AND/OR LIMERICKS

YEAR:	255 DAYS DOWN, 110 DAYS LEFT (UNLESS IT'S A LEAP YEAR [256/110])

SEPTEMBER 13

MONDAY	TUESDAY	WEDNESDAY	THURSDAY	FRIDAY	SATURDAY ☐
. . . . ☐ TODAY	. . . . ☐ TODAY	. . . . ☐ TODAY	. . . . ☐ TODAY	. . . . ☐ TODAY	☐ SUNDAY

IT'S NATIONAL PEANUT DAY
THE AVERAGE AMERICAN WILL EAT ABOUT 3,000 PB&Js IN THEIR LIFETIME.

NIALL HORAN WAS BORN IN 1993   TYLER PERRY WAS BORN IN 1969

7 AM

8 AM

9 AM

10 AM

11 AM

NOON

1 PM

2 PM

3 PM

4 PM

5 PM

6 PM

ON THIS DAY IN 1997: 'CANDLE IN THE WIND 1997' WAS RELEASED BY ELTON JOHN.

BRILLIANT AND/OR TERRIBLE IDEAS

256 DAYS DOWN, 109 DAYS LEFT (UNLESS IT'S A LEAP YEAR [257/109])   YEAR:

SEPTEMBER 14

MONDAY	TUESDAY	WEDNESDAY	THURSDAY	FRIDAY	SATURDAY ☐
. . . .	. . . .	. . . .	. . . .	. . . .	
☐ TODAY	☐ TODAY	☐ TODAY	☐ TODAY	☐ TODAY	☐ SUNDAY

IT'S NATIONAL COLORING DAY
COLORING UTILIZES BOTH HEMISPHERES OF THE BRAIN.

AMY WINEHOUSE WAS BORN IN 1983   SAM NEILL WAS BORN IN 1947

7 AM
. . . .
8 AM
. . . .
9 AM
. . . .
10 AM
. . . .
11 AM
. . . .
NOON
. . . .
1 PM
. . . .
2 PM
. . . .
3 PM
. . . .
4 PM
. . . .
5 PM
. . . .
6 PM

ON THIS DAY IN 1901: THE FIRST BODYBUILDING CONTEST WAS HELD IN LONDON.

NOTES AND/OR LIMERICKS

YEAR: 257 DAYS DOWN, 108 DAYS LEFT (UNLESS IT'S A LEAP YEAR [258/108])

SEPTEMBER 15

MONDAY	TUESDAY	WEDNESDAY	THURSDAY	FRIDAY	SATURDAY ☐
· · · · · · · ☐ TODAY	· · · · · · · ☐ TODAY	· · · · · · · ☐ TODAY	· · · · · · · ☐ TODAY	· · · · · · · ☐ TODAY	☐ SUNDAY

IT'S INTERNATIONAL DOT DAY

POINTILLISM IS PAINTING WITH DOTS INSTEAD OF BRUSH STROKES.

TOM HARDY WAS BORN IN 1977   PRINCE HARRY WAS BORN IN 1984

7 AM

8 AM

9 AM

10 AM

11 AM

NOON

1 PM

2 PM

3 PM

4 PM

5 PM

6 PM

ON THIS DAY IN 1997: THE GOOGLE.COM DOMAIN NAME WAS REGISTERED.

BRILLIANT AND/OR TERRIBLE IDEAS

258 DAYS DOWN, 107 DAYS LEFT (UNLESS IT'S A LEAP YEAR [259/107])   YEAR:

SEPTEMBER 16

MONDAY	TUESDAY	WEDNESDAY	THURSDAY	FRIDAY	SATURDAY ☐
. . . .	. . . .	. . . .	. . . .	. . . .	☐
☐ TODAY	☐ TODAY	☐ TODAY	☐ TODAY	☐ TODAY	SUNDAY

IT'S NATIONAL GUACAMOLE DAY
GUACAMOLE LITERALLY TRANSLATES TO 'AVOCADO SAUCE.'

B.B. KING WAS BORN IN 1925   AMY POEHLER WAS BORN IN 197'

7 AM
. . . .
                                                                                        8 AM
. . . .
9 AM
. . . .
                                                                                       10 AM
11 AM
. . . .
                                                                                        NOON
. . . .
1 PM
. . . .
                                                                                        2 PM
3 PM
. . . .
                                                                                        4 PM
. . . .
5 PM
. . . .
                                                                                        6 PM

ON THIS DAY IN 1996: 'JUDGE JUDY' PREMIERED ON CBS.

NOTES AND/OR LIMERICKS

YEAR: 259 DAYS DOWN, 106 DAYS LEFT (UNLESS IT'S A LEAP YEAR [260/106])

		WRITE IN THE DATES BELOW (AND SHADE IN TODAY)			
MONDAY	TUESDAY	WEDNESDAY	THURSDAY	FRIDAY	SATURDAY ☐
☐ TODAY	☐ TODAY	☐ TODAY	☐ TODAY	☐ TODAY	☐ SUNDAY

IT'S NATIONAL APPLE DUMPLING DAY
THE CRABAPPLE IS THE ONLY VARIETY NATIVE TO NORTH AMERICA.

PATRICK MAHOMES WAS BORN IN 1995   ELVIRA WAS BORN IN 1951

7 AM

8 AM

9 AM

10 AM

11 AM

NOON

1 PM

2 PM

3 PM

4 PM

5 PM

6 PM

ON THIS DAY IN 1849: HARRIET TUBMAN ESCAPED FROM SLAVERY.

BRILLIANT AND/OR TERRIBLE IDEAS

260 DAYS DOWN, 105 DAYS LEFT (UNLESS IT'S A LEAP YEAR [261/105])   YEAR:

SEPTEMBER 18

MONDAY	TUESDAY	WEDNESDAY	THURSDAY	FRIDAY	SATURDAY ☐
· · · · · · · ·	· · · · · · · ·	· · · · · · · ·	· · · · · · · ·	· · · · · · · ·	☐
☐ TODAY	☐ TODAY	☐ TODAY	☐ TODAY	☐ TODAY	SUNDAY

IT'S WORLD BAMBOO DAY
CERTAIN TYPES CAN GROW 35 INCHES IN A SINGLE DAY.

JASON SUDEIKIS WAS BORN IN 1975   JAMES GANDOLFINI WAS BORN IN 1961

7 AM

· ·
8 AM
· ·
9 AM

· ·
10 AM
· ·
11 AM

· ·
NOON
· ·
1 PM

· ·
2 PM
· ·
3 PM

· ·
4 PM
· ·
5 PM

· ·
6 PM

ON THIS DAY IN 1970: JIMI HENDRIX DIED IN LONDON AT THE AGE OF 27.

NOTES AND/OR LIMERICKS

YEAR: 261 DAYS DOWN, 104 DAYS LEFT (UNLESS IT'S A LEAP YEAR [262/104])

SEPTEMBER 19

WRITE IN THE DATES BELOW (AND SHADE IN TODAY)

MONDAY	TUESDAY	WEDNESDAY	THURSDAY	FRIDAY	SATURDAY ☐
. . . .	. . . .	. . . .	. . . .	. . . .	
☐ TODAY	☐ TODAY	☐ TODAY	☐ TODAY	☐ TODAY	☐ SUNDAY

IT'S INTERNATIONAL TALK LIKE A PIRATE DAY
WHICH WAS PROBABLY THE SAME AS HOW EVERYONE ELSE SPOKE.

JEREMY IRONS WAS BORN IN 1948   JIMMY FALLON WAS BORN IN 1974

7 AM
. . . .
8 AM
. . . .
9 AM
. . . .
10 AM
. . . .
11 AM
. . . .
NOON
. . . .
1 PM
. . . .
2 PM
. . . .
3 PM
. . . .
4 PM
. . . .
5 PM
. . . .
6 PM

ON THIS DAY IN 1947: JACKIE ROBINSON WAS NAMED 'ROOKIE OF THE YEAR.'

BRILLIANT AND/OR TERRIBLE IDEAS

262 DAYS DOWN, 103 DAYS LEFT (UNLESS IT'S A LEAP YEAR [263/103])   YEAR:

SEPTEMBER 20

IT'S NATIONAL PEPPERONI PIZZA DAY
IN ITALIAN 'PEPPERONI' ACTUALLY MEANS 'PEPPER.'

GEORGE R.R. MARTIN WAS BORN IN 1948   SOPHIA LOREN WAS BORN IN 193

7 AM

8 AM

9 AM

10 AM

11 AM

NOON

1 PM

2 PM

3 PM

4 PM

5 PM

6 PM

ON THIS DAY IN 1999: 'LAW AND ORDER: SVU' PREMIERED ON NBC.

NOTES AND/OR LIMERICKS

YEAR: 263 DAYS DOWN, 102 DAYS LEFT (UNLESS IT'S A LEAP YEAR [264/102])

SEPTEMBER 21

MONDAY	TUESDAY	WEDNESDAY	THURSDAY	FRIDAY	SATURDAY ☐
. . . .	. . . .	. . . .	. . . .	. . . .	
☐ TODAY	☐ TODAY	☐ TODAY	☐ TODAY	☐ TODAY	☐ SUNDAY

WRITE IN THE DATES BELOW (AND SHADE IN TODAY)

IT'S MINIATURE GOLF DAY
IN THE 1920s, THERE WERE OVER 150 ROOFTOP COURSES IN NYC.

THAN COEN WAS BORN IN 1957   BILL MURRAY WAS BORN IN 1950

7 AM

8 AM

9 AM

10 AM

11 AM

NOON

1 PM

2 PM

3 PM

4 PM

5 PM

6 PM

ON THIS DAY IN 1996: JOHN F. KENNEDY JR. MARRIED CAROLYN BESSETTE.

BRILLIANT AND/OR TERRIBLE IDEAS

264 DAYS DOWN, 101 DAYS LEFT (UNLESS IT'S A LEAP YEAR [265/101])

YEAR:

SEPTEMBER 22

IT'S NATIONAL ELEPHANT APPRECIATION DAY
THEY ARE AFRAID OF BEES...BUT THEN AGAIN, SO ARE WE.

JOAN JETT WAS BORN IN 1958   BILLIE PIPER WAS BORN IN 198

7 AM
. . . .
                                                                                          8 A
. . . .
9 AM
. . . .
                                                                                          10 A
. . . .
11 AM
. . . .
                                                                                          NOO
. . . .
1 PM
. . . .
                                                                                          2 P
. . . .
3 PM
. . . .
                                                                                          4 P
. . . .
5 PM
. . . .
                                                                                          6 P

ON THIS DAY IN 1994: 'FRIENDS' PREMIERED ON NBC.

NOTES AND/OR LIMERICKS

| YEAR: | | 265 DAYS DOWN, 100 DAYS LEFT (UNLESS IT'S A LEAP YEAR [266/100]) |

SEPTEMBER 23

IT'S NATIONAL GREAT AMERICAN POT PIE DAY
GEEZ, CALM DOWN GUYS. JUST 'POT PIE' WOULD HAVE BEEN FINE.

OHN COLTRANE WAS BORN IN 1926   MELANIE BRIDGES WAS BORN IN 1977

7 AM
. . . .
AM
. . . .
9 AM
. . . .
O AM
. . . .
11 AM
. . . .
OON
. . . .
1 PM
. . . .
PM
. . . .
3 PM
. . . .
PM
. . . .
5 PM
. . . .
PM

ON THIS DAY IN 1994: 'THE SHAWSHANK REDEMPTION' WAS RELEASED.

BRILLIANT AND/OR TERRIBLE IDEAS

SEPTEMBER 24

IT'S NATIONAL PUNCTUATION DAY
THE ACTUAL TERM FOR THE # SYMBOL IS AN OCTOTHORPE.

JIM HENSON WAS BORN IN 1936   NIA VARDALOS WAS BORN IN 196

7 AM
. . . .
                                                                              8 A
. . . .
9 AM
. . . .
                                                                              10 A
. . . .
11 AM
. . . .
                                                                              NOO
. . . .
1 PM
. . . .
                                                                              2 P
. . . .
3 PM
. . . .
                                                                              4 P
. . . .
5 PM
. . . .
                                                                              6 P

ON THIS DAY IN 1961: THE FINAL EPISODE OF 'I LOVE LUCY' AIRED.

NOTES AND/OR LIMERICKS																											

YEAR:	267 DAYS DOWN, 98 DAYS LEFT (UNLESS IT'S A LEAP YEAR [268/98])

SEPTEMBER 25

WRITE IN THE DATES BELOW (AND SHADE IN TODAY)

MONDAY	TUESDAY	WEDNESDAY	THURSDAY	FRIDAY	SATURDAY ☐
. . . .	. . . .	. . . .	. . . .	. . . .	☐
☐ TODAY	☐ TODAY	☐ TODAY	☐ TODAY	☐ TODAY	☐ SUNDAY

IT'S NATIONAL COMIC BOOK DAY

IN 1954 CONGRESS INVESTIGATED THEIR EFFECT ON JUVENILE DELINQUENCY.

DONALD GLOVER WAS BORN IN 1983   MARK HAMILL WAS BORN IN 1951

7 AM

AM

9 AM

10 AM

11 AM

NOON

1 PM

PM

3 PM

PM

5 PM

PM

ON THIS DAY IN 2018: BILL COSBY WAS SENTENCED TO PRISON FOR 3-10 YEARS.

BRILLIANT AND/OR TERRIBLE IDEAS

268 DAYS DOWN, 97 DAYS LEFT (UNLESS IT'S A LEAP YEAR [269/97])   YEAR:

SEPTEMBER 26

MONDAY	TUESDAY	WEDNESDAY	THURSDAY	FRIDAY	SATURDAY ☐
. . . .	. . . .	. . . .	. . . .	. . . .	
☐ TODAY	☐ TODAY	☐ TODAY	☐ TODAY	☐ TODAY	☐ SUNDAY

IT'S LUMBERJACK DAY
LOGGING IS 33 TIMES MORE DANGEROUS THAN THE AVERAGE JOB.

SERENA WILLIAMS WAS BORN IN 1981   OLIVIA NEWTON-JOHN WAS BORN IN 194

7 AM
. . . .
8 A
. . . .
9 AM
. . . .
10 A
. . . .
11 AM
. . . .
NOO
. . . .
1 PM
. . . .
2 P
. . . .
3 PM
. . . .
4 P
. . . .
5 PM
. . . .
6 P

ON THIS DAY IN 1969: 'THE BRADY BUNCH' AIRED ON NBC.

NOTES AND/OR LIMERICKS

YEAR: 269 DAYS DOWN, 96 DAYS LEFT (UNLESS IT'S A LEAP YEAR [270/96])

SEPTEMBER 27

MONDAY	TUESDAY	WEDNESDAY	THURSDAY	FRIDAY	SATURDAY ☐
. . . . ☐ TODAY	. . . . ☐ TODAY	. . . . ☐ TODAY	. . . . ☐ TODAY	. . . . ☐ TODAY	☐ SUNDAY

IT'S NATIONAL CHOCOLATE MILK DAY
7% OF AMERICANS THINK CHOCOLATE MILK COMES FROM BROWN COWS.

RIL LAVIGNE WAS BORN IN 1984   JENNA ORTEGA WAS BORN IN 2002

7 AM

AM

9 AM

AM

11 AM

NOON

1 PM

PM

3 PM

PM

5 PM

PM

ON THIS DAY IN 1937: THE FIRST SANTA CLAUS TRAINING SCHOOL OPENED IN NYC.

BRILLIANT AND/OR TERRIBLE IDEAS

270 DAYS DOWN, 95 DAYS LEFT (UNLESS IT'S A LEAP YEAR [271/95])   YEAR:

SEPTEMBER 28

MONDAY	TUESDAY	WEDNESDAY	THURSDAY	FRIDAY	SATURDAY
. . . .	. . . .	. . . .	. . . .	. . . .	
☐ TODAY	☐ TODAY	☐ TODAY	☐ TODAY	☐ TODAY	☐ SUNDA

IT'S NATIONAL GOOD NEIGHBOR DAY
MR. ROGERS SUFFERED FROM RED-GREEN COLOR BLINDNESS.

BRIGETTE BARDOT WAS BORN IN 1934   NAOMI WATTS WAS BORN IN 19

7 AM
. . . .
                                                                        8 A
. . . .
9 AM
. . . .
                                                                        10 A
. . . .
11 AM
. . . .
                                                                        NOC
. . . .
1 PM
. . . .
                                                                        2 P
. . . .
3 PM
. . . .
                                                                        4 P
. . . .
5 PM
. . . .
                                                                        6 P

ON THIS DAY IN 2020: THE COVID-19 GLOBAL DEATH TOLL PASSED 1 MILLION.

NOTES AND/OR LIMERICKS

YEAR: 271 DAYS DOWN, 94 DAYS LEFT (UNLESS IT'S A LEAP YEAR [272/94])

SEPTEMBER 29

MONDAY	TUESDAY	WEDNESDAY	THURSDAY	FRIDAY	SATURDAY ☐
. . . .	. . . .	. . . .	. . . .	. . . .	
☐ TODAY	☐ TODAY	☐ TODAY	☐ TODAY	☐ TODAY	☐ SUNDAY

IT'S NATIONAL COFFEE DAY
THE WORLD'S FIRST WEBCAM WATCHED A COFFEE POT.

KEVIN DURANT WAS BORN IN 1988   HALSEY WAS BORN IN 1994

7 AM

8 AM

9 AM

10 AM

11 AM

NOON

1 PM

2 PM

3 PM

4 PM

5 PM

6 PM

ON THIS DAY IN 2021: BRITNEY SPEARS' FATHER IS SUSPENDED AS HER CONSERVATOR.

BRILLIANT AND/OR TERRIBLE IDEAS

272 DAYS DOWN, 93 DAYS LEFT (UNLESS IT'S A LEAP YEAR [273/93])   YEAR:

SEPTEMBER 30

IT'S EXTRA VIRGIN OLIVE OIL DAY
RIPENESS IS THE ONLY DIFFERENCE BETWEEN BLACK AND GREEN OLIVES.

MARION COTILLARD WAS BORN IN 1975   TRUMAN CAPOTE WAS BORN IN 1924

7 AM

8 AM

9 AM

10 AM

11 AM

NOON

1 PM

2 PM

3 PM

4 PM

5 PM

6 PM

ON THIS DAY IN 1946: 22 NAZI LEADERS WERE FOUND GUILTY OF WAR CRIMES.

NOTES AND/OR LIMERICKS

YEAR: 273 DAYS DOWN, 92 DAYS LEFT (UNLESS IT'S A LEAP YEAR [274/92])

LISTS, NOTES & MEMOIRS

WAYS THIS MONTH WAS GREAT
'IT ENDED' IS A VALID ANSWER

1
2
3
4
5
6
7
8
9
10
11
12
13
14

WAYS THAT IT WASN'T
USE ADDITIONAL PAPER IF NEEDED

1
2
3
4
5
6
7
8
9
10
11
12
13
14

PEOPLE THAT I PLAN ON HAUNTING SOME DAY
USE FIGURE 1 FOR ANY NECESSARY VISUAL AIDS

FIG. 1

1
2
3

4
5
6

IT'S OFFICIALLY

× OCTOBER ×

OF THE YEAR

☐ ☐ ☐ ☐

MONTH TEN

. . . .

. . . .

. . . .

OCTOBER AT A GLANCE

CONGRATULATIONS, YOU MADE IT
TO THE MONTH OF OCTOBER

✖

CELEBRATE, IT'S:

NTL. CRIME PREVENTION MONTH

BAT APPRECIATION MONTH

NTL. DENTAL HYGIENE MONTH

NATIONAL PIZZA MONTH

SQUIRREL AWARENESS MONTH

OFFICIAL SYMBOLS:

BIRTHSTONE: OPAL

FLOWERS: MARIGOLD & COSMO

TREES: ROWAN, MAPLE, & WALNUT

LIBRA (SEP 23 / OCT 22)

SCORPIO (OCT 23 / NOV 21)

✖

A FEW DATES TO KNOW*
LIKE, IMPORTANT ONES.

✖

SUKKOT
(JUDAISM)
15TH DAY OF THE HEBREW MONTH
OF TISHREI (COULD BE SEPTEMBER
OR OCTOBER)

NATIONAL
COMING OUT DAY
OCTOBER 11TH

INDIGENOUS PEOPLES' DAY
SECOND MONDAY OF OCTOBER

COLUMBUS DAY
SECOND MONDAY OF OCTOBER

CANADIAN THANKSGIVING
SECOND MONDAY IN OCTOBER

DUSSEHRA
(HINDUISM)
10TH DAY OF THE MONTH OF
ASHWIN IN THE HINDU CALENDAR
(SEPTEMBER OR OCTOBER)

MILVIAN BRIDGE DAY
(CHRISTIAN)
OCTOBER 28TH

HALLOWEEN
OCTOBER 31ST

MARK YOUR CALENDAR ✖ IT'S RIGHT OVER THERE

*A DISCLAIMER OF SORTS

HEY THERE. WE HERE AT BRASS MONKEY LIKE TO JOKE AROUND...BUT WE ALSO WANT TO TAKE A
MINUTE TO RECOGNIZE JUST A FEW OF THE MANY HOLIDAYS & EVENTS THAT ARE IMPORTANT TO OUR
FRIENDS AROUND THE GLOBE (AND AT HOME). YOU MAY BE DIFFERENT THAN US. WE MAY HAVE
NEVER MET. BUT WE LOVE YOU ALL THE SAME.

SO, WITH ALL OF THAT SAID, IF YOU HAVEN'T HEARD OF A DAY, PLEASE LOOK IT UP. LEARNING
ABOUT AND APPRECIATING CULTURES DIFFERENT THAN YOURS IS REALLY IMPORTANT...WAY MORE SO
THAN POSTING A FEW 'STRAWBERRY JAM DAY' VIDEOS ON TIKTOK. DON'T GET US WRONG, THERE IS
PLENTY OF ROOM FOR BOTH. JUST PLEASE DO BOTH.

OCTOBER AT A GLANCE

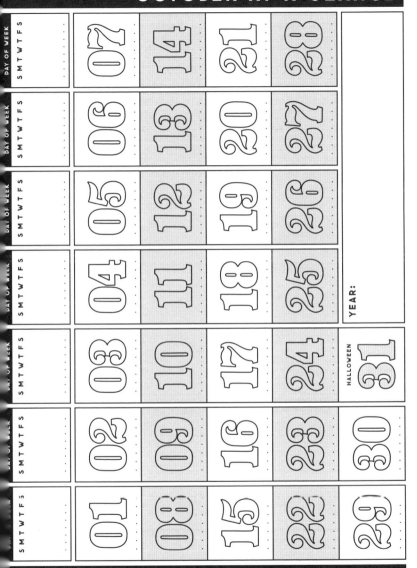

DAY OF WEEK — S M T W T F S

01	02	03	04	05	06	07
08	09	10	11	12	13	14
15	16	17	18	19	20	21
22	23	24	25	26	27	28
29	30	31 HALLOWEEN				

YEAR:

WELL, WHAT ARE YOU WAITING FOR?

✖ START PLANNING. IN THE CALENDAR ABOVE, WE'VE MARKED THE MORE COMMON U.S. HOLIDAYS ALREADY (THE ONES THAT ARE DATED, THAT IS). SO USE THE LIST TO THE LEFT TO FILL IN THE REST...LIKE ALL OF THE ONES THAT CHANGE DATES FROM YEAR TO YEAR, FOR EXAMPLE. ✖

LISTS, NOTES & MEMOIRS

FOODS WITH MISLEADING NAMES
OR SOME BORING TO-DO LIST

1
2
3
4
5
6
7
8
9
10
11
12
13
14

NAMES THAT SOUND LIKE FOOD
OR A GROCERY LIST OR SOMETHING

1
2
3
4
5
6
7
8
9
10
11
12
13
14

WORST IDEAS FOR SEXY HALLOWEEN COSTUMES
USE FIGURE 1 FOR ANY NECESSARY VISUAL AIDS

FIG. 1

1
2
3

4
5
6

MONDAY	TUESDAY	WEDNESDAY	THURSDAY	FRIDAY	SATURDAY ☐
. . . . ☐ TODAY	. . . . ☐ TODAY	. . . . ☐ TODAY	. . . . ☐ TODAY	. . . . ☐ TODAY	☐ SUNDAY

WRITE IN THE DATES BELOW (AND SHADE IN TODAY)

IT'S INTERNATIONAL MUSIC DAY
IN 2016, MOZART SOLD MORE CDs THAN BEYONCÉ.

JULIE ANDREWS WAS BORN IN 1935   BRIE LARSON WAS BORN IN 1989

7 AM

8 AM

9 AM

10 AM

11 AM

NOON

1 PM

2 PM

3 PM

4 PM

5 PM

6 PM

ON THIS DAY IN 1971: WALT DISNEY WORLD OPENED IN ORLANDO, FLORIDA.

BRILLIANT AND/OR TERRIBLE IDEAS

274 DAYS DOWN, 91 DAYS LEFT (UNLESS IT'S A LEAP YEAR [275/91])   YEAR:

OCTOBER 2

IT'S WORLD DAY FOR FARMED ANIMALS
GOATS AND SHEEP DON'T HAVE ANY TEETH ON THEIR UPPER JAW.

ANNIE LIEBOVITZ WAS BORN IN 1949   KELLY RIPA WAS BORN IN 1970

7 AM
. . . .
                                                                                    8 AM
. . . .
9 AM
. . . .
                                                                                    10 AM
. . . .
11 AM
. . . .
                                                                                    NOON
. . . .
1 PM
. . . .
                                                                                    2 PM
. . . .
3 PM
. . . .
                                                                                    4 PM
. . . .
5 PM
. . . .
                                                                                    6 PM

ON THIS DAY IN 1967: THURGOOD MARSHALL JOINED THE U.S. SUPREME COURT.

NOTES AND/OR LIMERICKS

YEAR: 275 DAYS DOWN, 90 DAYS LEFT (UNLESS IT'S A LEAP YEAR [276/90])

OCTOBER 3

MONDAY	TUESDAY	WEDNESDAY	THURSDAY	FRIDAY	SATURDAY ☐
☐ TODAY	☐ TODAY	☐ TODAY	☐ TODAY	☐ TODAY	☐ SUNDAY

IT'S NATIONAL BOYFRIEND DAY
THE TERM 'BOYFRIEND' BECAME POPULAR IN THE EARLY 1900s.

GWEN STEFANI WAS BORN IN 1969   ALICIA VIKANDER WAS BORN IN 1988

7 AM

8 AM

9 AM

10 AM

11 AM

NOON

1 PM

2 PM

3 PM

4 PM

5 PM

6 PM

ON THIS DAY IN 2018: A SINGLE BOTTLE OF WHISKEY SOLD FOR $1.1 MILLION.

BRILLIANT AND/OR TERRIBLE IDEAS

276 DAYS DOWN, 89 DAYS LEFT (UNLESS IT'S A LEAP YEAR [277/89])   YEAR:

OCTOBER 4

MONDAY	TUESDAY	WEDNESDAY	THURSDAY	FRIDAY	SATURDAY ☐
· · · · · · · · ·	· · · · · · · · ·	· · · · · · · · ·	· · · · · · · · ·	· · · · · · · · ·	
☐ TODAY	☐ TODAY	☐ TODAY	☐ TODAY	☐ TODAY	☐ SUNDAY

IT'S NATIONAL CINNAMON ROLL DAY
SWEDISH PEOPLE EAT AN AVERAGE OF 316 CINNAMON ROLLS PER YEAR.

DAKOTA JOHNSON WAS BORN IN 1989   CHRISTOPH WALTZ WAS BORN IN 1956

7 AM
· ·
8 AM
· ·
9 AM
· ·
10 AM
· ·
11 AM
· ·
NOON
· ·
1 PM
· ·
2 PM
· ·
3 PM
· ·
4 PM
· ·
5 PM
· ·
6 PM

ON THIS DAY IN 2006: WIKILEAKS WAS LAUNCHED BY JULIAN ASSANGE.

NOTES AND/OR LIMERICKS

YEAR: 277 DAYS DOWN, 88 DAYS LEFT (UNLESS IT'S A LEAP YEAR [278/88])

OCTOBER 5

MONDAY	TUESDAY	WEDNESDAY	THURSDAY	FRIDAY	SATURDAY ☐
. . . .	. . . .	. . . .	. . . .	. . . .	☐
☐ TODAY	☐ TODAY	☐ TODAY	☐ TODAY	☐ TODAY	SUNDAY

IT'S NATIONAL GET FUNKY DAY
CELEBRATE BY LISTENING TO JAMES BROWN AND EATING SOME CAMEMBERT.

NEIL DEGRASSE TYSON WAS BORN IN 1958   KATE WINSLET WAS BORN IN 1975

7 AM

8 AM

9 AM

10 AM

11 AM

NOON

1 PM

2 PM

3 PM

4 PM

5 PM

6 PM

ON THIS DAY IN 1962: THE FIRST JAMES BOND FILM, 'DR. NO' WAS RELEASED.

BRILLIANT AND/OR TERRIBLE IDEAS

278 DAYS DOWN, 87 DAYS LEFT (UNLESS IT'S A LEAP YEAR [279/87])   YEAR:

OCTOBER 6

IT'S GARLIC LOVERS DAY
THE STICKY JUICE IN THE CLOVES CAN BE USED AS AN ADHESIVE.

ELIZABETH SHUE WAS BORN IN 1963   ADDISON RAE WAS BORN IN 2000

7 AM
. . . .
                                                                              8 AM
. . . .
9 AM
. . . .
                                                                              10 AM
11 AM
. . . .
                                                                              NOON
. . . .
1 PM
. . . .
                                                                              2 PM
3 PM
. . . .
                                                                              4 PM
. . . .
5 PM
. . . .
                                                                              6 PM

ON THIS DAY IN 1993: MICHAEL JORDAN RETIRED FROM THE NBA (THE FIRST TIME).

NOTES AND/OR LIMERICKS

YEAR: 279 DAYS DOWN, 86 DAYS LEFT (UNLESS IT'S A LEAP YEAR [280/86])

		WRITE IN THE DATES BELOW (AND SHADE IN TODAY)			
MONDAY	**TUESDAY**	**WEDNESDAY**	**THURSDAY**	**FRIDAY**	**SATURDAY** ☐
. . . . ☐ TODAY	. . . . ☐ TODAY	. . . . ☐ TODAY	. . . . ☐ TODAY	. . . . ☐ TODAY	☐ **SUNDAY**

IT'S NATIONAL BATHTUB DAY
ARCHIMEDES DISCOVERED THE PHYSICS OF DISPLACEMENT WHILE BATHING.

TONI BRAXTON WAS BORN IN 1967   YO-YO MA WAS BORN IN 1955

7 AM

8 AM

9 AM

10 AM

11 AM

NOON

1 PM

2 PM

3 PM

4 PM

5 PM

6 PM

ON THIS DAY IN 1959: THE FIRST PHOTO OF THE FAR SIDE OF THE MOON IS SHARED.

BRILLIANT AND/OR TERRIBLE IDEAS

280 DAYS DOWN, 85 DAYS LEFT (UNLESS IT'S A LEAP YEAR [281/85])   YEAR:

OCTOBER 8

WRITE IN THE DATES BELOW (AND SHADE IN TODAY)

MONDAY	TUESDAY	WEDNESDAY	THURSDAY	FRIDAY	SATURDAY ☐
. . . .	. . . .	. . . .	. . . .	. . . .	
☐ TODAY	☐ TODAY	☐ TODAY	☐ TODAY	☐ TODAY	☐ SUNDAY

IT'S NATIONAL PIEROGI DAY

THE WORD PIEROGI IS ALREADY PLURAL. THE SINGULAR FORM IS 'PIEROG.'

SIGOURNEY WEAVER WAS BORN IN 1949   BRUNO MARS WAS BORN IN 1985

7 AM

. . . .

8 AM

. . . .

9 AM

. . . .

10 AM

. . . .

11 AM

. . . .

NOON

. . . .

1 PM

. . . .

2 PM

. . . .

3 PM

. . . .

4 PM

. . . .

5 PM

. . . .

6 PM

ON THIS DAY IN 1945: THE MICROWAVE OVEN WAS PATENTED.

NOTES AND/OR LIMERICKS

YEAR: 281 DAYS DOWN, 84 DAYS LEFT (UNLESS IT'S A LEAP YEAR [282/84])

OCTOBER 9

IT'S NATIONAL MOLDY CHEESE DAY
THE MOLD IN BLUE CHEESE IS A STRAIN OF PENICILLIUM.

BELLA HADID WAS BORN IN 1996   JOHN LENNON WAS BORN IN 1940

7 AM

8 AM

9 AM

10 AM

11 AM

NOON

1 PM

2 PM

3 PM

4 PM

5 PM

6 PM

ON THIS DAY IN 2012: MALALA YOUSAFZAI WAS SHOT 3 TIMES BY A TALIBAN GUNMAN.

BRILLIANT AND/OR TERRIBLE IDEAS

282 DAYS DOWN, 83 DAYS LEFT (UNLESS IT'S A LEAP YEAR [283/83])   YEAR:

OCTOBER 10

MONDAY	TUESDAY	WEDNESDAY	THURSDAY	FRIDAY	SATURDAY ☐
. . . .	. . . .	. . . .	. . . .	. . . .	
☐ TODAY	☐ TODAY	☐ TODAY	☐ TODAY	☐ TODAY	☐ SUNDAY

IT'S NATIONAL TUXEDO DAY

BOTH WILLIAM SHAKESPEARE AND BEETHOVEN HAD PET TUXEDO CATS.

TANYA TUCKER WAS BORN IN 1958   MARIO LOPEZ WAS BORN IN 197

7 AM
. . . .
                                                                            8 AM
. . . .
9 AM
. . . .
                                                                            10 A
. . . .
11 AM
. . . .
                                                                            NOO
. . . .
1 PM
. . . .
                                                                            2 P
. . . .
3 PM
. . . .
                                                                            4 P
. . . .
5 PM
. . . .
                                                                            6 P

ON THIS DAY IN 1961: 'THE BOB NEWHART SHOW' PREMIERED ON NBC.

NOTES AND/OR LIMERICKS

YEAR: | 283 DAYS DOWN, 82 DAYS LEFT (UNLESS IT'S A LEAP YEAR [284/82])

OCTOBER 11

WRITE IN THE DATES BELOW (AND SHADE IN TODAY)					
MONDAY	TUESDAY	WEDNESDAY	THURSDAY	FRIDAY	SATURDAY ☐
. . . . ☐ TODAY	. . . . ☐ TODAY	. . . . ☐ TODAY	. . . . ☐ TODAY	. . . . ☐ TODAY	☐ SUNDAY

IT'S NATIONAL COMING OUT DAY
WE SUPPORT YOU.

LUKE PERRY WAS BORN IN 1966   CARDI B. WAS BORN IN 1992

7 AM

8 AM

9 AM

10 AM

11 AM

NOON

1 PM

2 PM

3 PM

4 PM

5 PM

PM

ON THIS DAY IN 1975: 'SATURDAY NIGHT LIVE' PREMIERED ON NBC.

BRILLIANT AND/OR TERRIBLE IDEAS

284 DAYS DOWN, 81 DAYS LEFT (UNLESS IT'S A LEAP YEAR [285/81])   YEAR:

OCTOBER 12

MONDAY	TUESDAY	WEDNESDAY	THURSDAY	FRIDAY	SATURDAY ☐
. . . . ☐ TODAY	. . . . ☐ TODAY	. . . . ☐ TODAY	. . . . ☐ TODAY	. . . . ☐ TODAY	☐ SUNDAY

IT'S NATIONAL PULLED PORK DAY
PIGS OUTNUMBER PEOPLE 2 TO 1 IN DENMARK.

HUGH JACKMAN WAS BORN IN 1968   KIRK CAMERON WAS BORN IN 1970

7 AM

8 AM

9 AM

10 AM

11 AM

NOON

1 PM

2 PM

3 PM

4 PM

5 PM

6 PM

ON THIS DAY IN 1810: THE FIRST OKTOBERFEST WAS CELEBRATED IN GERMANY.

NOTES AND/OR LIMERICKS

YEAR: 285 DAYS DOWN, 80 DAYS LEFT (UNLESS IT'S A LEAP YEAR [286/80])

OCTOBER 13

MONDAY	TUESDAY	WEDNESDAY	THURSDAY	FRIDAY	SATURDAY ☐
. . . .	. . . .	. . . .	. . . .	. . . .	☐
☐ TODAY	☐ TODAY	☐ TODAY	☐ TODAY	☐ TODAY	☐ SUNDAY

IT'S TREAT YO' SELF DAY
PARKS AND REC WAS ORIGINALLY TITLED 'PUBLIC SERVICE.'

PAUL SIMON WAS BORN IN 1941   NANCY KERRIGAN WAS BORN IN 1969

7 AM

8 AM

9 AM

10 AM

11 AM

NOON

1 PM

2 PM

3 PM

4 PM

5 PM

6 PM

ON THIS DAY IN 2016: BOB DYLAN WON THE NOBEL PRIZE FOR LITERATURE.

BRILLIANT AND/OR TERRIBLE IDEAS

286 DAYS DOWN, 79 DAYS LEFT (UNLESS IT'S A LEAP YEAR [287/79])   YEAR:

OCTOBER 14

it's national lowercase day

BENJAMIN FRANKLIN REPORTEDLY WANTED TO BANISH THE LETTER C.

E.E. CUMMINGS WAS BORN IN 1894   RALPH LAUREN WAS BORN IN 1939

7 AM
. . . .
8 AM
. . . .
9 AM
. . . .
10 AM
. . . .
11 AM
. . . .
NOON
. . . .
1 PM
. . . .
2 PM
. . . .
3 PM
. . . .
4 PM
. . . .
5 PM
. . . .
6 PM

ON THIS DAY IN 1982: PRESIDENT REAGAN DECLARED 'A WAR ON DRUGS.'

NOTES AND/OR LIMERICKS

YEAR: | 287 DAYS DOWN, 78 DAYS LEFT (UNLESS IT'S A LEAP YEAR [288/78])

OCTOBER 15

WRITE IN THE DATES BELOW (AND SHADE IN TODAY)

MONDAY	TUESDAY	WEDNESDAY	THURSDAY	FRIDAY	SATURDAY ☐
☐ TODAY	☐ TODAY	☐ TODAY	☐ TODAY	☐ TODAY	☐ SUNDAY

IT'S NATIONAL GROUCH DAY
OSCAR THE GROUCH MADE HIS DEBUT ON 'SESAME STREET' IN 1969.

PENNY MARSHALL WAS BORN IN 1943   EMERIL LAGASSE WAS BORN IN 1959

7 AM

AM

9 AM

O AM

11 AM

OON

1 PM

PM

3 PM

PM

5 PM

PM

ON THIS DAY IN 1987: BOB BARKER STOPPED DYING HIS HAIR.

BRILLIANT AND/OR TERRIBLE IDEAS

288 DAYS DOWN, 77 DAYS LEFT (UNLESS IT'S A LEAP YEAR [289/77])   YEAR:

OCTOBER 16

MONDAY	TUESDAY	WEDNESDAY	THURSDAY	FRIDAY	SATURDAY ☐
. . . . ☐ TODAY	. . . . ☐ TODAY	. . . . ☐ TODAY	. . . . ☐ TODAY	. . . . ☐ TODAY	☐ SUNDAY

IT'S WORLD SPINE DAY
MORE THAN 98% OF EARTH'S ANIMALS DON'T HAVE ONE.

ANGELA LANSBURY WAS BORN IN 1925   NAOMI OSAKA WAS BORN IN 199

7 AM
. . . .
                                                                                    8 A
. . . .
9 AM
. . . .
                                                                                    10 A
11 AM
. . . .
                                                                                    NOO
. . . .
1 PM
. . . .
                                                                                    2 P
. . . .
3 PM
. . . .
                                                                                    4 P
. . . .
5 PM
. . . .
                                                                                    6 P

ON THIS DAY IN 1950: 'THE LION, THE WITCH, AND THE WARDROBE' WAS PUBLISHED.

NOTES AND/OR LIMERICKS

YEAR: 289 DAYS DOWN, 76 DAYS LEFT (UNLESS IT'S A LEAP YEAR [290/76])

OCTOBER 17

MONDAY	TUESDAY	WEDNESDAY	THURSDAY	FRIDAY	SATURDAY ☐
☐ TODAY	☐ TODAY	☐ TODAY	☐ TODAY	☐ TODAY	☐ SUNDAY

IT'S BLACK POETRY DAY
JUPITER HAMMON WAS THE FIRST AFRICAN AMERICAN POET TO BE PUBLISHED.

EVEL KNIEVEL WAS BORN IN 1938   NORM MACDONALD WAS BORN IN 1959

7 AM

8 AM

9 AM

10 AM

11 AM

NOON

1 PM

2 PM

3 PM

4 PM

5 PM

6 PM

ON THIS DAY IN 1957: 'JAILHOUSE ROCK' STARRING ELVIS PREMIERED IN MEMPHIS.

BRILLIANT AND/OR TERRIBLE IDEAS

290 DAYS DOWN, 75 DAYS LEFT (UNLESS IT'S A LEAP YEAR [291/75])

YEAR:

OCTOBER 18

MONDAY	TUESDAY	WEDNESDAY	THURSDAY	FRIDAY	SATURDAY ☐
. . . .	. . . .	. . . .	. . . .	. . . .	☐
☐ TODAY	☐ TODAY	☐ TODAY	☐ TODAY	☐ TODAY	SUNDAY

IT'S NATIONAL NO BEARD DAY

THE LAST U.S. PRESIDENT TO HAVE FACIAL HAIR WAS WILLIAM TAFT.

ZAC EFRON WAS BORN IN 1987   NE-YO WAS BORN IN 197

7 AM
. . . .
                                                                                    8 AM
. . . .
9 AM
. . . .
                                                                                    10 AM
. . . .
11 AM
. . . .
                                                                                    NOON
. . . .
1 PM
. . . .
                                                                                    2 P
. . . .
3 PM
. . . .
                                                                                    4 P
. . . .
5 PM
. . . .
                                                                                    6 P

ON THIS DAY IN 1952: THE FIRST ISSUE OF 'MAD MAGAZINE' IS PUBLISHED.

NOTES AND/OR LIMERICKS

YEAR: 291 DAYS DOWN, 74 DAYS LEFT (UNLESS IT'S A LEAP YEAR [292/74])

OCTOBER 19

IT'S NATIONAL SEAFOOD BISQUE DAY
IT'S EITHER DELICIOUS OR DEADLY DEPENDING ON YOUR ALLERGIES.

REBECCA FERGUSON WAS BORN IN 1983   JON FAVREAU WAS BORN IN 1966

7 AM

8 AM

9 AM

10 AM

11 AM

NOON

1 PM

2 PM

3 PM

4 PM

5 PM

6 PM

ON THIS DAY IN 1960: MARTIN LUTHER KING JR. IS ARRESTED IN ATLANTA.

BRILLIANT AND/OR TERRIBLE IDEAS

292 DAYS DOWN, 73 DAYS LEFT (UNLESS IT'S A LEAP YEAR [293/73])   YEAR:

OCTOBER 20

IT'S INTERNATIONAL CHEFS DAY
BEFORE INA GARTEN WAS A CHEF SHE WROTE NUCLEAR ENERGY POLICIES.

SNOOP DOGG WAS BORN IN 1971   JOHN KRASINSKI WAS BORN IN 197

7 AM
. . . .
                                                                          8 A
. . . .
9 AM
. . . .
                                                                          10 A
. . . .
11 AM
. . . .
                                                                          NOO
. . . .
1 PM
. . . .
                                                                          2 P
. . . .
3 PM
. . . .
                                                                          4 P
. . . .
5 PM
. . . .
                                                                          6 P

ON THIS DAY IN 1951: CBS STARTED USING THE 'EYEBALL' LOGO.

NOTES AND/OR LIMERICKS

YEAR: 293 DAYS DOWN, 72 DAYS LEFT (UNLESS IT'S A LEAP YEAR [294/72])

OCTOBER 21

WRITE IN THE DATES BELOW (AND SHADE IN TODAY)

MONDAY	TUESDAY	WEDNESDAY	THURSDAY	FRIDAY	SATURDAY ☐
. . . .	. . . .	. . . .	. . . .	. . . .	
☐ TODAY	☐ TODAY	☐ TODAY	☐ TODAY	☐ TODAY	☐ SUNDAY

IT'S INTERNATIONAL DAY OF THE NACHO
THE DISH WAS CREATED BY A MAN IN MEXICO NAMED, WELL, NACHO.

UDGE JUDY WAS BORN IN 1942   CARRIE FISHER WAS BORN IN 1956

7 AM

AM

9 AM

 AM

11 AM

OON

1 PM

PM

3 PM

PM

5 PM

PM

ON THIS DAY IN 1959: THE GUGGENHEIM MUSEUM OPENED IN NEW YORK CITY.

BRILLIANT AND/OR TERRIBLE IDEAS

294 DAYS DOWN, 71 DAYS LEFT (UNLESS IT'S A LEAP YEAR [295/71]   YEAR:

OCTOBER 22

MONDAY	TUESDAY	WEDNESDAY	THURSDAY	FRIDAY	SATURDAY ☐
. . . .	. . . .	. . . .	. . . .	. . . .	
☐ TODAY	☐ TODAY	☐ TODAY	☐ TODAY	☐ TODAY	☐ SUNDAY

IT'S INTERNATIONAL CAPS LOCK DAY
WE MADE THIS BOOK IN ITS HONOR.

JEFF GOLDBLUM WAS BORN IN 1952   CHRISTOPHER LLOYD WAS BORN IN 193

7 AM
. . . .
                                                                          8 A
. . . .
9 AM
. . . .
                                                                          10 A
. . . .
11 AM
. . . .
                                                                          NOO
. . . .
1 PM
. . . .
                                                                          2 P
. . . .
3 PM
. . . .
                                                                          4 P
. . . .
5 PM
. . . .
                                                                          6 P

ON THIS DAY IN 1969: PAUL MCCARTNEY DENIED RUMORS OF HIS OWN DEATH.

NOTES AND/OR LIMERICKS

YEAR:	295 DAYS DOWN, 70 DAYS LEFT (UNLESS IT'S A LEAP YEAR [296/70])

OCTOBER 23

MONDAY	TUESDAY	WEDNESDAY	THURSDAY	FRIDAY	SATURDAY ☐
☐ TODAY	☐ TODAY	☐ TODAY	☐ TODAY	☐ TODAY	☐ SUNDAY

IT'S NATIONAL CROC DAY
THEY WERE ORIGINALLY DESIGNED AS A BOATING SHOE.

PELÉ WAS BORN IN 1940   EMILIA CLARKE WAS BORN IN 1986

7 AM

AM

9 AM

10 AM

11 AM

NOON

1 PM

PM

3 PM

PM

5 PM

PM

ON THIS DAY IN 2001: THE FIRST APPLE iPOD WAS RELEASED.

BRILLIANT AND/OR TERRIBLE IDEAS

296 DAYS DOWN, 69 DAYS LEFT (UNLESS IT'S A LEAP YEAR [297/69])

YEAR:

OCTOBER 24

MONDAY	TUESDAY	WEDNESDAY	THURSDAY	FRIDAY	SATURDAY ☐
. . . .	. . . .	. . . .	. . . .	. . . .	☐
☐ TODAY	☐ TODAY	☐ TODAY	☐ TODAY	☐ TODAY	SUNDAY

IT'S NATIONAL BOLOGNA DAY
AROUND 1,632 PEOPLE IN THE U.S. HAVE THE LAST NAME 'BOLOGNA.'

DRAKE WAS BORN IN 1986   KEVIN KLINE WAS BORN IN 194

7 AM
. . . .
                                                                                    8 A
. . . .
9 AM
. . . .
                                                                                   10 A
. . . .
11 AM
. . . .
                                                                                    NOO
. . . .
1 PM
. . . .
                                                                                    2 P
. . . .
3 PM
. . . .
                                                                                    4 P
. . . .
5 PM
. . . .
                                                                                    6 P

ON THIS DAY IN 1926: HARRY HOUDINI PERFORMED FOR THE LAST TIME.

NOTES AND/OR LIMERICKS

| YEAR: | 297 DAYS DOWN, 68 DAYS LEFT (UNLESS IT'S A LEAP YEAR [298/68]) |

OCTOBER 25

WRITE IN THE DATES BELOW (AND SHADE IN TODAY)

MONDAY	TUESDAY	WEDNESDAY	THURSDAY	FRIDAY	SATURDAY ☐
☐ TODAY	☐ TODAY	☐ TODAY	☐ TODAY	☐ TODAY	☐ SUNDAY

IT'S WORLD PASTA DAY
BEFORE MACHINERY, PASTA WAS KNEADED BY FOOT.

PABLO PICASSO WAS BORN IN 1881   KATY PERRY WAS BORN IN 1984

7 AM

8 AM

9 AM

10 AM

11 AM

NOON

1 PM

2 PM

3 PM

4 PM

5 PM

6 PM

ON THIS DAY IN 1962: NELSON MANDELA WAS SENTENCED TO 5 YEARS IN PRISON.

BRILLIANT AND/OR TERRIBLE IDEAS

298 DAYS DOWN, 67 DAYS LEFT (UNLESS IT'S A LEAP YEAR [299/67])

YEAR:

OCTOBER 26

MONDAY	TUESDAY	WEDNESDAY	THURSDAY	FRIDAY	SATURDAY ☐
☐ TODAY	☐ TODAY	☐ TODAY	☐ TODAY	☐ TODAY	☐ SUNDAY

IT'S NATIONAL PUMPKIN DAY

THE FIRST JACK O' LANTERNS WERE MADE OUT OF TURNIPS.

RITA WILSON WAS BORN IN 1956   SETH MACFARLANE WAS BORN IN 1973

7 AM

. . . .

8 AM

. . . .

9 AM

. . . .

10 AM

. . . .

11 AM

. . . .

NOON

. . . .

1 PM

. . . .

2 PM

. . . .

3 PM

. . . .

4 PM

. . . .

5 PM

. . . .

6 PM

ON THIS DAY IN 1949: THE U.S. MINIMUM WAGE INCREASED TO 75 CENTS.

NOTES AND/OR LIMERICKS

YEAR: | 299 DAYS DOWN, 66 DAYS LEFT (UNLESS IT'S A LEAP YEAR [300/66])

OCTOBER 27

MONDAY	TUESDAY	WEDNESDAY	THURSDAY	FRIDAY	SATURDAY ☐
. . . .	. . . .	. . . .	. . . .	. . . .	
☐ TODAY	☐ TODAY	☐ TODAY	☐ TODAY	☐ TODAY	☐ SUNDAY

IT'S NATIONAL BLACK CAT DAY
IN SCOTLAND AND JAPAN THEY ARE ACTUALLY A SIGN OF GOOD LUCK.

JOHN CLEESE WAS BORN IN 1939   SYLVIA PLATH WAS BORN IN 1932

7 AM
. . . .
8 AM
. . . .
9 AM
. . . .
10 AM
. . . .
11 AM
. . . .
NOON
. . . .
1 PM
. . . .
2 PM
. . . .
3 PM
. . . .
4 PM
. . . .
5 PM
. . . .
6 PM

ON THIS DAY IN 1985: THE KANSAS CITY ROYALS WON THE WORLD SERIES.

BRILLIANT AND/OR TERRIBLE IDEAS

300 DAYS DOWN, 65 DAYS LEFT (UNLESS IT'S A LEAP YEAR [301/65])   YEAR:

OCTOBER 28

MONDAY	TUESDAY	WEDNESDAY	THURSDAY	FRIDAY	SATURDAY ☐
. . . .	. . . .	. . . .	. . . .	. . . .	
☐ TODAY	☐ TODAY	☐ TODAY	☐ TODAY	☐ TODAY	☐ SUNDAY

IT'S INTERNATIONAL ANIMATION DAY
THE PIXAR LAMP IS NAMED 'LUXO JUNIOR.'

FRANK OCEAN WAS BORN IN 1987   JOAQUIN PHOENIX WAS BORN IN 1974

7 AM
. . . .
                                                                                        8 AM
. . . .
9 AM
. . . .
                                                                                        10 AM
. . . .
11 AM
. . . .
                                                                                        NOON
. . . .
1 PM
. . . .
                                                                                        2 PM
. . . .
3 PM
. . . .
                                                                                        4 PM
. . . .
5 PM
. . . .
                                                                                        6 PM

ON THIS DAY IN 1965: CONSTRUCTION ON THE ST. LOUIS ARCH WAS COMPLETED.

NOTES AND/OR LIMERICKS

YEAR: 301 DAYS DOWN, 64 DAYS LEFT (UNLESS IT'S A LEAP YEAR [302/64])

OCTOBER 29

MONDAY	TUESDAY	WEDNESDAY	THURSDAY	FRIDAY	SATURDAY ☐
☐ TODAY	☐ TODAY	☐ TODAY	☐ TODAY	☐ TODAY	☐ SUNDAY

IT'S NATIONAL OATMEAL DAY

QUAKER OATS WAS THE FIRST COMPANY TO PUT RECIPES ON PACKAGING.

WINONA RYDER WAS BORN IN 1971   BOB ROSS WAS BORN IN 1942

7 AM

8 AM

9 AM

10 AM

11 AM

NOON

1 PM

2 PM

3 PM

4 PM

5 PM

6 PM

ON THIS DAY IN 1998: JOHN GLENN BECAME THE OLDEST PERSON TO GO TO SPACE.

BRILLIANT AND/OR TERRIBLE IDEAS

302 DAYS DOWN, 63 DAYS LEFT (UNLESS IT'S A LEAP YEAR [303/63])   YEAR:

OCTOBER 30

IT'S NATIONAL CANDY CORN DAY
IT WAS ORIGINALLY CALLED 'CHICKEN FEED.'

HENRY WINKLER WAS BORN IN 1945   ASHLEY GRAHAM WAS BORN IN 198

7 AM
. . . .
                                                                              8 AM
. . . .
9 AM
. . . .
                                                                              10 AM
. . . .
11 AM
. . . .
                                                                              NOON
. . . .
1 PM
. . . .
                                                                              2 PM
. . . .
3 PM
. . . .
                                                                              4 PM
. . . .
5 PM
. . . .
                                                                              6 PM

ON THIS DAY IN 2003: 'WICKED' FIRST PREMIERED ON BROADWAY.

NOTES AND/OR LIMERICKS

YEAR: 303 DAYS DOWN, 62 DAYS LEFT (UNLESS IT'S A LEAP YEAR [304/62])

	WRITE IN THE DATES BELOW (AND SHADE IN TODAY)				
MONDAY	**TUESDAY**	**WEDNESDAY**	**THURSDAY**	**FRIDAY**	**SATURDAY** ☐
. . . . ☐ TODAY	. . . . ☐ TODAY	. . . . ☐ TODAY	. . . . ☐ TODAY	. . . . ☐ TODAY	☐ **SUNDAY**

IT'S HALLOWEEN
OH, AND IT'S NATIONAL DOORBELL DAY.

PIPER PERABO WAS BORN IN 1976   WILLOW SMITH WAS BORN IN 2000

7 AM

8 AM

9 AM

10 AM

11 AM

NOON

1 PM

2 PM

3 PM

4 PM

5 PM

6 PM

ON THIS DAY IN 1994: VENUS WILLIAMS MADE HER PROFESSIONAL DEBUT AT 14.

BRILLIANT AND/OR TERRIBLE IDEAS

304 DAYS DOWN, 61 DAYS LEFT (UNLESS IT'S A LEAP YEAR [305/61])   YEAR:

IT'S OFFICIALLY

✕ NOVEMBER ✕

OF THE YEAR

MONTH ELEVEN

. . . .

. . . .

. . . .

NOVEMBER AT A GLANCE

CONGRATULATIONS, YOU MADE IT
TO THE MONTH OF NOVEMBER

✖

CELEBRATE, IT'S:

NTL. NOVEL WRITING MONTH

ADOPT A SENIOR PET MONTH

NATIONAL GRATITUDE MONTH

BANANA PUDDING LOVERS MONTH

SPINACH AND SQUASH MONTH

OFFICIAL SYMBOLS:

BIRTHSTONE: TOPAZ

FLOWER: CHRYSANTHEMUM

TREES: WALNUT, CHESTNUT, & ASH

SCORPIO (OCT 23 / NOV 21)

SAGITTARIUS (NOV 22 / DEC 21)

✖

A FEW DATES TO KNOW*
LIKE, IMPORTANT ONES.

✖

DAY OF THE DEAD
(MEXICAN)
NOVEMBER 1ST & 2ND

ELECTION DAY
FIRST TUESDAY OF NOVEMBER

DIWALI
(HINDUISM)
STARTS ON THE 15TH DAY OF
THE HINDU MONTH OF KARTIK
(OCTOBER OR NOVEMBER)

VETERANS DAY
NOVEMBER 11TH

**TRANSGENDER DAY
OF REMEMBRANCE**
NOVEMBER 20TH

THANKSGIVING
FOURTH THURSDAY OF NOVEMBER

**NATIVE AMERICAN
HERITAGE DAY**
FRIDAY AFTER THANKSGIVING

**DAYLIGHT SAVING
TIME ENDS**
FIRST SUNDAY OF NOVEMBER

MARK YOUR CALENDAR ✖ IT'S RIGHT OVER THERE

---

*A DISCLAIMER OF SORTS

HEY THERE. WE HERE AT BRASS MONKEY LIKE TO JOKE AROUND...BUT WE ALSO WANT TO TAKE A
MINUTE TO RECOGNIZE JUST A FEW OF THE MANY HOLIDAYS & EVENTS THAT ARE IMPORTANT TO OUR
FRIENDS AROUND THE GLOBE (AND AT HOME). YOU MAY BE DIFFERENT THAN US. WE MAY HAVE
NEVER MET. BUT WE LOVE YOU ALL THE SAME.

SO, WITH ALL OF THAT SAID, IF YOU HAVEN'T HEARD OF A DAY, PLEASE LOOK IT UP. LEARNING
ABOUT AND APPRECIATING CULTURES DIFFERENT THAN YOURS IS REALLY IMPORTANT...WAY MORE SO
THAN POSTING A FEW 'STRAWBERRY JAM DAY' VIDEOS ON TIKTOK. DON'T GET US WRONG, THERE IS
PLENTY OF ROOM FOR BOTH. JUST PLEASE DO BOTH.

NOVEMBER AT A GLANCE

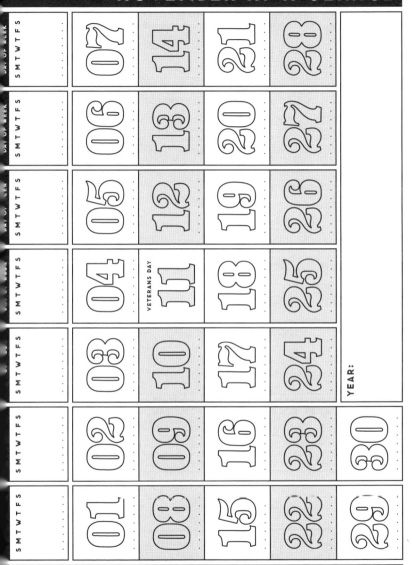

S M T W F S	S M T W F S	S M T W F S	S M T W F S	S M T W F S	S M T W F S	S M T W F S
07	06	05	04	03	02	01
14	13	12	11 VETERANS DAY	10	09	08
21	20	19	18	17	16	15
28	27	26	25	24	23	22
			YEAR:		30	29

WELL, WHAT ARE YOU WAITING FOR?

✖ START PLANNING. IN THE CALENDAR ABOVE, WE'VE MARKED THE MORE COMMON U.S. HOLIDAYS ALREADY (THE ONES THAT ARE DATED, THAT IS). SO USE THE LIST TO THE LEFT TO FILL IN THE REST...LIKE ALL OF THE ONES THAT CHANGE DATES FROM YEAR TO YEAR, FOR EXAMPLE. ✖

LISTS, NOTES & MEMOIRS

MOVIES SO BAD THEY'RE GOOD
OR SOME BORING TO-DO LIST

1
2
3
4
5
6
7
8
9
10
11
12
13
14

MOVIES SO BAD THEY'RE BAD
OR A GROCERY LIST OR SOMETHING

1
2
3
4
5
6
7
8
9
10
11
12
13
14

MORE ACCURATE NAMES FOR POPULAR COCKTAILS
USE FIGURE 1 FOR ANY NECESSARY VISUAL AIDS

FIG. 1

1
2
3

4
5
6

NOVEMBER 1

MONDAY	TUESDAY	WEDNESDAY	THURSDAY	FRIDAY	SATURDAY ☐
☐ TODAY	☐ TODAY	☐ TODAY	☐ TODAY	☐ TODAY	☐ SUNDAY

IT'S INTERNATIONAL SCENTED CANDLE DAY
WE'RE GETTING A HEADACHE JUST THINKING ABOUT IT.

AISHWARYA RAI WAS BORN IN 1973   PENN BADGLEY WAS BORN IN 1986

7 AM

8 AM

9 AM

10 AM

11 AM

NOON

1 PM

2 PM

3 PM

4 PM

5 PM

6 PM

ON THIS DAY IN 2015: THE KANSAS CITY ROYALS WON THE WORLD SERIES.

BRILLIANT AND/OR TERRIBLE IDEAS

305 DAYS DOWN, 60 DAYS LEFT (UNLESS IT'S A LEAP YEAR [306/60])

YEAR:

NOVEMBER 2

MONDAY	TUESDAY	WEDNESDAY	THURSDAY	FRIDAY	SATURDAY ☐
. . . .	. . . .	. . . .	. . . .	. . . .	
☐ TODAY	☐ TODAY	☐ TODAY	☐ TODAY	☐ TODAY	☐ SUNDAY

IT'S NATIONAL DEVILED EGG DAY
THE DISH WAS DUBBED 'DEVILED EGGS' IN 1786.

DAVID SCHWIMMER WAS BORN IN 1966   SHAH RUKH KHAN WAS BORN IN 1965

7 AM
. . . .
8 AM
. . . .
9 AM
. . . .
10 AM
. . . .
11 AM
. . . .
NOON
. . . .
1 PM
. . . .
2 PM
. . . .
3 PM
. . . .
4 PM
. . . .
5 PM
. . . .
6 PM

ON THIS DAY IN 2003: 'ARRESTED DEVELOPMENT' DEBUTED ON FOX.

NOTES AND/OR LIMERICKS

YEAR: 306 DAYS DOWN, 59 DAYS LEFT (UNLESS IT'S A LEAP YEAR [307/59])

NOVEMBER 3

MONDAY	TUESDAY	WEDNESDAY	THURSDAY	FRIDAY	SATURDAY ☐
. . . . ☐ TODAY	. . . . ☐ TODAY	. . . . ☐ TODAY	. . . . ☐ TODAY	. . . . ☐ TODAY	☐ SUNDAY

IT'S CLICHÉ DAY
GET OUT THERE AND GIVE IT ONE HUNDRED AND TEN PERCENT.

DOLPH LUNDGREN WAS BORN IN 1957   CHARLES BRONSON WAS BORN IN 1921

7 AM

8 AM

9 AM

10 AM

11 AM

NOON

1 PM

2 PM

3 PM

4 PM

5 PM

6 PM

ON THIS DAY IN 1988: GERALDO RIVERA'S NOSE WAS BROKEN ON SET.

BRILLIANT AND/OR TERRIBLE IDEAS

NOVEMBER 4

MONDAY	TUESDAY	WEDNESDAY	THURSDAY	FRIDAY	SATURDAY ☐
. . . .	. . . .	. . . .	. . . .	. . . .	☐ SUNDAY
☐ TODAY	☐ TODAY	☐ TODAY	☐ TODAY	☐ TODAY	☐

IT'S NATIONAL CANDY DAY

SNICKERS WERE NAMED AFTER ONE OF FRANK MARS' FAVORITE HORSES.

KATHY GRIFFIN WAS BORN IN 1960   SEAN COMBS WAS BORN IN 1969

7 AM
. . . .
                                                                             8 AM
. . . .
9 AM
. . . .
                                                                            10 AM
. . . .
11 AM
. . . .
                                                                             NOON
. . . .
1 PM
. . . .
                                                                             2 PM
. . . .
3 PM
. . . .
                                                                             4 PM
. . . .
5 PM
. . . .
                                                                             6 PM

ON THIS DAY IN 1922: THE ENTRANCE TO KING TUTANKHAMUN'S TOMB WAS FOUND.

NOTES AND/OR LIMERICKS

YEAR:	308 DAYS DOWN, 57 DAYS LEFT (UNLESS IT'S A LEAP YEAR [309/57])

NOVEMBER 5

MONDAY	TUESDAY	WEDNESDAY	THURSDAY	FRIDAY	SATURDAY ☐
. . . .	. . . .	. . . .	. . . .	. . . .	☐ SUNDAY
☐ TODAY	☐ TODAY	☐ TODAY	☐ TODAY	☐ TODAY	☐

IT'S NATIONAL LOVE YOUR RED HAIR DAY
THE ODDS OF HAVING BLUE EYES WITH RED HAIR IS 0.17 PERCENT.

FAMKE JANSSEN WAS BORN IN 1964   TILDA SWINTON WAS BORN IN 1960

7 AM

8 AM

9 AM

10 AM

11 AM

NOON

1 PM

2 PM

3 PM

4 PM

5 PM

6 PM

ON THIS DAY IN 1935: PARKER BROTHERS RELEASED THE GAME 'MONOPOLY.'

BRILLIANT AND/OR TERRIBLE IDEAS

309 DAYS DOWN, 56 DAYS LEFT (UNLESS IT'S A LEAP YEAR [310/56])   YEAR:

NOVEMBER 6

WRITE IN THE DATES BELOW (AND SHADE IN TODAY)

MONDAY	TUESDAY	WEDNESDAY	THURSDAY	FRIDAY	SATURDAY ☐
. . . .	. . . .	. . . .	. . . .	. . . .	☐
☐ TODAY	☐ TODAY	☐ TODAY	☐ TODAY	☐ TODAY	SUNDAY

IT'S NATIONAL SAXOPHONE DAY
IT'S THE ONLY INSTRUMENT TO BE INVENTED BY A SINGLE PERSON.

SALLY FIELD WAS BORN IN 1946   EMMA STONE WAS BORN IN 198

7 AM
. . . .
8 A
. . . .
9 AM
. . . .
10 A
. . . .
11 AM
. . . .
NOO
. . . .
1 PM
. . . .
2 P
. . . .
3 PM
. . . .
4 P
. . . .
5 PM
. . . .
6 P

ON THIS DAY IN 1975: 'GOOD MORNING AMERICA' PREMIERED ON ABC.

NOTES AND/OR LIMERICKS

YEAR:	310 DAYS DOWN, 55 DAYS LEFT (UNLESS IT'S A LEAP YEAR [311/55])

NOVEMBER 7

IT'S BITTERSWEET CHOCOLATE WITH ALMONDS DAY
BITTERSWEET CHOCOLATE WITHOUT ALMONDS CAN GO TO HELL.

LORDE WAS BORN IN 1996   JONI MITCHELL WAS BORN IN 1943

7 AM

8 AM

9 AM

10 AM

11 AM

NOON

1 PM

2 PM

3 PM

4 PM

5 PM

6 PM

ON THIS DAY IN 1991: MAGIC JOHNSON ANNOUNCED HE WAS HIV-POSITIVE.

BRILLIANT AND/OR TERRIBLE IDEAS

311 DAYS DOWN, 54 DAYS LEFT (UNLESS IT'S A LEAP YEAR [312/54])   YEAR:

NOVEMBER 8

MONDAY	TUESDAY	WEDNESDAY	THURSDAY	FRIDAY	SATURDAY ☐
· · · · · · · ·	· · · · · · · ·	· · · · · · · ·	· · · · · · · ·	· · · · · · · ·	
☐ TODAY	☐ TODAY	☐ TODAY	☐ TODAY	☐ TODAY	☐ SUNDAY

IT'S COOK SOMETHING BOLD AND PUNGENT DAY
THE AVERAGE PERSON CONSUMES AROUND 2 POUNDS OF GARLIC EVERY YEAR.

GORDON RAMSAY WAS BORN IN 1966   PARKER POSEY WAS BORN IN 1968

7 AM
· ·
8 AM
· ·
9 AM
· ·
10 AM
· ·
11 AM
· ·
NOON
· ·
1 PM
· ·
2 PM
· ·
3 PM
· ·
4 PM
· ·
5 PM
· ·
6 PM

ON THIS DAY IN 1966: RONALD REAGAN WAS ELECTED GOVERNOR OF CALIFORNIA.

NOTES AND/OR LIMERICKS

YEAR:	312 DAYS DOWN, 53 DAYS LEFT (UNLESS IT'S A LEAP YEAR [313/53])

NOVEMBER 9

MONDAY	TUESDAY	WEDNESDAY	THURSDAY	FRIDAY	SATURDAY ☐
. . . .	. . . .	. . . .	. . . .	. . . .	
☐ TODAY	☐ TODAY	☐ TODAY	☐ TODAY	☐ TODAY	☐ SUNDAY

IT'S NATIONAL FRIED CHICKEN SANDWICH DAY
IN A SURVEY, 16% OF PEOPLE SAID THEY WOULD MARRY A CHICKEN SANDWICH.

LOU FERRIGNO WAS BORN IN 1951   ERIC DANE WAS BORN IN 1972

7 AM

8 AM

9 AM

10 AM

11 AM

NOON

1 PM

PM

3 PM

PM

5 PM

PM

ON THIS DAY IN 1967: THE FIRST ISSUE OF 'ROLLING STONE' WAS PUBLISHED.

BRILLIANT AND/OR TERRIBLE IDEAS

313 DAYS DOWN, 52 DAYS LEFT (UNLESS IT'S A LEAP YEAR [314/52])   YEAR:

NOVEMBER 10

MONDAY	TUESDAY	WEDNESDAY	THURSDAY	FRIDAY	SATURDAY
. . . .	. . . .	. . . .	. . . .	. . . .	
☐ TODAY	☐ TODAY	☐ TODAY	☐ TODAY	☐ TODAY	☐ SUNDA

IT'S SESAME STREET DAY
OSCAR THE GROUCH WAS ORIGINALLY ORANGE.

TRACY MORGAN WAS BORN IN 1968   SINBAD WAS BORN IN 19

7 AM
. . . .
8 A
. . . .
9 AM
. . . .
10 A
. . . .
11 AM
. . . .
NOC
. . . .
1 PM
. . . .
2 P
. . . .
3 PM
. . . .
4 P
. . . .
5 PM
. . . .
6 P

ON THIS DAY IN 1989: THE BERLIN WALL BEGAN TO COME DOWN.

NOTES AND/OR LIMERICKS

| YEAR: | 314 DAYS DOWN, 51 DAYS LEFT (UNLESS IT'S A LEAP YEAR [315/51]) |

NOVEMBER 11

MONDAY	TUESDAY	WEDNESDAY	THURSDAY	FRIDAY	SATURDAY ☐
. . . .	. . . .	. . . .	. . . .	. . . .	
☐ TODAY	☐ TODAY	☐ TODAY	☐ TODAY	☐ TODAY	☐ SUNDAY

IT'S VETERANS DAY
IT'S ALSO NATIONAL ORIGAMI DAY.

DEMI MOORE WAS BORN IN 1962   STANLEY TUCCI WAS BORN IN 1960

7 AM

AM

9 AM

10 AM

11 AM

NOON

1 PM

PM

3 PM

PM

5 PM

PM

ON THIS DAY IN 1994: BILL GATES BOUGHT DA VINCI'S 'CODEX' FOR $30M.

BRILLIANT AND/OR TERRIBLE IDEAS

315 DAYS DOWN, 50 DAYS LEFT (UNLESS IT'S A LEAP YEAR [316/50])   YEAR:

NOVEMBER 12

IT'S NATIONAL HAPPY HOUR DAY
IRONICALLY, THEY BECAME POPULAR DURING PROHIBITION.

RYAN GOSLING WAS BORN IN 1980   GRACE KELLY WAS BORN IN 192

7 AM

. . . .

8 A

. . . .

9 AM

. . . .

10 A

. . . .

11 AM

. . . .

NOO

. . . .

1 PM

. . . .

2 P

. . . .

3 PM

. . . .

4 P

. . . .

5 PM

. . . .

6 P

ON THIS DAY IN 1954: THE ELLIS ISLAND IMMIGRATION CENTER WAS CLOSED.

NOTES AND/OR LIMERICKS

YEAR: 316 DAYS DOWN, 49 DAYS LEFT (UNLESS IT'S A LEAP YEAR [317/49])

NOVEMBER 13

MONDAY	TUESDAY	WEDNESDAY	THURSDAY	FRIDAY	SATURDAY ☐
. . . .	. . . .	. . . .	. . . .	. . . .	
☐ TODAY	☐ TODAY	☐ TODAY	☐ TODAY	☐ TODAY	☐ SUNDAY

IT'S START A RUMOR DAY
DEMI MOORE GAVE BIRTH TO RUMER WILLIS IN KENTUCKY.

JOE MANTEGNA WAS BORN IN 1947   GERARD BUTLER WAS BORN IN 1969

7 AM

8 AM

9 AM

10 AM

11 AM

NOON

1 PM

2 PM

3 PM

4 PM

5 PM

6 PM

ON THIS DAY IN 1940: WALT DISNEY RELEASED 'FANTASIA.'

BRILLIANT AND/OR TERRIBLE IDEAS

317 DAYS DOWN, 48 DAYS LEFT (UNLESS IT'S A LEAP YEAR [318/48])   YEAR:

NOVEMBER 14

MONDAY	TUESDAY	WEDNESDAY	THURSDAY	FRIDAY	SATURDAY ☐
. . . .	. . . .	. . . .	. . . .	. . . .	
☐ TODAY	☐ TODAY	☐ TODAY	☐ TODAY	☐ TODAY	☐ SUNDAY

IT'S NATIONAL PICKLE DAY
CLEOPATRA CLAIMED THAT PICKLES MADE HER BEAUTIFUL.

CLAUDE MONET WAS BORN IN 1840   JOSH DUHAMEL WAS BORN IN 197

7 AM
. . . .
8 AM
. . . .
9 AM
. . . .
10 A
. . . .
11 AM
. . . .
NOO
. . . .
1 PM
. . . .
2 P
. . . .
3 PM
. . . .
4 P
. . . .
5 PM
. . . .
6 P

ON THIS DAY IN 1851: 'MOBY DICK' BY HERMAN MELVILLE WAS PUBLISHED.

NOTES AND/OR LIMERICKS

| YEAR: | | 318 DAYS DOWN, 47 DAYS LEFT (UNLESS IT'S A LEAP YEAR [319/47]) |

NOVEMBER 15

WRITE IN THE DATES BELOW (AND SHADE IN TODAY)

MONDAY	TUESDAY	WEDNESDAY	THURSDAY	FRIDAY	SATURDAY ☐
☐ TODAY	☐ TODAY	☐ TODAY	☐ TODAY	☐ TODAY	☐ SUNDAY

IT'S STEVE IRWIN DAY
THE ONE ANIMAL HE WAS NERVOUS AROUND WERE PARROTS.

GEORGIA O'KEEFE WAS BORN IN 1887   SHAILENE WOODLEY WAS BORN IN 1991

7 AM

8 AM

9 AM

10 AM

11 AM

NOON

1 PM

2 PM

3 PM

4 PM

5 PM

6 PM

ON THIS DAY IN 1969: THE FIRST WENDY'S HAMBURGERS OPENED IN COLUMBUS, OHIO.

BRILLIANT AND/OR TERRIBLE IDEAS

319 DAYS DOWN, 46 DAYS LEFT (UNLESS IT'S A LEAP YEAR [320/46])   YEAR:

NOVEMBER 16

IT'S NATIONAL FAST FOOD DAY
CHIPOTLE BUYS SOME OF THEIR AVOCADOS FROM JASON MRAZ.

PETE DAVIDSON WAS BORN IN 1993   LISA BONET WAS BORN IN 196

7 AM
. . . .
8 A
. . . .
9 AM
. . . .
10 A
. . . .
11 AM
. . . .
NOO
. . . .
1 PM
. . . .
2 P
. . . .
3 PM
. . . .
4 P
. . . .
5 PM
. . . .
6 P

ON THIS DAY IN 1907: OKLAHOMA BECAME THE 46TH STATE OF THE U.S.

NOTES AND/OR LIMERICKS

YEAR:	320 DAYS DOWN, 45 DAYS LEFT (UNLESS IT'S A LEAP YEAR [321/45])

NOVEMBER 17

MONDAY	TUESDAY	WEDNESDAY	THURSDAY	FRIDAY	SATURDAY ☐
. . . . ☐ TODAY	. . . . ☐ TODAY	. . . . ☐ TODAY	. . . . ☐ TODAY	. . . . ☐ TODAY	☐ SUNDAY

IT'S NATIONAL BAKLAVA DAY
THE EARLIEST KNOWN VERSION IS FROM ASSYRIA IN 700 BC.

RUPAUL WAS BORN IN 1960   RACHEL MCADAMS WAS BORN IN 1978

7 AM

8 AM

9 AM

10 AM

11 AM

NOON

1 PM

2 PM

3 PM

4 PM

5 PM

6 PM

ON THIS DAY IN 1978: THE 'STAR WARS HOLIDAY SPECIAL' AIRED—FOR THE ONLY TIME.

BRILLIANT AND/OR TERRIBLE IDEAS

321 DAYS DOWN, 44 DAYS LEFT (UNLESS IT'S A LEAP YEAR [322/44])   YEAR:

NOVEMBER 18

MONDAY	TUESDAY	WEDNESDAY	THURSDAY	FRIDAY	SATURDAY ☐
. . . .	. . . .	. . . .	. . . .	. . . .	
☐ TODAY	☐ TODAY	☐ TODAY	☐ TODAY	☐ TODAY	☐ SUNDAY

IT'S MICKEY MOUSE DAY
HIS FIRST APPEARANCE WAS IN 'STEAMBOAT WILLY' IN 1928.

SOJOURNER TRUTH WAS BORN IN 1797   OWEN WILSON WAS BORN IN 196

7 AM
. . . .
  8 A

. . . .
9 AM
. . . .
  10 A

. . . .
11 AM
. . . .
  NOO

. . . .
1 PM
. . . .
  2 P

. . . .
3 PM
. . . .
  4 P

. . . .
5 PM
. . . .
  6 P

ON THIS DAY IN 1993: VINCE MCMAHON WAS CHARGED WITH STEROID DISTRIBUTION.

NOTES AND/OR LIMERICKS

YEAR:	322 DAYS DOWN, 43 DAYS LEFT (UNLESS IT'S A LEAP YEAR [323/43])

NOVEMBER 19

WRITE IN THE DATES BELOW (AND SHADE IN TODAY)

MONDAY	TUESDAY	WEDNESDAY	THURSDAY	FRIDAY	SATURDAY ☐
. . . . ☐ TODAY	. . . . ☐ TODAY	. . . . ☐ TODAY	. . . . ☐ TODAY	. . . . ☐ TODAY	☐ SUNDAY

IT'S NATIONAL PLAY MONOPOLY DAY
THE FIRST MONOPOLY CHAMPIONSHIP TOOK PLACE IN 1991.

MEG RYAN WAS BORN IN 1961   JODIE FOSTER WAS BORN IN 1962

7 AM

8 AM

9 AM

10 AM

11 AM

NOON

1 PM

2 PM

3 PM

4 PM

5 PM

6 PM

ON THIS DAY IN 1991: TROJAN AIRED THE FIRST CONDOM AD ON NETWORK TV.

BRILLIANT AND/OR TERRIBLE IDEAS

323 DAYS DOWN, 42 DAYS LEFT (UNLESS IT'S A LEAP YEAR [324/42])   YEAR:

NOVEMBER 20

MONDAY	TUESDAY	WEDNESDAY	THURSDAY	FRIDAY	SATURDAY ☐
. . . .	. . . .	. . . .	. . . .	. . . .	
☐ TODAY	☐ TODAY	☐ TODAY	☐ TODAY	☐ TODAY	☐ SUNDAY

IT'S NATIONAL ABSURDITY DAY
MICHAEL BAY DIRECTED THE FIRST 'GO MILK?' AD.

JOEL MCHALE WAS BORN IN 1971   BO DEREK WAS BORN IN 1956

7 AM
. . . .
8 AM
. . . .
9 AM
. . . .
10 AM
. . . .
11 AM
. . . .
NOON
. . . .
1 PM
. . . .
2 PM
. . . .
3 PM
. . . .
4 PM
. . . .
5 PM
. . . .
6 PM

ON THIS DAY IN 1973: 'A CHARLIE BROWN THANKSGIVING' AIRED ON CBS.

NOTES AND/OR LIMERICKS

YEAR:	324 DAYS DOWN, 41 DAYS LEFT (UNLESS IT'S A LEAP YEAR [325/41])

NOVEMBER 21

MONDAY	TUESDAY	WEDNESDAY	THURSDAY	FRIDAY	SATURDAY ☐
☐ TODAY	☐ TODAY	☐ TODAY	☐ TODAY	☐ TODAY	☐ SUNDAY

IT'S NATIONAL STUFFING DAY
CONTROVERSIAL OPINION, BUT WE'LL PASS ON SOGGY BUTT BREAD.

BJÖRK WAS BORN IN 1965   GOLDIE HAWN WAS BORN IN 1945

7 AM

8 AM

9 AM

10 AM

11 AM

NOON

1 PM

2 PM

3 PM

4 PM

5 PM

6 PM

ON THIS DAY IN 1959: JACK BENNY AND RICHARD NIXON PLAYED A MUSICAL DUET.

BRILLIANT AND/OR TERRIBLE IDEAS

325 DAYS DOWN, 40 DAYS LEFT (UNLESS IT'S A LEAP YEAR [326/40])   YEAR:

NOVEMBER 22

WRITE IN THE DATES BELOW (AND SHADE IN TODAY)

MONDAY	TUESDAY	WEDNESDAY	THURSDAY	FRIDAY	SATURDAY ☐
. . . . ☐ TODAY	. . . . ☐ TODAY	. . . . ☐ TODAY	. . . . ☐ TODAY	. . . . ☐ TODAY	☐ . SUNDAY

IT'S NATIONAL CRANBERRY RELISH DAY
AMERICANS CONSUME 400 MILLION POUNDS OF CRANBERRIES ON THANKSGIVING.

MARK RUFFALO WAS BORN IN 1967   HAILEY BIEBER WAS BORN IN 1996

7 AM
. . . .
                                                                              8 AM
. . . .
9 AM
. . . .
                                                                              10 AM
. . . .
11 AM
. . . .
                                                                              NOON
. . . .
1 PM
. . . .
                                                                              2 PM
. . . .
3 PM
. . . .
                                                                              4 PM
. . . .
5 PM
. . . .
                                                                              6 PM

ON THIS DAY IN 1954: THE HUMANE SOCIETY OF THE U.S. WAS FORMED.

NOTES AND/OR LIMERICKS

YEAR: | 326 DAYS DOWN, 39 DAYS LEFT (UNLESS IT'S A LEAP YEAR [327/39])

NOVEMBER 23

MONDAY	TUESDAY	WEDNESDAY	THURSDAY	FRIDAY	SATURDAY ☐
. . . . ☐ TODAY	. . . . ☐ TODAY	. . . . ☐ TODAY	. . . . ☐ TODAY	. . . . ☐ TODAY	☐ SUNDAY

IT'S NATIONAL ESPRESSO DAY

IN ITALY, YOU CAN PURCHASE 'POCKET ESPRESSO' IN TO-GO POUCHES.

VINCENT CASSEL WAS BORN IN 1966   MILEY CYRUS WAS BORN IN 1992

7 AM
. . . .
8 AM
. . . .
9 AM
. . . .
10 AM
. . . .
11 AM
. . . .
NOON
. . . .
1 PM
. . . .
2 PM
. . . .
3 PM
. . . .
4 PM
. . . .
5 PM
. . . .
6 PM

ON THIS DAY IN 1991: FREDDIE MERCURY CONFIRMED HIS AIDS DIAGNOSIS.

BRILLIANT AND/OR TERRIBLE IDEAS

327 DAYS DOWN, 38 DAYS LEFT (UNLESS IT'S A LEAP YEAR [328/38])   YEAR:

NOVEMBER 24

MONDAY	TUESDAY	WEDNESDAY	THURSDAY	FRIDAY	SATURDAY ☐
. . . . ☐ TODAY	. . . . ☐ TODAY	. . . . ☐ TODAY	. . . . ☐ TODAY	. . . . ☐ TODAY	☐ SUNDAY

IT'S CELEBRATE YOUR UNIQUE TALENT DAY
1 PERCENT OF PEOPLE CAN LICK THEIR ELBOW WITH THEIR TONGUE.

SARAH HYLAND WAS BORN IN 1990   COLIN HANKS WAS BORN IN 197

7 AM
. . . .
8 A

. . . .
9 AM
. . . .
10 A

. . . .
11 AM
. . . .
NOO

. . . .
1 PM
. . . .
2 P

. . . .
3 PM
. . . .
4 P

. . . .
5 PM
. . . .
6 P

ON THIS DAY IN 1971: D.B. COOPER ESCAPED VIA PARACHUTE WITH $200K IN RANSOM.

NOTES AND/OR LIMERICKS

YEAR:	328 DAYS DOWN, 37 DAYS LEFT (UNLESS IT'S A LEAP YEAR [329/37])

NOVEMBER 25

MONDAY	TUESDAY	WEDNESDAY	THURSDAY	FRIDAY	SATURDAY ☐
☐ TODAY	☐ TODAY	☐ TODAY	☐ TODAY	☐ TODAY	☐ SUNDAY

IT'S NATIONAL PARFAIT DAY
THIS DESSERT'S NAME WAS DERIVED FROM THE FRENCH WORD FOR 'PERFECT.'

AMY GRANT WAS BORN IN 1960   CHRISTINA APPLEGATE WAS BORN IN 1971

7 AM

8 AM

9 AM

10 AM

11 AM

NOON

1 PM

2 PM

3 PM

4 PM

5 PM

6 PM

ON THIS DAY IN 1963: THE FUNERAL FOR PRESIDENT JOHN F. KENNEDY WAS HELD.

BRILLIANT AND/OR TERRIBLE IDEAS

329 DAYS DOWN, 36 DAYS LEFT (UNLESS IT'S A LEAP YEAR [330/36])

YEAR:

NOVEMBER 26

IT'S GOOD GRIEF DAY
IN THE 1980s, SALLY WAS VOICED BY FERGIE.

RITA ORA WAS BORN IN 1990   TINA TURNER WAS BORN IN 1939

7 AM

8 AM

9 AM

10 AM

11 AM

NOON

1 PM

2 PM

3 PM

4 PM

5 PM

6 PM

ON THIS DAY IN 2003: THE CONCORDE COMPLETED ITS FINAL FLIGHT.

NOTES AND/OR LIMERICKS																							

YEAR: ____   330 DAYS DOWN, 35 DAYS LEFT (UNLESS IT'S A LEAP YEAR [331/35])

NOVEMBER 27

MONDAY	TUESDAY	WEDNESDAY	THURSDAY	FRIDAY	SATURDAY ☐
☐ TODAY	☐ TODAY	☐ TODAY	☐ TODAY	☐ TODAY	☐ SUNDAY

IT'S NATIONAL ELECTRIC GUITAR DAY
IN 2001, CHRIS BLACK MARRIED HIS STRATOCASTER NAMED FENDA.

BRUCE LEE WAS BORN IN 1940   JIMI HENDRIX WAS BORN IN 1942

7 AM

8 AM

9 AM

10 AM

11 AM

NOON

1 PM

2 PM

3 PM

4 PM

5 PM

6 PM

ON THIS DAY IN 2005: 50 CENT AND AEROSMITH HEADLINED A BAT MITZVAH.

BRILLIANT AND/OR TERRIBLE IDEAS

331 DAYS DOWN, 34 DAYS LEFT (UNLESS IT'S A LEAP YEAR [332/34])   YEAR:

NOVEMBER 28

MONDAY	TUESDAY	WEDNESDAY	THURSDAY	FRIDAY	SATURDAY ☐
. . . . ☐ TODAY	. . . . ☐ TODAY	. . . . ☐ TODAY	. . . . ☐ TODAY	. . . . ☐ TODAY	☐ SUNDAY

IT'S NATIONAL FRENCH TOAST DAY
IN GERMAN, IT'S CALLED 'ARME RITTER' WHICH MEANS 'POOR KNIGHTS.'

JON STEWART WAS BORN IN 1962   KAREN GILLAN WAS BORN IN 1987

7 AM
. . . .
8 AM
. . . .
9 AM
. . . .
10 AM
. . . .
11 AM
. . . .
NOON
. . . .
1 PM
. . . .
2 PM
. . . .
3 PM
. . . .
4 PM
. . . .
5 PM
. . . .
6 PM

ON THIS DAY IN 1994: SERIAL KILLER JEFFERY DAHMER WAS KILLED IN PRISON.

NOTES AND/OR LIMERICKS

YEAR: 332 DAYS DOWN, 33 DAYS LEFT (UNLESS IT'S A LEAP YEAR [333/33])

NOVEMBER 29

MONDAY	TUESDAY	WEDNESDAY	THURSDAY	FRIDAY	SATURDAY ☐
. . . . ☐ TODAY	. . . . ☐ TODAY	. . . . ☐ TODAY	. . . . ☐ TODAY	. . . . ☐ TODAY	☐ SUNDAY

IT'S SQUARE DANCING DAY
WAS EVERYONE ELSE FORCED TO LEARN HOW IN MIDDLE SCHOOL?

ANNA FARIS WAS BORN IN 1976   DON CHEADLE WAS BORN IN 1964

7 AM

8 AM

9 AM

10 AM

11 AM

NOON

1 PM

2 PM

3 PM

4 PM

5 PM

6 PM

ON THIS DAY IN 1972: ATARI REVEALED THEIR ARCADE GAME 'PONG.'

BRILLIANT AND/OR TERRIBLE IDEAS

333 DAYS DOWN, 32 DAYS LEFT (UNLESS IT'S A LEAP YEAR [334/32])   YEAR:

NOVEMBER 30

MONDAY	TUESDAY	WEDNESDAY	THURSDAY	FRIDAY	SATURDAY ☐
. . . . ☐ TODAY	. . . . ☐ TODAY	. . . . ☐ TODAY	. . . . ☐ TODAY	. . . . ☐ TODAY	☐ SUNDAY

IT'S NATIONAL MASON JAR DAY
SAFELY PRESERVES FOOD AND REFRESHES HIPSTERS.

CHRISSY TEIGEN WAS BORN IN 1985   BEN STILLER WAS BORN IN 1965

7 AM
. . . .
                                                                              8 AM
. . . .
9 AM
. . . .
                                                                              10 AM
. . . .
11 AM
. . . .
                                                                              NOON
. . . .
1 PM
. . . .
                                                                              2 PM
. . . .
3 PM
. . . .
                                                                              4 PM
. . . .
5 PM
. . . .
                                                                              6 PM

ON THIS DAY IN 2004: AFTER 74 CONSECUTIVE WINS ON 'JEOPARDY!' KEN JENNINGS LOST.

NOTES AND/OR LIMERICKS

YEAR: 334 DAYS DOWN, 31 DAYS LEFT (UNLESS IT'S A LEAP YEAR [335/31])

LISTS, NOTES & MEMOIRS

WAYS THIS MONTH WAS GREAT
'IT ENDED' IS A VALID ANSWER

1
2
3
4
5
6
7
8
9
10
11
12
13
14

WAYS THAT IT WASN'T
USE ADDITIONAL PAPER IF NEEDED

1
2
3
4
5
6
7
8
9
10
11
12
13
14

THE WORST COMPLIMENTS THAT I'VE EVER RECEIVED
USE FIGURE 1 FOR ANY NECESSARY VISUAL AIDS

FIG. 1

1   4

2   5

3   6

ORIGINALLY THE TENTH MONTH OF THE YEAR (IN THE ROMAN CALENDAR).

IT'S OFFICIALLY

✖ DECEMBER ✖

OF THE YEAR

MONTH TWELVE

. . . .

. . . .

. . . .

ITS NAME COMES FROM THE LATIN WORD 'DECEM' (MEANING TEN).

DECEMBER AT A GLANCE

CONGRATULATIONS, YOU MADE IT
TO THE MONTH OF DECEMBER

✖

CELEBRATE, IT'S:

UNIVERSAL HUMAN RIGHTS MONTH

NATIONAL PEAR MONTH

NATIONAL CAR DONATION MONTH

AIDS AWARENESS MONTH

SPIRITUAL LITERACY MONTH

OFFICIAL SYMBOLS:

BIRTHSTONE: TURQUOISE

FLOWERS: NARCISSUS & HOLLY

TREES: HORNBEAM, FIG, & BEECH

SAGITTARIUS (NOV 22 / DEC 21)

CAPRICORN (DEC 22 / JAN 19)

✖

A FEW DATES TO KNOW*
LIKE, IMPORTANT ONES.

✖

WORLD AIDS DAY
DECEMBER 1ST

FEAST OF OUR LADY OF GUADALUPE
(MEXICAN)
DECEMBER 12TH

START OF WINTER
(WINTER SOLSTICE)
DECEMBER 21ST
(OR 22ND)

CHRISTMAS DAY
DECEMBER 25TH

HANUKKAH
(JUDAISM)
STARTS ON THE 25TH DAY OF
THE HEBREW MONTH OF KISLEV
(USUALLY DECEMBER)

BOXING DAY
(UNITED KINGDOM)
DECEMBER 26TH

KWANZAA
STARTS ON DECEMBER 26TH

NEW YEAR'S EVE
DECEMBER 31ST

MARK YOUR CALENDAR ✖ IT'S RIGHT OVER THERE

---

*A DISCLAIMER OF SORTS

HEY THERE. WE HERE AT BRASS MONKEY LIKE TO JOKE AROUND...BUT WE ALSO WANT TO TAKE A MINUTE TO RECOGNIZE JUST A FEW OF THE MANY HOLIDAYS & EVENTS THAT ARE IMPORTANT TO OUR FRIENDS AROUND THE GLOBE (AND AT HOME). YOU MAY BE DIFFERENT THAN US. WE MAY HAVE NEVER MET. BUT WE LOVE YOU ALL THE SAME.

SO, WITH ALL OF THAT SAID, IF YOU HAVEN'T HEARD OF A DAY, PLEASE LOOK IT UP. LEARNING ABOUT AND APPRECIATING CULTURES DIFFERENT THAN YOURS IS REALLY IMPORTANT...WAY MORE SO THAN POSTING A FEW 'STRAWBERRY JAM DAY' VIDEOS ON TIKTOK. DON'T GET US WRONG, THERE IS PLENTY OF ROOM FOR BOTH. JUST PLEASE DO BOTH.

DECEMBER AT A GLANCE

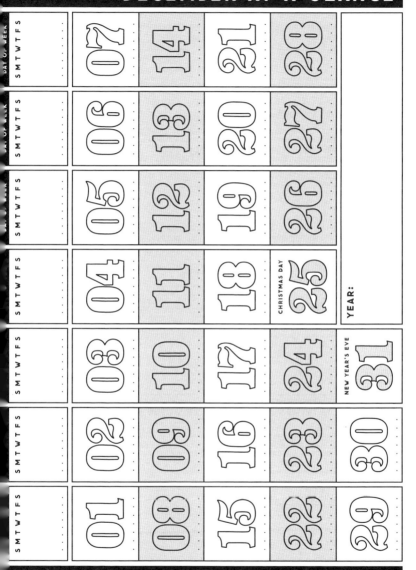

S M T W T F S	S M T W T F S	S M T W T F S	S M T W T F S	S M T W T F S	S M T W T F S	S M T W T F S
07	06	05	04	03	02	01
14	13	12	11	10	09	08
21	20	19	18	17	16	15
28	27	26	CHRISTMAS DAY 25	NEW YEAR'S EVE 24	23	22
				31	30	29

YEAR:

WELL, WHAT ARE YOU WAITING FOR?

✗ START PLANNING. IN THE CALENDAR ABOVE, WE'VE MARKED THE MORE COMMON U.S. HOLIDAYS ALREADY (THE ONES THAT ARE DATED, THAT IS). SO USE THE LIST TO THE LEFT TO FILL IN THE REST...LIKE ALL OF THE ONES THAT CHANGE DATES FROM YEAR TO YEAR, FOR EXAMPLE. ✗

LISTS, NOTES & MEMOIRS

THE BEST GIFTS I'VE GIVEN
OR SOME BORING TO-DO LIST

1
2
3
4
5
6
7
8
9
10
11
12
13
14

THE WORST GIFTS I'VE RECEIVED
OR A GROCERY LIST OR SOMETHING

1
2
3
4
5
6
7
8
9
10
11
12
13
14

CHRISTMAS SONGS THAT ARE WORSE THAN TORTURE
USE FIGURE 1 FOR ANY NECESSARY VISUAL AIDS

FIG. 1

1
2
3

4
5
6

DECEMBER 1

WRITE IN THE DATES BELOW (AND SHADE IN TODAY)

MONDAY	TUESDAY	WEDNESDAY	THURSDAY	FRIDAY	SATURDAY ☐
. . . .	. . . .	. . . .	. . . .	. . . .	
☐ TODAY	☐ TODAY	☐ TODAY	☐ TODAY	☐ TODAY	☐ SUNDAY

IT'S NATIONAL CHRISTMAS LIGHTS DAY
THOMAS EDISON SHOWCASED THE FIRST LIT CHRISTMAS TREE IN 1882.

RICHARD PRYOR WAS BORN IN 1940   BETTE MIDLER WAS BORN IN 1945

7 AM

8 AM

9 AM

10 AM

11 AM

NOON

1 PM

2 PM

3 PM

4 PM

5 PM

6 PM

ON THIS DAY IN 1955: ROSA PARKS WAS ARRESTED, IGNITING THE BUS BOYCOTT.

BRILLIANT AND/OR TERRIBLE IDEAS

335 DAYS DOWN, 30 DAYS LEFT (UNLESS IT'S A LEAP YEAR [336/30])   YEAR:

DECEMBER 2

MONDAY	TUESDAY	WEDNESDAY	THURSDAY	FRIDAY	SATURDAY ☐
. . . .	. . . .	. . . .	. . . .	. . . .	
☐ TODAY	☐ TODAY	☐ TODAY	☐ TODAY	☐ TODAY	☐ SUNDAY

IT'S NATIONAL BASKETBALL DAY
THE AVERAGE NBA PLAYER HAS A VERTICAL LEAP OF 28 INCHES.

LUCY LIU WAS BORN IN 1968   BRITNEY SPEARS WAS BORN IN 198

7 AM
. . . .
                                                                                    8 A

. . . .
9 AM
. . . .
                                                                                    10 A

. . . .
11 AM
. . . .
                                                                                    NOO

. . . .
1 PM
. . . .
                                                                                    2 P

. . . .
3 PM
. . . .
                                                                                    4 P

. . . .
5 PM
. . . .
                                                                                    6 P

ON THIS DAY IN 1997: 'GOOD WILL HUNTING' WAS RELEASED.

NOTES AND/OR LIMERICKS

YEAR:	336 DAYS DOWN, 29 DAYS LEFT (UNLESS IT'S A LEAP YEAR [337/29])

DECEMBER 3

MONDAY	TUESDAY	WEDNESDAY	THURSDAY	FRIDAY	SATURDAY ☐
. . . .	. . . .	. . . .	. . . .	. . . .	
☐ TODAY	☐ TODAY	☐ TODAY	☐ TODAY	☐ TODAY	☐ SUNDAY

IT'S NATIONAL GREEN BEAN CASSEROLE DAY
THE ORIGINAL RECIPE IS IN THE NATIONAL INVENTOR'S HALL OF FAME.

AMANDA SEYFRIED WAS BORN IN 1985   BRENDAN FRASER WAS BORN IN 1968

7 AM

8 AM

9 AM

10 AM

11 AM

NOON

1 PM

2 PM

3 PM

4 PM

5 PM

6 PM

ON THIS DAY IN 1976: AN ASSASSINATION ATTEMPT WAS MADE ON BOB MARLEY.

BRILLIANT AND/OR TERRIBLE IDEAS

337 DAYS DOWN, 28 DAYS LEFT (UNLESS IT'S A LEAP YEAR [338/28])   YEAR:

DECEMBER 4

WRITE IN THE DATES BELOW (AND SHADE IN TODAY)

MONDAY	TUESDAY	WEDNESDAY	THURSDAY	FRIDAY	SATURDAY ☐
. . . .	. . . .	. . . .	. . . .	. . . .	
☐ TODAY	☐ TODAY	☐ TODAY	☐ TODAY	☐ TODAY	☐ SUNDAY

IT'S NATIONAL DICE DAY
THE DOTS ON TRADITIONAL DICE ARE KNOWN AS 'PIPS.'

JAY-Z WAS BORN IN 1969   FRED ARMISEN WAS BORN IN 196

7 AM
. . . .
                                                                                    8 AM
. . . .
9 AM
. . . .
                                                                                    10 AM
. . . .
11 AM
. . . .
                                                                                    NOO
. . . .
1 PM
. . . .
                                                                                    2 P
. . . .
3 PM
. . . .
                                                                                    4 P
. . . .
5 PM
. . . .
                                                                                    6 P

ON THIS DAY IN 1980: LED ZEPPELIN OFFICIALLY DISBANDED.

NOTES AND/OR LIMERICKS

YEAR: | 338 DAYS DOWN, 27 DAYS LEFT (UNLESS IT'S A LEAP YEAR [339/27])

DECEMBER 5

MONDAY	TUESDAY	WEDNESDAY	THURSDAY	FRIDAY	SATURDAY ☐
. . . .	. . . .	. . . .	. . . .	. . . .	
☐ TODAY	☐ TODAY	☐ TODAY	☐ TODAY	☐ TODAY	☐ SUNDAY

IT'S NATIONAL BLUE JEANS DAY
LEVI STRAUSS RECEIVED A PATENT FOR JEANS IN 1873.

RANKIE MUNIZ WAS BORN IN 1985   MARGARET CHO WAS BORN IN 1968

7 AM

. . . .

AM

. . . .

9 AM

. . . .

O AM

. . . .

11 AM

. . . .

OON

. . . .

1 PM

. . . .

PM

. . . .

3 PM

. . . .

PM

. . . .

5 PM

. . . .

PM

ON THIS DAY IN 1933: PROHIBITION ENDED (THANKS TO THE 21ST AMENDMENT).

BRILLIANT AND/OR TERRIBLE IDEAS

DECEMBER 6

MONDAY	TUESDAY	WEDNESDAY	THURSDAY	FRIDAY	SATURDAY ☐
. . . . ☐ TODAY	. . . . ☐ TODAY	. . . . ☐ TODAY	. . . . ☐ TODAY	. . . . ☐ TODAY	☐ SUNDAY

IT'S NATIONAL PAWNBROKERS DAY
SAINT NICHOLAS (YES, THAT ONE) IS THE PATRON SAINT OF PAWNBROKERS.

JUDD APATOW WAS BORN IN 1967   SARAH RAFFERTY WAS BORN IN 197

7 AM
. . . .
8 A
. . . .
9 AM
. . . .
10 A
. . . .
11 AM
. . . .
NOO
. . . .
1 PM
. . . .
2 P
. . . .
3 PM
. . . .
4 P
. . . .
5 PM
. . . .
6 P

ON THIS DAY IN 1964: THE SONG 'RUDOLPH THE RED-NOSED REINDEER' DEBUTED.

NOTES AND/OR LIMERICKS

| YEAR: | | 340 DAYS DOWN, 25 DAYS LEFT (UNLESS IT'S A LEAP YEAR [341/25]) |

DECEMBER 7

WRITE IN THE DATES BELOW (AND SHADE IN TODAY)

MONDAY	TUESDAY	WEDNESDAY	THURSDAY	FRIDAY	SATURDAY ☐
☐ TODAY	☐ TODAY	☐ TODAY	☐ TODAY	☐ TODAY	☐ SUNDAY

IT'S NATIONAL COTTON CANDY DAY
IT WAS INVENTED BY A DENTIST IN 1897.

MILY BROWNING WAS BORN IN 1988   NICHOLAS HOLT WAS BORN IN 1989

7 AM

AM

9 AM

) AM

11 AM

OON

1 PM

PM

3 PM

PM

5 PM

PM

ON THIS DAY IN 1941: PEARL HARBOR, HAWAII, WAS ATTACKED BY JAPAN.

BRILLIANT AND/OR TERRIBLE IDEAS

341 DAYS DOWN, 24 DAYS LEFT (UNLESS IT'S A LEAP YEAR [342/24])   YEAR:

DECEMBER 8

MONDAY	TUESDAY	WEDNESDAY	THURSDAY	FRIDAY	SATURDAY ☐
. . . .	. . . .	. . . .	. . . .	. . . .	☐
☐ TODAY	☐ TODAY	☐ TODAY	☐ TODAY	☐ TODAY	SUNDAY

IT'S NATIONAL BROWNIE DAY
ACCORDING TO OUR CORRECT OPINION, CENTER PIECES ARE THE BEST.

NICKI MINAJ WAS BORN IN 1982   IAN SOMERHALDER WAS BORN IN 197

7 AM
. . . .
                                                                        8 A
. . . .
9 AM
. . . .
                                                                        10 A
. . . .
11 AM
. . . .
                                                                        NOO
. . . .
1 PM
. . . .
                                                                        2 P
. . . .
3 PM
. . . .
                                                                        4 P
. . . .
5 PM
. . . .
                                                                        6 F

ON THIS DAY IN 1995: THE GRATEFUL DEAD ANNOUNCED THEIR BREAK UP.

NOTES AND/OR LIMERICKS

YEAR: 342 DAYS DOWN, 23 DAYS LEFT (UNLESS IT'S A LEAP YEAR [343/23])

DECEMBER 9

MONDAY	TUESDAY	WEDNESDAY	THURSDAY	FRIDAY	SATURDAY ☐
. . . .	. . . .	. . . .	. . . .	. . . .	
☐ TODAY	☐ TODAY	☐ TODAY	☐ TODAY	☐ TODAY	☐ SUNDAY

WRITE IN THE DATES BELOW (AND SHADE IN TODAY)

IT'S NATIONAL LLAMA DAY
WHEN AGITATED, THEY CAN SPIT DISTANCES OVER 15 FEET.

JOHN MALKOVICH WAS BORN IN 1953   JUDI DENCH WAS BORN IN 1934

7 AM

8 AM

9 AM

10 AM

11 AM

NOON

1 PM

2 PM

3 PM

4 PM

5 PM

6 PM

ON THIS DAY IN 1965: 'A CHARLIE BROWN CHRISTMAS' PREMIERED.

BRILLIANT AND/OR TERRIBLE IDEAS

343 DAYS DOWN, 22 DAYS LEFT (UNLESS IT'S A LEAP YEAR [344/22])   YEAR:

DECEMBER 10

MONDAY	TUESDAY	WEDNESDAY	THURSDAY	FRIDAY	SATURDAY
. . . . ☐ TODAY	. . . . ☐ TODAY	. . . . ☐ TODAY	. . . . ☐ TODAY	. . . . ☐ TODAY	☐ SUNDA

IT'S DEWEY DECIMAL SYSTEM DAY
MELVIL DEWEY CREATED THE SYSTEM AT 21 WHILE WORKING IN A LIBRARY.

EMILY DICKINSON WAS BORN IN 1830   RAVEN-SYMONÉ WAS BORN IN 19

7 AM
. . . .

8 A
. . . .

9 AM
. . . .

10 A
. . . .

11 AM
. . . .

NO
. . . .

1 PM
. . . .

2
. . . .

3 PM
. . . .

4
. . . .

5 PM
. . . .

6

ON THIS DAY IN 1967: OTIS REDDING WAS KILLED IN A PLANE CRASH.

NOTES AND/OR LIMERICKS

YEAR:	344 DAYS DOWN, 21 DAYS LEFT (UNLESS IT'S A LEAP YEAR [345/21])

DECEMBER 11

MONDAY	TUESDAY	WEDNESDAY	THURSDAY	FRIDAY	SATURDAY ☐
. . . . ☐ TODAY	. . . . ☐ TODAY	. . . . ☐ TODAY	. . . . ☐ TODAY	. . . . ☐ TODAY	☐ SUNDAY

IT'S INTERNATIONAL MOUNTAIN DAY
ON AVERAGE, 6 PEOPLE DIE EVERY YEAR TRYING TO CLIMB MT. EVEREST.

EY MYSTERIO WAS BORN IN 1974   HAILEE STEINFELD WAS BORN IN 1996

7 AM

AM

9 AM

) AM

11 AM

ЭON

1 PM

PM

3 PM

PM

5 PM

PM

ON THIS DAY IN 1769: VENETIAN BLINDS WERE PATENTED BY EDWARD BEVAN.

BRILLIANT AND/OR TERRIBLE IDEAS

345 DAYS DOWN, 20 DAYS LEFT (UNLESS IT'S A LEAP YEAR [346/20])

YEAR:

DECEMBER 12

WRITE IN THE DATES BELOW (AND SHADE IN TODAY)

MONDAY	TUESDAY	WEDNESDAY	THURSDAY	FRIDAY	SATURDAY
. . . .	. . . .	. . . .	. . . .	. . . .	
☐ TODAY	☐ TODAY	☐ TODAY	☐ TODAY	☐ TODAY	☐ SUNDAY

IT'S NATIONAL POINSETTIA DAY
NAMED AFTER JOEL R. POINSETT, THE FIRST U.S. AMBASSADOR TO MEXICO.

FRANK SINATRA WAS BORN IN 1915   MAYIM BIALIK WAS BORN IN 19

7 AM
. . . .
                                                                          8 A
. . . .
9 AM
. . . .
                                                                          10 A
. . . .
11 AM
. . . .
                                                                          NO
. . . .
1 PM
. . . .
                                                                          2 F
. . . .
3 PM
. . . .
                                                                          4
. . . .
5 PM
. . . .
                                                                          6

ON THIS DAY IN 1987: 'FAITH' BY GEORGE MICHAEL HIT NUMBER 1.

NOTES AND/OR LIMERICKS

| YEAR: | 346 DAYS DOWN, 19 DAYS LEFT (UNLESS IT'S A LEAP YEAR [347/19]) |

DECEMBER 13

MONDAY	TUESDAY	WEDNESDAY	THURSDAY	FRIDAY	SATURDAY ☐
☐ TODAY	☐ TODAY	☐ TODAY	☐ TODAY	☐ TODAY	☐ SUNDAY

IT'S NATIONAL VIOLIN DAY
THE ACT OF PLAYING BURNS APPROXIMATELY 170 CALORIES PER HOUR.

AMIE FOXX WAS BORN IN 1967   TAYLOR SWIFT WAS BORN IN 1989

7 AM

. . . .
 AM
. . . .

9 AM

. . . .
0 AM
. . . .

11 AM

. . . .
OON
. . . .

1 PM

. . . .
PM
. . . .

3 PM

. . . .
PM
. . . .

5 PM

. . . .
PM

ON THIS DAY IN 1950: JAMES DEAN BEGAN HIS CAREER IN A PEPSI COMMERCIAL.

BRILLIANT AND/OR TERRIBLE IDEAS

347 DAYS DOWN, 18 DAYS LEFT (UNLESS IT'S A LEAP YEAR [348/18])   YEAR:

DECEMBER 14

MONDAY	TUESDAY	WEDNESDAY	THURSDAY	FRIDAY	SATURDAY ☐
. . . .	. . . .	. . . .	. . . .	. . . .	
☐ TODAY	☐ TODAY	☐ TODAY	☐ TODAY	☐ TODAY	☐ SUNDAY

IT'S ROAST CHESTNUTS DAY
ROASTING OVER AN OPEN FIRE? SCORE THE SKINS SO THEY DON'T EXPLODE.

PATTY DUKE WAS BORN IN 1946   VANESSA HUDGENS WAS BORN IN 198

7 AM
. . . .
8 AM
. . . .
9 AM
. . . .
10 A
. . . .
11 AM
. . . .
NOO
. . . .
1 PM
. . . .
2 P
. . . .
3 PM
. . . .
4 P
. . . .
5 PM
. . . .
6 P

ON THIS DAY IN 2008: AN IRAQI JOURNALIST THREW A SHOE AT GEORGE W. BUSH.

NOTES AND/OR LIMERICKS

YEAR: 348 DAYS DOWN, 17 DAYS LEFT (UNLESS IT'S A LEAP YEAR [349/17])

WRITE IN THE DATES BELOW (AND SHADE IN TODAY)					
MONDAY	TUESDAY	WEDNESDAY	THURSDAY	FRIDAY	SATURDAY ☐
. . . .	. . . .	. . . .	. . . .	. . . .	
☐ TODAY	☐ TODAY	☐ TODAY	☐ TODAY	☐ TODAY	☐ SUNDAY

IT'S NATIONAL WEAR YOUR PEARLS DAY
KOKICHI MIKIMOTO CREATED CULTURED PEARLS IN 1893.

ON JOHNSON WAS BORN IN 1949   MAUDE APATOW WAS BORN IN 1997

7 AM

AM

9 AM

0 AM

11 AM

OON

1 PM

PM

3 PM

PM

5 PM

PM

ON THIS DAY IN 2001: THE TOWER OF PISA REOPENED AFTER $27M IN REPAIRS.

BRILLIANT AND/OR TERRIBLE IDEAS

349 DAYS DOWN, 16 DAYS LEFT (UNLESS IT'S A LEAP YEAR [350/16])   YEAR:

DECEMBER 16

MONDAY	TUESDAY	WEDNESDAY	THURSDAY	FRIDAY	SATURDAY ☐
. . . .	. . . .	. . . .	. . . .	. . . .	
☐ TODAY	☐ TODAY	☐ TODAY	☐ TODAY	☐ TODAY	☐ SUNDAY

IT'S STUPID TOY DAY
HOT WHEELS ARE THE HIGHEST-GROSSING TOY OF ALL TIME.

KRYSTEN RITTER WAS BORN IN 1981   BENJAMIN BRATT WAS BORN IN 196

7 AM
. . . .
8 A
. . . .
9 AM
. . . .
10 A
. . . .
11 AM
. . . .
NOO
. . . .
1 PM
. . . .
2 P
. . . .
3 PM
. . . .
4 P
. . . .
5 PM
. . . .
6 P

ON THIS DAY IN 1773: THE BOSTON TEA PARTY TOOK PLACE.

NOTES AND/OR LIMERICKS

YEAR: | 350 DAYS DOWN, 15 DAYS LEFT (UNLESS IT'S A LEAP YEAR [351/15])

DECEMBER 17

MONDAY	TUESDAY	WEDNESDAY	THURSDAY	FRIDAY	SATURDAY ☐
☐ TODAY	☐ TODAY	☐ TODAY	☐ TODAY	☐ TODAY	☐ SUNDAY

IT'S NATIONAL MAPLE SYRUP DAY
IN 2012, THIEVES STOLE 6 MILLION LBS OF IT (WORTH $18 MILLION).

ILLA JOVOVICH WAS BORN IN 1975   SARAH PAULSON WAS BORN IN 1974

7 AM

AM

9 AM

AM

11 AM

OON

1 PM

PM

3 PM

PM

5 PM

PM

ON THIS DAY IN 1892: THE FIRST ISSUE OF 'VOGUE' MAGAZINE WAS PUBLISHED.

BRILLIANT AND/OR TERRIBLE IDEAS

351 DAYS DOWN, 14 DAYS LEFT (UNLESS IT'S A LEAP YEAR [352/14])

YEAR:

DECEMBER 18

MONDAY	TUESDAY	WEDNESDAY	THURSDAY	FRIDAY	SATURDAY ☐
. . . .	. . . .	. . . .	. . . .	. . . .	☐
☐ TODAY	☐ TODAY	☐ TODAY	☐ TODAY	☐ TODAY	SUNDAY

IT'S NATIONAL TWIN DAY
1 TO 2 PERCENT OF ALL FRATERNAL TWINS HAVE DIFFERENT DADS.

BILLIE EILISH WAS BORN IN 2001   BRAD PITT WAS BORN IN 196

7 AM
. . . .
                                                                                      8 A
. . . .
9 AM
. . . .
                                                                                      10 A
. . . .
11 AM
. . . .
                                                                                      NOO
. . . .
1 PM
. . . .
                                                                                      2 P
. . . .
3 PM
. . . .
                                                                                      4 P
. . . .
5 PM
. . . .
                                                                                      6 P

ON THIS DAY IN 1997: COMEDIAN CHRIS FARLEY DIED OF AN OVERDOSE.

NOTES AND/OR LIMERICKS

YEAR:	352 DAYS DOWN, 13 DAYS LEFT (UNLESS IT'S A LEAP YEAR [353/13])

DECEMBER 19

MONDAY	TUESDAY	WEDNESDAY	THURSDAY	FRIDAY	SATURDAY ☐
. . . .	. . . .	. . . .	. . . .	. . . .	
☐ TODAY	☐ TODAY	☐ TODAY	☐ TODAY	☐ TODAY	☐ SUNDAY

IT'S NATIONAL HARD CANDY DAY
HARD CANDIES WITH MINT AND LEMON WERE ORIGINALLY USED MEDICINALLY.

ALYSSA MILANO WAS BORN IN 1972   JAKE GYLLENHAAL WAS BORN IN 1980

7 AM

AM

9 AM

O AM

11 AM

OON

1 PM

PM

3 PM

PM

5 PM

PM

ON THIS DAY IN 1986: 'LITTLE SHOP OF HORRORS' DEBUTED IN THEATERS.

BRILLIANT AND/OR TERRIBLE IDEAS

353 DAYS DOWN, 12 DAYS LEFT (UNLESS IT'S A LEAP YEAR [354/12])   YEAR:

DECEMBER 20

WRITE IN THE DATES BELOW (AND SHADE IN TODAY)

MONDAY	TUESDAY	WEDNESDAY	THURSDAY	FRIDAY	SATURDAY ☐
. . . .	. . . .	. . . .	. . . .	. . . .	
☐ TODAY	☐ TODAY	☐ TODAY	☐ TODAY	☐ TODAY	☐ SUNDAY

IT'S NATIONAL GAMES DAY
THE FOLDING CHESSBOARD WAS INVENTED BY A PRIEST IN 1125.

JONAH HILL WAS BORN IN 1983   DICK WOLF WAS BORN IN 194

7 AM
. . . .
8 A
. . . .
9 AM
. . . .
10 A
. . . .
11 AM
. . . .
NOO
. . . .
1 PM
. . . .
2 P
. . . .
3 PM
. . . .
4 P
. . . .
5 PM
. . . .
6 P

ON THIS DAY IN 1957: ELVIS PRESLEY WAS DRAFTED (HE WOULD SERVE FOR 2 YEARS).

NOTES AND/OR LIMERICKS

YEAR: 354 DAYS DOWN, 11 DAYS LEFT (UNLESS IT'S A LEAP YEAR [355/11])

DECEMBER 21

WRITE IN THE DATES BELOW (AND SHADE IN TODAY)

MONDAY	TUESDAY	WEDNESDAY	THURSDAY	FRIDAY	SATURDAY ☐
. . . .	. . . .	. . . .	. . . .	. . . .	
☐ TODAY	☐ TODAY	☐ TODAY	☐ TODAY	☐ TODAY	☐ SUNDAY

IT'S NATIONAL CROSSWORD PUZZLE DAY
THE FIRST NEW YORK TIMES CROSSWORD PUZZLE WAS PUBLISHED IN 1930.

SAMUEL L. JACKSON WAS BORN IN 1948   STEVEN YEUN WAS BORN IN 1983

7 AM

. . . .

8 AM

. . . .

9 AM

. . . .

10 AM

. . . .

11 AM

. . . .

NOON

. . . .

1 PM

. . . .

2 PM

. . . .

3 PM

. . . .

4 PM

. . . .

5 PM

. . . .

6 PM

ON THIS DAY IN 2012: THE WORLD ENDED (ACCORDING TO THE MAYAN CALENDAR).

BRILLIANT AND/OR TERRIBLE IDEAS

355 DAYS DOWN, 10 DAYS LEFT (UNLESS IT'S A LEAP YEAR [356/10])   YEAR:

DECEMBER 22

MONDAY	TUESDAY	WEDNESDAY	THURSDAY	FRIDAY	SATURDAY ☐
. . . .	. . . .	. . . .	. . . .	. . . .	
☐ TODAY	☐ TODAY	☐ TODAY	☐ TODAY	☐ TODAY	☐ SUNDAY

IT'S NATIONAL COOKIE EXCHANGE DAY
YOU KNOW WHAT TO DO: 1408 W. 12TH ST. KANSAS CITY, MO 64101.

MEGHAN TRAINOR WAS BORN IN 1993   JORDIN SPARKS WAS BORN IN 1989

7 AM

. . . .
8 AM

9 AM

. . . .
10 AM

11 AM

. . . .
NOON

1 PM

. . . .
2 PM

3 PM

. . . .
4 PM

5 PM

. . . .
6 PM

ON THIS DAY IN 1808: LUDWIG VAN BEETHOVEN'S FIFTH SYMPHONY PREMIERED.

NOTES AND/OR LIMERICKS

YEAR:	356 DAYS DOWN, 9 DAYS LEFT (UNLESS IT'S A LEAP YEAR [357/9])

DECEMBER 23

MONDAY	TUESDAY	WEDNESDAY	THURSDAY	FRIDAY	SATURDAY ☐
. . . . ☐ TODAY	. . . . ☐ TODAY	. . . . ☐ TODAY	. . . . ☐ TODAY	. . . . ☐ TODAY	☐ SUNDAY

IT'S FESTIVUS

WRITER DAN O'KEEFE BASED IT ON HIS FATHER'S REAL TRADITION.

EDDIE VEDDER WAS BORN IN 1964   FINN WOLFHARD WAS BORN IN 2002

7 AM

8 AM

9 AM

10 AM

11 AM

NOON

1 PM

2 PM

3 PM

4 PM

5 PM

6 PM

ON THIS DAY IN 1888: VINCENT VAN GOGH CUT OFF PART OF HIS LEFT EAR.

BRILLIANT AND/OR TERRIBLE IDEAS

357 DAYS DOWN, 8 DAYS LEFT (UNLESS IT'S A LEAP YEAR [358/8])

YEAR:

DECEMBER 24

MONDAY	TUESDAY	WEDNESDAY	THURSDAY	FRIDAY	SATURDAY ☐
. . . .	. . . .	. . . .	. . . .	. . . .	
☐ TODAY	☐ TODAY	☐ TODAY	☐ TODAY	☐ TODAY	☐ SUNDAY

IT'S CHRISTMAS EVE
OH, AND NATIONAL EGGNOG DAY.

AVA GARDNER WAS BORN IN 1922   RYAN SEACREST WAS BORN IN 1974

7 AM
. . . .
                                                                              8 AM
. . . .
9 AM
. . . .
                                                                              10 AM
11 AM
. . . .
                                                                              NOON
. . . .
1 PM
. . . .
                                                                              2 PM
. . . .
3 PM
. . . .
                                                                              4 PM
. . . .
5 PM
. . . .
                                                                              6 PM

ON THIS DAY IN 1955: NORAD TRACKED SANTA FOR THE FIRST TIME.

NOTES AND/OR LIMERICKS

YEAR:	358 DAYS DOWN, 7 DAYS LEFT (UNLESS IT'S A LEAP YEAR [359/7])

DECEMBER 25

MONDAY	TUESDAY	WEDNESDAY	THURSDAY	FRIDAY	SATURDAY ☐
☐ TODAY	☐ TODAY	☐ TODAY	☐ TODAY	☐ TODAY	☐ SUNDAY

IT'S CHRISTMAS DAY
BUT DON'T FORGET ABOUT NATIONAL PUMPKIN PIE DAY.

SISSY SPACEK WAS BORN IN 1949   HUMPHREY BOGART WAS BORN IN 1899

7 AM

8 AM

9 AM

10 AM

11 AM

NOON

1 PM

2 PM

3 PM

4 PM

5 PM

6 PM

ON THIS DAY IN 1959: RINGO STARR GOT HIS FIRST DRUM SET.

BRILLIANT AND/OR TERRIBLE IDEAS

DECEMBER 26

WRITE IN THE DATES BELOW (AND SHADE IN TODAY)

MONDAY	TUESDAY	WEDNESDAY	THURSDAY	FRIDAY	SATURDAY ☐
. . . . ☐ TODAY	. . . . ☐ TODAY	. . . . ☐ TODAY	. . . . ☐ TODAY	. . . . ☐ TODAY	☐ SUNDAY

IT'S NATIONAL CANDY CANE DAY
THEY WERE FIRST INVENTED IN GERMANY IN 1670.

KIT HARRINGTON WAS BORN IN 1986   CHRIS DAUGHTRY WAS BORN IN 1979

7 AM
. . . .
8 AM
. . . .
9 AM
. . . .
10 AM
. . . .
11 AM
. . . .
NOON
. . . .
1 PM
. . . .
2 PM
. . . .
3 PM
. . . .
4 PM
. . . .
5 PM
. . . .
6 PM

ON THIS DAY IN 1966: THE FIRST DAY OF THE FIRST KWANZA WAS CELEBRATED.

NOTES AND/OR LIMERICKS

YEAR:	360 DAYS DOWN, 5 DAYS LEFT (UNLESS IT'S A LEAP YEAR [361/5])

DECEMBER 27

WRITE IN THE DATES BELOW (AND SHADE IN TODAY)

MONDAY	TUESDAY	WEDNESDAY	THURSDAY	FRIDAY	SATURDAY ☐
. . . .	. . . .	. . . .	. . . .	. . . .	
☐ TODAY	☐ TODAY	☐ TODAY	☐ TODAY	☐ TODAY	☐ SUNDAY

IT'S MAKE CUT-OUT SNOWFLAKES DAY
IN 1988, A SCIENTIST FOUND TWO IDENTICAL SNOW CRYSTALS.

MARLENE DIETRICH WAS BORN IN 1901   HAYLEY WILLIAMS WAS BORN IN 1988

7 AM

8 AM

9 AM

10 AM

11 AM

NOON

1 PM

2 PM

3 PM

4 PM

5 PM

6 PM

ON THIS DAY IN 1932: RADIO CITY MUSIC HALL OPENED IN NEW YORK CITY.

BRILLIANT AND/OR TERRIBLE IDEAS

361 DAYS DOWN, 4 DAYS LEFT (UNLESS IT'S A LEAP YEAR [362/4])

YEAR:

DECEMBER 28

WRITE IN THE DATES BELOW (AND SHADE IN TODAY)

MONDAY	TUESDAY	WEDNESDAY	THURSDAY	FRIDAY	SATURDAY ☐
. . . .	. . . .	. . . .	. . . .	. . . .	☐
☐ TODAY	☐ TODAY	☐ TODAY	☐ TODAY	☐ TODAY	SUNDAY

IT'S NATIONAL CARD PLAYING DAY
A DECK CAN BE ARRANGED MORE WAYS THAN THERE ARE ATOMS ON EARTH.

MAGGIE SMITH WAS BORN IN 1934   JOHN LEGEND WAS BORN IN 1978

7 AM
. . . .
8 AM
. . . .
9 AM
. . . .
10 AM
. . . .
11 AM
. . . .
NOON
. . . .
1 PM
. . . .
2 PM
. . . .
3 PM
. . . .
4 PM
. . . .
5 PM
. . . .
6 PM

ON THIS DAY IN 2007: MISCHA BARTON WAS ARRESTED IN WEST HOLLYWOOD.

NOTES AND/OR LIMERICKS

YEAR:	362 DAYS DOWN, 3 DAYS LEFT (UNLESS IT'S A LEAP YEAR [363/3])

DECEMBER 29

MONDAY	TUESDAY	WEDNESDAY	THURSDAY	FRIDAY	SATURDAY ☐
. . . . ☐ TODAY	. . . . ☐ TODAY	. . . . ☐ TODAY	. . . . ☐ TODAY	. . . . ☐ TODAY	☐ SUNDAY

IT'S INTERNATIONAL CELLO DAY
YO-YO MA HAS SIX HONORARY DOCTORATES.

JUDE LAW WAS BORN IN 1972   MARY TYLER MOORE WAS BORN IN 1936

7 AM

8 AM

9 AM

10 AM

11 AM

NOON

1 PM

2 PM

3 PM

4 PM

5 PM

6 PM

ON THIS DAY IN 1862: THE MODERN BOWLING BALL WAS INVENTED.

BRILLIANT AND/OR TERRIBLE IDEAS

363 DAYS DOWN, 2 DAYS LEFT (UNLESS IT'S A LEAP YEAR [364/2])   YEAR:

DECEMBER 30

WRITE IN THE DATES BELOW (AND SHADE IN TODAY)

MONDAY	TUESDAY	WEDNESDAY	THURSDAY	FRIDAY	SATURDAY ☐
. . . .	. . . .	. . . .	. . . .	. . . .	☐
☐ TODAY	☐ TODAY	☐ TODAY	☐ TODAY	☐ TODAY	SUNDAY

IT'S NATIONAL BICARBONATE OF SODA DAY
IT CAN DO EVERYTHING FROM POLISH SILVER TO TENDERIZE MEAT.

LEBRON JAMES WAS BORN IN 1984   ELLIE GOULDING WAS BORN IN 198

7 AM
. . . .
                                                                            8 A
. . . .
9 AM
. . . .
                                                                           10 A
. . . .
11 AM
. . . .
                                                                            NOO
. . . .
1 PM
. . . .
                                                                            2 P
. . . .
3 PM
. . . .
                                                                            4 P
. . . .
5 PM
. . . .
                                                                            6 P

ON THIS DAY IN 2011: THIS DAY NEVER HAPPENED IN SAMOA DUE TO A TIME ZONE CHANGE.

NOTES AND/OR LIMERICKS

YEAR: 364 DAYS DOWN, 1 DAYS LEFT (UNLESS IT'S A LEAP YEAR [365/1])

DECEMBER 31

MONDAY	TUESDAY	WEDNESDAY	THURSDAY	FRIDAY	SATURDAY ☐
. . . . ☐ TODAY	. . . . ☐ TODAY	. . . . ☐ TODAY	. . . . ☐ TODAY	. . . . ☐ TODAY	☐ SUNDAY

IT'S NEW YEAR'S EVE
OH, AND NATIONAL CHAMPAGNE DAY.

NTHONY HOPKINS WAS BORN IN 1937   HUNTER SCHAFER WAS BORN IN 1998

7 AM

AM

9 AM

) AM

11 AM

OON

1 PM

PM

3 PM

PM

5 PM

PM

ON THIS DAY IN 1907: THE FIRST ANNUAL BALL DROP WAS HELD IN TIMES SQUARE.

BRILLIANT AND/OR TERRIBLE IDEAS

365 DAYS DOWN, 0 DAYS LEFT (UNLESS IT'S A LEAP YEAR [366/0])   YEAR: